VANISHING LEGAL JUSTICE

A full trial has become an uncommon phenomenon in many legal systems, replaced largely by promotion of settlement and plea bargaining. This book uncovers today's judicial role in this radically changed legal setting using multiple methods.

Over five years, researchers analyzed court dockets, studied judges in action, and conducted interviews with judges and lawyers. This book, which spans several legal cultures, follows in the footsteps of the "vanishing trial phenomenon," probing its existence beyond common law systems. In doing so, it provides insights into the changing judicial role and the metamorphosis of legal systems.

Offering a new perspective on possible futures of legal systems, including the use of artificial intelligence, the authors provide a rich context for legal scholars and policymakers to redesign the architecture of conflicts. Moreover, they introduce new jurisprudential perspectives on the relationship between law and conflict resolution, with an emphasis on the judicial role.

MICHAL ALBERSTEIN, SJD (Harvard University), is Dean of the Faculty of Law at Bar-Ilan University, Israel. A renowned expert in conflict resolution, she has received numerous academic honors and authored several books. This book's findings were made possible by a prestigious five-year grant she received from the European Research Council.

NOFIT AMIR, PhD, is a lawyer, mediator, and researcher in comparative law. Her research examines the evolving role of judges through a comparative lens, focusing on judges in different places and time periods.

VANISHING LEGAL JUSTICE

The Changing Role of Judges in an Era of Settlements and Plea Bargains

MICHAL ALBERSTEIN
Bar-Ilan University
NOFIT AMIR
Bar-Ilan University

CAMBRIDGE
UNIVERSITY PRESS

CAMBRIDGE
UNIVERSITY PRESS

Shaftesbury Road, Cambridge CB2 8EA, United Kingdom

One Liberty Plaza, 20th Floor, New York, NY 10006, USA

477 Williamstown Road, Port Melbourne, VIC 3207, Australia

314–321, 3rd Floor, Plot 3, Splendor Forum, Jasola District Centre, New Delhi – 110025, India

103 Penang Road, #05-06/07, Visioncrest Commercial, Singapore 238467

Cambridge University Press is part of Cambridge University Press & Assessment, a department of the University of Cambridge.

We share the University's mission to contribute to society through the pursuit of education, learning and research at the highest international levels of excellence.

www.cambridge.org
Information on this title: www.cambridge.org/9781316517994

DOI: 10.1017/9781009049313

When citing this work, please include a reference to the DOI 10.1017/9781009049313

First published 2025

A catalogue record for this publication is available from the British Library

A Cataloging-in-Publication data record for this book is available from the Library of Congress

ISBN 978-1-316-51799-4 Hardback

This book is dedicated to our children:
Dor, Shir, and Ron-Dov Alberstein-Davidovitch
Hila, Maya, and Tamar Amir

CONTENTS

PREFACE

This book is part of a long journey to study the transformation of legal institutions across legal cultures. The shift in emphasis from trial to consensual resolutions – a phenomenon known as "the vanishing trial" – raises many questions regarding the role of judges and legal systems as a whole. We were fortunate to receive European Research Council (ERC) grant to look into these questions, and specifically to comparatively study the changing role of judges in an age of vanishing trials. The five-year research project included a variety of methods – from "on the ground" courtroom observations to statistical analyses as well as comparative and theoretical work. It enabled us to gather a community of dedicated scholars, judges, practitioners, and students who participated in seminars, conducted interviews and observations, wrote academic papers, and engaged in conversations on the new roles of judges and the philosophy of promoting settlement in the shadow of authority. This book provides a panoramic yet short overview of our research findings and offers a glimpse into rich data and scholarship that reveal, overall, the transformed essence of legal justice today, as well as the decline of traditional adjudication in favor of abbreviated proceedings and consent-based dispositions.

We thank the ERC for supporting this research. Deep thanks also go to our colleagues and friends who formed our research community and team: Michal Roness, Dr. Nourit Zimerman, Dr. Ayelet Sela, Dr. Hadas Cohen, Dr. Dana Rosen, Dr. Beatrice Coscas-Wiliiams, Dr. Yosef Zohar, Adv. Ronit Cohen, Adv. and mediator Sari Luz-Kanner, Dr. Amos Gabrieli, and Adv. Gideon Fisher. We thank our Italian partner Prof. Paula Lucarelli together with her colleague Dr. Laura Ristori. We thank Dr. Diana Richards from the United Kingdom. We thank the many students and judges who took part in this journey. Last but definitely not least, we thank our spouses, Nadav Davidovitch and Gideon Amir, for their support and inspiration, and dedicate this book to our children in hope for new horizons of legal justice.

As heated debates take place regarding the power structure of democracies and the role of the Supreme Court within them, no one has taken notice of the fact that lower courts – the courts called upon by individuals to salve wounds and create peace and security in society – are undergoing dramatic change. We believe that lower courts are the foundation for legal justice, and that a full understanding of their transformation is essential to capture the role of the Supreme Court as well.

As the dynamic nature of legal systems unfolds in this book, one finds that the judges of today are neither the judges of yesterday nor the judges of tomorrow. This book shines a cross-cultural light on the transformation of their roles and uncovers how this transformation is altering legal systems as a whole.

TABLE OF CASES

European Cases

Apicella v. Italy, no. 64890/01, 2006.
A.P. v. Italy, no. 35265/97, 1999.
Bottazzi v. Italy, no. 34884/97, 1999.
Di Mauro v. Italy, no. 34256/96, 1999.
Ferrari v. Italy, no. 33440/96, 1999.

European Legislation

Article 185 bis CPC. (It.).
Article 249 of the Treaty of the Functioning of the European Union (Treaty of Rome) (1957).
CPR, 2021, part 3.1(m) (Eng.).
CPR, 2021, part 44.13(1) (Eng.).
Legal Decree No. 206/2021 (2021) (It.).
Article 2041 c.c. (It.).
D.Lgs. 4 Marzo 2010, n.28 (It.).

UK Legislation

Criminal Justice Act 2003, Section 144. (UK).
Criminal Procedure Rules (2015), Pre-trial procedure, Rule 3.3. (UK).
Human Rights Act of 1998, art. 6 (Eng.).
Practice Direction 3.16(2) of the Civil Procedure Rules, 2024.
UK Civil Procedure Rules (CPR), 1998.
UK Ministry of Justice, The Practice Direction for Pre-Action Conduct and Protocols, Section 1.8., 2015.

US Cases

Bielski v. Coinbase (N.D. Cal. 2022) https://casetext.com/case/bielski-v-coinbase-inc.
Bowers v. Northern Two Cayes Co. Ltd, 2016 WL 3647339 at pp. 2 (W.D.N.C. Cir. 2016).

Faretta v. California, 422 U.S. 806 (1975).
Johnson v. Dentsply Sirona, Inc., 2017 WL 4295420 (N.D. Okla. 2017).
Neary v. Regents of the Univ. of Cal., 10 Cal. Rptr. 2d 859, 864, 865 (Cal. 1992).
Yahoo!, Inc. v. Microsoft Corp., 983 F.Supp. 2d 310 (S.D.N.Y.2013).

US Legislation

Article 17.1 Federal Rules of Criminal Procedure Committee Notes—2002 Amendment.
Code of Judicial Conduct for U.S. Judges Canon 3(A)(4) (Admin. Office of the Courts 2014).
FED. R. CIV. P. 16 (C)(2)(I) (1993).
Oregon's Uniform Trial Court Rules (UTCR) 2023.

Israeli Cases

CA 5120/16 The State of Israel vs. Credit Lines Israel, Financial Services (2019).
CivA 5860/16 Facebook Inc. v. Ohad Ben Hamu (2018).
CivC 19-08-31612 Linoy Bar Gefen vs. Twitter Inc. (2021).
CSA 1168/02 Falah vs. Civil Service Authority (2008).
HCJ 532/71 Bahmoutzki v. State of Israel (1972).
HCJ 288/89 Cohen v. Oshiyot Insurance Co. Ltd. (1989).
HCJ 4810/15 Interior Ministry vs. ICM Investments (2015).
HCJ 8417/13 John Doe v. State of Israel (2013).
HCJ 1958/98 State of Israel v. John Doe (2002).
RCA 288/89 Ushiyot Insurance Company v. Cohen (1989).
Tel Aviv District Court, 65143-12-15 Alias v. Verint Systems Ltd. (2016).

Israeli Legislation

Israel Civil Procedure Rules 2018.
Israel Civil Procedure Rules 1984.
Israel Courts Act (Consolidated Version) 1984.
Israel Courts Regulations (Mediation), 1993. Revised 2019.

Introduction

The roles of judges have changed dramatically in recent decades. To date, in many legal systems, most cases settle or end through plea bargaining, in a phenomenon that has been called "the vanishing trial."[1] The greater part of judges' time is spent on managing cases and encouraging parties to reach consensual solutions.

True to its name, the vanishing trial phenomenon encompasses nearly all civil and criminal cases. In the United States, only 1 percent of filed civil cases reach trial, and only 2 percent of criminal cases go through a full trial. In England, more than half of all civil courts have been shut down in the past two decades, and only a small minority of cases are decided through trial. This phenomenon – which has hardly been researched outside the United States – is sweeping across the globe and is not limited to common law systems. The mode of change differs, but the effect is similar – a significant drop in the rate of trial that is accompanied by hardly any public notice. It is a reverse sleight of hand: In many places, trial has nearly vanished but is still perceived by onlookers to take center stage.

What is the role of judges, lawyers, and legal systems in general when only a negligible number of civil and criminal cases are decided by a judge? What are the underlying goals and principles of justice systems? How do legal cultures grapple with the contradiction, at times, between settlement and their founding principles? Has the emphasis on settlement led to a consensual spirit of dispute resolution? Finally, how does this changed context affect the end user, and especially the common litigant not as well versed as repeat players in the dynamic changes that legal systems are undergoing?

These questions led to a five-year research project commissioned by the European Research Council, whose findings are described in this

[1] Marc Galanter, *The Vanishing Trial: An Examination of Trials and Related Matters in Federal and State Courts*, 1 J. EMPIR. LEG. STUD. 459 (2004).

book. The research was conducted in three legal systems – England and Wales, Israel, and Italy – and addressed both the civil and the criminal setting of settlements. The overarching goal of the project was to understand the role of judges and courts in promoting settlement. The US legal system, from whence the overriding preference for settlement was exported to other countries (as we show in this book), was often the point of comparison for our findings and was also a part of this study.

To understand what judges do in an era of vanishing trials, we examined regulation, interviewed judges and lawyers, observed hundreds of pretrial hearings, and analyzed court dockets. We found a host of recurring judicial practices such as direct facilitation of negotiation between the parties, using costs and procedure to promote settlement, prediction, quasi-arbitration, negative portrayal of trial, and narrow mediation-like techniques. We also found correlations between the type of judicial intervention and case trajectories.

By comparing the changing roles of judges in different legal systems, this book conceptualizes the main challenges facing legal systems and uncovers the gaps between (1) the traditional judicial role and its present form, (2) law in the books and law in action, and (3) the goals of conflict resolution and their actual attainment. Moreover, it proposes possible ways forward at a critical point in time, when the meaning of the judicial role has been destabilized and not yet reformulated – and technology, which aims to automate legal processes, is poised to fill this vacuum.

In Part I of the book, we comparatively describe the transformation of legal systems through vanishing trials and the development of multi-door legal systems that resulted from a variety of abbreviated procedures. We describe and analyze the regulatory framework in which judges operate to promote settlement and repeated court reforms aiming to incentivize judges' behavior and increase settlement rates across the research countries. We explore new melds of adversarial-inquisitorial justice that have developed during this transformation, and the resultant blurring of lines between adversarial and inquisitorial legal cultures. As a result, we offer a more contemporary and relevant way to classify legal systems and track their transformation.

In Part II, we uncover the gap between judicial conflict resolution (JCR) in books and in action, since some activities that are allowed judges by law are not actually exercised, and the implementation of norms differs across cultures and individual judges. To reach our findings, we had to surmount a data challenge: Courts were generally not cooperative in providing information. Gleaning data regarding the mode of disposition of cases and the milestones leading to the disposition of the case is extremely difficult. We describe the lean and unforthcoming narrative of courts and explain the multi-methods approach taken in the study to deal with this challenge, uncovering actual judicial settlement practices through (1) an analysis of court dockets with regard to the distribution and relationship between case types, legal procedure, and modes of disposition; (2) observation of hundreds of pretrial hearings and systematical description of their activities in the courtroom; and (3) the uncovering of judges' and lawyers' narratives through interviews and inviting them to seminars. The cross-boundary narratives of judges and lawyers about their roles in relation to settlement are pools of data from which we gained deep insights into different perspectives on the judicial role. We integrated our findings, which included a host of recurring judicial practices, variations between what is written in regulation and actual practice, as well as the links between the multiple methods and the reflections they offer upon each other to create a multifaceted image of the judicial role.

The third and final part of the book is both theoretical and prescriptive in nature, combining research findings into theoretical insights and practical recommendations on the future of court systems and the judicial role. *Theoretically*, we develop a jurisprudence of judicial conflict resolution and a current conceptualization of the role of judges. Judicial activities may be conceptualized along the lines of generic modes of conflict resolution such as negotiation, mediation, arbitration, and restorative justice, as well as other non-adversarial practices. In addition, judicial discretion in court settlement hearings may entail legal as well as conflict considerations and requires new guidelines. The combination of judicial authority and mediation – often perceived as a contradiction in terms – is explored. In addition, we explore a nascent form of mediation – authoritative mediation – which shows promise and poses ethical questions as a new form of law. *Prescriptively,* we suggest practical steps to the creation of meaningful judicial roles in an age of consensual resolutions, and discuss contemporary visions for online processing of resolution of complaints, including artificial intelligence, and the questions they raise regarding law and the judicial role.

After describing the transformation of legal systems and the insights gained into the diverging possibilities the future holds, we show that legal systems have reached a critical conjuncture. The choices policymakers make at this critical point in time will define the meaning of legal justice for years to come.

PART I

Vanishing Trials, Transformed Legal Systems

1

Judicial Role in Transition

1.1 Rise of the Settlement Judge in the United States

Settlement has always been the end result of some disputes, yet until recent decades it was not officially incentivized by legal systems. In the early twentieth century, the pretrial conference was introduced in the USA as a forum to prepare cases for trial. The idea was that before the presentation of evidence, a judge could make sure all requirements were met and clarify the main issues to make trial more efficient. With time, the pretrial became a forum for judicial settlement practices.

In 1983, the judicial settlement role was formally introduced into legislation after decades of practice.[1] Rule 16 (Pretrial Conferences; Scheduling; Management) of the Federal Rules of Civil Procedure was amended to specifically include the discussion of settlement possibilities during pretrial conferences. Moreover, Rule 16 lists settlement of the case as a purpose for calling a conference: "In any action, the court may in its discretion direct the attorneys for the parties. . .to appear before it for a conference or conferences before trial for such purposes as. . . (5) facilitating the settlement of case."

In recent decades, the pretrial has become the main court setting for the discussion of cases in the USA, largely displacing trial.[2] By the time the vanishing trial phenomenon was observed and commented upon, the rate of trial in the USA was 1.8 percent of filed cases.[3] In his 2004 landmark article, Marc Galanter documented a general decline of adjudicated cases from the early twentieth century, and a more precipitous decline in the 1980s and 1990s. In 2019, the civil trial rate was below

[1] Cheryl L. Roberto, *Limits of Judicial Authority in Pretrial Settlement under Rule 16 of the Federal Rules of Civil Procedure*, 2 OHIO ST. J. DISP. RESOL. 311 (1987).

[2] Marc Galanter, *The Vanishing Trial: An Examination of Trials and Related Matters in Federal and State Courts*, 1 J. EMPIR. LEG. STUD. 459 (2004); Edson R. Sunderland, *Theory and Practice of Pre-Trial Procedure*, 36 MICH. L. REV. 215(1937).

[3] Galanter, *supra* note 2.

1 percent.[4] The criminal trial rate is less than 2 percent due to parallel trends in the criminal legal system that have put plea bargaining at the forefront of prosecutors' efforts. Settlement has become the modal legal outcome.[5]

1.1.1 Why Settlement?

The precipitous decline in trial that Galanter commented upon is often attributed to trends taking place in the 1970s. At that time, the US legal system was searching for ways to stem high caseloads due to a "litigation explosion."[6] Concurrently, the Critical Legal Studies movement, which viewed adjudication as inextricably tied with politics and underlying biases, was beginning to gain acceptance.[7] In addition, the Alternative Dispute Resolution (ADR) movement was offering an alternative view of justice, emphasizing the need for broader, consensual resolutions to conflict. Thus, efficiency concerns merged with critical and alternative views of the judicial process to deflect cases from adjudication.

That, at least, is the common explanation. Some have proposed that the "litigation explosion" of the 1970s was, in fact, not an explosion at all,[8] and that one had to look elsewhere to explain the falling rate of adjudication – namely, to the judges themselves, who had lost faith in their own profession.[9] As one judge put it, "We should at least consider the idea that judges, told often enough that their decisionmaking is crucially informed by their politics, will begin to believe what they hear

4 U.S. Courts Judicial Business Report, Table C-4 (2019). https://www.uscourts.gov/judicial-business-2019-tables [https://perma.cc/L8FJ-4L4C].

5 Theodore Eisenberg & Charlotte Lanvers, *What Is the Settlement Rate and Why Should We Care*, 6 J. EMPIRICAL LEGAL STUD. 111, 112 (2009) (citing settlement as the "modal civil outcome").

6 Austin Sarat, *The Litigation Explosion, Access to Justice, and Court Reform: Examining the Critical Assumptions*, 37 RUTGERS L. REV. 319 (1985).

7 For background on the Critical Legal Studies (CLS) movement, which emerged during the 1970s, see MARK KELMAN, A GUIDE TO CRITICAL LEGAL STUDIES (1987).

8 Sarat, *supra* note 6.

9 Marc Galanter, *A World Without Trials*, J. DISP. RESOL. 7, 10 (2006) 16–17 (noting "the ascendance of a judicial ideology that commends intensive judicial case management and active promotion of settlements, which are defined as a superior result. The primary role of courts, in this emerging view, is less enunciating and enforcing public norms and more facilitating the resolution of disputes. Elements of this perspective had been around for decades, but in the 1970s it was embraced by administrators in the federal judiciary and soon became the dominant view"; the primary force behind this change of vision, in his opinion, consists of corporate and government repeat players that seek to evade accountability).

and to respond accordingly."[10] According to one hypothesis, criticism of the judicial role, which began long before the 1970s,[11] may in itself have been enough to persuade judges that settlement was the better outcome, to be promoted and sought in the courtroom.[12]

The tactics pretrial judges[13] use to encourage parties to reach settlement in civil justice are varied – from leveraging procedure and time schedule to negotiating the case themselves.[14] With the consent of the parties, judges may meet with the parties separately in their chambers, taking offers from one party to another until reaching an agreed-upon offer.[15] One study, based on interviews and surveys of lawyers and judges, documented more than 70 judicial settlement practices.[16]

In criminal justice, plea bargaining constitutes the most common form of case disposition in the USA. In 2018, only 2 percent of federal criminal cases went to trial, and the percentages for most state courts were comparable.[17] The merits of plea bargaining lie in clearing high

[10] Harry T. Edwards, *The Judicial Function and the Elusive Goal of Principled Decisionmaking*, 1991 WIS. L. REV. 837, 855 (1991).

[11] The view of the judicial function as the deciding of cases according to their legal merit has long come under intensive scrutiny, with legal realism making its debut in the nineteenth century in Europe and the USA. G. Edward White, *From Sociological Jurisprudence to Realism: Jurisprudence and Social Change in Early Twentieth-Century America*, 58 VA. L. REV. 999 (1972); Heikki Pihlajamaki, *Against Metaphysics in Law: The Historical Background of American and Scandinavian Legal Realism Compared*, 52 AM. J. COMP. L. 469 (2004).

[12] Galanter, *supra* note 2.

[13] The term "pretrial judges" here includes federal judges, state judges, and magistrates.

[14] For a description of judicial settlement practices and the questions they raise, *see* Ellen E. Deason, *Beyond Managerial Judges: Appropriate Roles in Settlement*, 78 OHIO ST. L.J. 73 (2017); William P. Lynch, *Why Settle for Less: Improving Settlement Conferences in Federal Court*, 94 WASH. L. REV. 1233 (2019); Marc Galanter, *A Settlement Judge, Not a Trial Judge: Judicial Mediation in the United States*, 12 J.L. & SOC'Y 1 (1985); Nancy A. Welsh, *Magistrate Judges, Settlement, and Procedural Justice*, 16 NEV. L.J. 983 (2016).

[15] The US Code of Judicial Conduct allows judges to engage in *ex parte* communications with parties when discussing settlement, with the consent of the parties; CODE OF JUDICIAL CONDUCT FOR U.S. JUDGES CANON 3(A)(4) (ADMIN. OFFICE OF THE COURTS 2014).

[16] James A. Wall, Dale E. Rude & Lawrence F. Schiller, *Judicial Participation in Settlement*, 1984 MO. J. DISP. RESOL. 25 (1984). *See also* John C. Cratsley, *Judicial Ethics and Judicial Settlement Practices: Time for Two Strangers to Meet*, 21 OHIO ST. J. DISP. RESOL. 569 (2006).

[17] For federal court figures, *see* UNITED STATES COURTS, U.S. DISTRICT COURTS – JUDICIAL BUSINESS (2018). For state court figures, *see* NICOLE WATERS, KATHRYN GENTHON, SARAH GIBSON & DIANE ROBINSON, COURT STATISTICS PROJECT DATAVIEWER (COURT STATISTICS PROJECT, 2019). *Cf.* an earlier report, U.S. DEPARTMENT OF JUSTICE, BUREAU OF JUSTICE ASSISTANCE, PLEA AND CHARGE

caseloads, though some studies have found that actual caseloads do not impact the number of pleas. Reducing the number of pleas even by a small fraction, it is believed, would "crash the system."[18]

State judges, other than in a handful of states that prohibit such judicial practice, can actively partake in the plea bargaining process between the prosecutor and defendant, making the pretrial or arraignment hearing a central forum for disposing of criminal cases; federal judges are prohibited from doing so, though some attempts have been made to change legislation in this regard.[19]

Due to the emphasis on settlement in both civil and criminal justice, the judicial role has become more managerial, overseeing the case if needed until the parties decide on the outcome themselves, usually in the pretrial phase.[20] Though not all pretrial judges subscribe to the role of the settlement or managerial judge, this mainstream phenomenon has

BARGAINING RESEARCH SUMMARY (2011), where a plea bargain rate of 90–95% was estimated. *See also* Galanter, *supra* note 9 at 10 ("From 1976 to 2002, the overall rate of criminal trials in courts of general jurisdiction in the 22 states for which data is available dropped from 8.5 percent of dispositions to 3.3 percent. The pattern of attrition resembles those in the federal courts, where criminal trials fell from 15.2 percent to 4.7 percent of dispositions in those years.")

18 RAM SUBRAMANIAN, LÉON DIGARD, I. I. MELVIN WASHINGTON & STEPHANIE SORAGE, IN THE SHADOWS: A REVIEW OF THE RESEARCH ON PLEA BARGAINING, VERA INSTITUTE OF JUSTICE, 35–38 (2020) https://www.vera.org/downloads/publications/in-the-shadows-pleabargaining.pdf.

19 Nancy J. King & Ronald F. Wright, *The Invisible Revolution in Plea Bargaining: Managerial Judging and Judicial Participation in Negotiations*, 95 TEX. L. REV. 325, 331–34 (2016). The criminal pretrial was set in Article 17.1 of the US Federal Rules of Criminal Procedure in the 1960s. According to Article 17.1 of Federal Rules of Criminal Procedure Committee Notes – 2002 Amendment, "On its own, or on a party's motion, the court may hold one or more pretrial conferences to promote a fair and expeditious trial. When a conference ends, the court must prepare and file a memorandum of any matters agreed to during the conference. The government may not use any statement made during the conference by the defendant or the defendant's attorney unless it is in writing and is signed by the defendant and the defendant's attorney." In problem-solving courts, which are relevant usually for minor offenses, the judge acts as a team manager with a host of specialists (e.g., social workers). This rare alternative, which is part of the plea system, as it can be accessed only by defendants who have pled guilty, focuses on rehabilitating the defendant. It is difficult to speak of broad judicial conflict resolution in this framework, as the victim, if there is one, is often not a part of the process.

20 Judith Resnik, *Managerial Judges*, 96 HARV. L. REV. 374 (1982); King, *id; Cf.* Albert W. Alschuler, *The Trial Judge's Role in Plea Bargaining, Part I*, 76 COLUM. L. REV. 1059 (1976) (studying judicial involvement in settlement decades ago and finding that open involvement in settlement was not common); *see also* John Paul Ryan & James J. Alfini, *Trial Judges' Participation in Plea Bargaining: An Empirical Perspective*, 13 LAW & SOC'Y REV. 479 (1979).

been gaining ground and intensity in the past decades, raising common dilemmas related to undue pressure in promoting settlement[21] and the appropriateness of the pretrial judge continuing to preside over the case in trial (where this is permitted). In criminal cases, the pretrial judge usually will not preside over the case, but this can happen in small localities.[22] The active stance of the pretrial judge has been reminiscent of some of the inquisitorial judges in continental legal systems, and scholars have interpreted it as a divergence from adversarialism.[23] The pros and cons of the settlement judge have been widely debated.[24]

1.1.2 *A Similar Fate: Alternative Dispute Resolution*

The term "mediation," which is the most well-known ADR process, may elicit expectations of a process that addresses the needs of litigants through dialogue. Unfortunately, ADR in major common law countries has generally gone through a similar process of falling from ideals to a bargaining reality. Much like the court system that has frequently adopted and promoted it, ADR often places efficiency concerns above its core values, such as face-to-face dialogue between the parties, which, with the popularity of caucusing, is quite rare.[25]

[21] Cratsley, *supra* note 16. Daisy Hurst Floyd, *Can the Judge Do That? The Need for a Clearer Judicial Role in Settlement*, ARIZ. STATE LAW J. 1–38 (1994). King & Wright, *supra* note 19.

[22] King & Wright, *supra* note 19.

[23] *Id.*, Resnik, *supra* note 20. Yet, traditionally, inquisitorial judges actively manage cases to reach the truth rather than to lead the parties to settle. By clarifying the issues to facilitate settlement, judges in (traditionally adversarial) common law systems may do the same.

[24] See, *e.g.*, Owen M. Fiss, *Against Settlement*, 93 YALE L.J. 1073 (1984); Tania Sourdin, *Five Reasons Why Judges Should Conduct Settlement Conferences*, 37 MONASH U. L. REV. 145 (2011). *See also* Cratsley, *supra* note 16; Resnik, *supra* note 20.

[25] Patrick G. Coy & Timothy Hedeen, *A Stage Model of Social Movement Co-optation: Community Mediation in the United States*, 46 SOC. Q. 405, 405 (2005) (noting that "community mediation has become increasingly institutionalized and has undergone various degrees of co-optation in its evolving relationship with the court system."); Nancy A. Welsh, *The Place of Court-Connected Mediation in a Democratic Justice System*, 5 CARDOZO J. CONFLICT RESOL. 117, 136–37 (2004); Tamara Relis, *Conseqeunces of Power*, 12 HARV. NEGOT. L. REV. 445 (2007) (noting that in malpractice mediation, the presence of the physician defendant is the exception rather than the rule); William R. Wood & Masahiro Suzuki, *Four Challenges in the Future of Restorative Justice*, 11(1) VICTIMS & OFFENDERS 149, 154–55 (2016) ("the future of restorative justice as we see it depends significantly on whether a focus on interactions between parties who have caused harm and those who have been harmed remain central to such a definition ... Perhaps the most frequently cited problem is the risk of restorative justice goals and 'best

The promotion of mediation by US and UK legal systems has led to a familiar cascade of co-optation.[26] Institutionalized mediation in England is targeted toward an efficient, speedy resolution of the case – much like adjudication or any other activity of the court.[27] It is often evaluative positional bargaining[28] – with mediators pointing out the weaknesses of each party's legal case – limited in time, and often conducted without dialogue between the parties. Mediators often shuttle between rooms (parties are not seated together) to negotiate a compromise.[29] In addition, parties may enter mediation merely as a necessary step to avoid cost shifting, since parties in the UK who refuse a mediation offer are exposed to cost sanctions.[30]

practice' being co-opted for other institutional or system goals and outcomes"). This is not to say that deeper forms of mediation do not exist at all, but rather they are not the common form. For different, deeper experiences, *see* JOSEPH P. FOLGER ET AL. (EDS.), TRANSFORMATIVE MEDIATION: A SOURCEBOOK – RESOURCES FOR CONFLICT INTERVENTION PRACTITIONERS AND PROGRAMS (2010).

26 Coy & Hedeen, *supra* note 25.; Carrie Menkel Meadow, *When Should I Be in the Middle? I've Looked at Life from Both Sides Now* in HOWARD GADLIN & NANCY A. WELSH (EDS.), EVOLUTION OF A FIELD: PERSONAL HISTORIES IN CONFLICT RESOLUTION, 421, 437 (2020) ("Another concern is the growing practice, in private mediation, for more evaluative, no-joint-session, shuttle-diplomacy forms of mediation. Major litigation, commercial, employment, and divorce mediation have now become professionalized, organized, and institutionalized as well as commercialized, so that in my home town of Los Angeles, the norm is now closer to dispute management by a mediator who shuttles back and forth between the parties, 'selling' solutions or settlements, without any or much quality face-to-face time.").

27 Sue Prince, *"Fine Words Butter No Parsnips": Can the Principle of Open Justice Survive the Introduction of an Online Court?* 38(1) CIV. JUST. Q. 111 (2019).

28 Nadja Alexander, *The Mediation Meta-Model: The Realities of Mediation Practice*, 12(6) ADR BULLETIN 126–31, 126 (2011) (presenting a spectrum of mediation practices, with positional bargaining on the one end, interest-based negotiation in the center, and dialogue-based discourse on the other end: "Interest-based negotiation and positional bargaining are both negotiation discourses and therefore outcome-oriented in nature; by contrast, the focus of dialogue is relational development and perspective sharing, rather than settlement or resolution.").

29 SIMON ROBERTS, A COURT IN THE CITY, 5 (2013); Prince, *supra* note 27.

30 HAZEL GENN, PAUL FENN, MARC MASON, ANDREW LANE, NADIA BECHAI, LAUREN GRAY & DEV VENCAPPA, TWISTING ARMS: COURT REFERRED AND COURT LINKED MEDIATION UNDER JUDICIAL PRESSURE (2007) (stating that demand for the voluntary ADR scheme at Central London increased significantly following the case of *Dunnett v. Railtrack* in 2002, which confirmed the power of the courts to deny a successful party legal costs following an unreasonable refusal to mediate, and that the rush to mediate was mitigated after the *Halsey* judgment in 2004, which offered a nuanced interpretation of "unreasonable." Since then, there have been further conflicting judicial decisions on the matter.).

Thus neither the positivist vision of the judge meting out justice nor the idyllic vision of mediation creating meaningful dialogue and agreement has materialized in the USA or UK. Instead, the most prevalent form of case disposition is often a bargain-like process ending in settlement. This is taken to the most extreme with the rise of "settlement mills"[31] – legal practices that deal with claims of their clients against insurance companies without involvement of courts on a massive scale, often with no involvement of the clients other than the signing of the settlement agreement.[32] In Italy and Israel, the co-optation of mediation in some frameworks is less extreme, and deeper forms of mediation are not rare. However, mediation is underused and disposes of only a small fraction of the cases.

1.1.3 *The Question*

To date, neither the normative values of adjudication nor the fundamental values of ADR (improved communication, relation-building, addressing needs and the broader conflict) prevail. In their stead is a drive for efficiency in both courts and mediation sessions, providing abbreviated justice – at best. Courts in many countries have adopted abbreviated modes of trial to save judicial bench time and mediators have adopted evaluative styles that are reminiscent of the selfsame abbreviated procedures of judges in court.

Judges, in this setting, are expected to manage cases until they settle rather than provide a reasoned decision on the dispute – though, as our research shows, some judges view higher horizons for their role, lending insights to possible new trajectories. As legal systems implement digital systems to cut litigation costs, and technological efforts aim to replace judges with AI, the question of the value and place of the judicial role has reached a critical crossroads.

1.2 Continental Law Countries

The transition to the settlement judge described in the preceding sections is not as accentuated in continental European countries. Continental law judges more commonly decide cases on their merits, as settlement is not

[31] Nora Freeman Engstrom, *Run-of-the-Mill Justice*, 22 GEO. J. LEGAL ETHICS 1485 (2009).
[32] Floyd, *supra* note 21.

as embedded in the legal culture as in common law jurisdictions.[33] Yet in continental law countries, too, judges have been encouraged through relatively recent reforms in civil justice to promote settlement between the parties and refer them to mediation when appropriate.[34] Whether this practice gathers momentum and turns into a full-fledged vanishing trial phenomenon remains to be seen.

The integration of settlement practices into the judicial role in continental law countries has occurred through an extensive web of borrowing – or "transplanting" – concepts from common law countries, especially the USA. Much borrowing occurs between legal systems, as has been widely commented upon in comparative literature: Today systems are often mixed.[35]

In continental Europe, various settlement transplants, as well as the introduction of abbreviated trials, have modified the inquisitorial nature of the judicial role, and shortened it significantly.[36] ADR, which began as an alternative movement in the USA in the 1970s, has been transplanted into most modern legal systems, resulting in both convergences and divergences between them, which put into question how close the legal systems have become. On the other receiving end, the common law judge becomes increasingly inquisitorial: making decisions on production of evidence, interrogating witnesses, and broadening discovery so that the adversarial nature of proceedings is modified and the facts are more easily discerned.[37] Thus, generally speaking, the two legal families have adopted the main backstops to protracted litigation from each other.

[33] *See* Pablo Cortes, *A Comparative Review of Offers to Settle: Would an Emerging Settlement Culture Pave the Way for Their Adoption in Continental Europe?* 32(1) CIV. JUST. Q. 42–67 (2013) (stating that the greater cost efficiency of continental law systems translates into a less pressing need to settle. Common law systems, in which litigation is usually more costly, incentivize litigants to avoid trial due to the large expenses involved in trial.).

[34] Nofit Amir & Michal Alberstein, *From Transplant to Disintegration? A Comparative Study of the Judicial Role,* 37(4) OHIO ST. J. DISP. RESOL. 555 (2022); Paola Lucarelli et al., *Fitting the Forum to the Fuss While Seeking the Truth: Lessons from Judicial Reforms in Italy,* 36 OHIO ST. J. DISP. RESOL. 213 (2020).

[35] Maximo Langer, *From Legal Transplants to Legal Translations: The Globalization of Plea Bargaining and the Americanization Thesis in Criminal Procedure,* 45 HARV. INT'L L.J. 1 (2004); Riccardo Montana, *Procedural Tradition in the Italian Criminal Justice System: The Semi-adversarial Reform in 1989 and the Inquisitorial Cultural Resistance to Adversarial Principles,* 20(4) INTNL. J. EVIDENCE & PROOF 289 (2016).

[36] Giulio Illuminati, *The Frustrated Turn to Adversarial Procedure in Italy (Italian Criminal Procedure Code of 1988)* WASH. UNIV. GLOBAL STUD. L. REV. 4 (2005).

[37] Resnik, *supra* note 20.

In the legal systems that we studied, legislative changes have been made to allow judges not only to refer cases to ADR but also to use ADR tools themselves to help parties resolve their cases. Though these tools could be viewed as broadening the judicial role, they are in fact being used in very narrow ways with the aim of limiting and sequestering the judicial role to a different extent in each legal system. By siphoning disputes out of the legal system (through judicial referral to dispute resolution or through pre-action requirements such as mandatory mediation), legal systems are undergoing different transformations. We show that these transformations could be part of a common linear trend toward disintegration of the judicial role.

Chapter 2 will show three different transformations of legal systems through settlement promotion – in fact, three different melds of adversarial and inquisitorial justice. Though the three legal systems transplanted the same ideas, implementation at this time varies greatly, and, in each, the judicial role is positioned differently to accommodate a settlement culture. In Italy, where settlement has begun to make its mark only in the past decade or so, the judicial role is still central. In Israel, settlement reforms have resulted in an emphasis on the pretrial stage, narrowing the judges' role. In England and Wales, the judicial role has become marginal in dealing with disputes, as cases are prevented from reaching court through a variety of means. Whether the judicial role will gradually disintegrate in the three jurisdictions is a question that is probed in the last section of Chapter 2.

2

The Comparative Landscape

2.1 Italy: Dawn of a Judicial Settlement Culture

2.1.1 Lightening the Load

The preferred outcome for cases in Italy has until recently been considered a judicial verdict.[1] This is changing with reforms introduced mainly since 2010 to reduce the colossal backlog of cases[2]: In 2009, Italy had nearly six million civil cases pending.[3] The legal system was slow, and every year the state had to disburse millions of euros to citizens as compensation for violation of L. 89/2001 (so called "Legge Pinto"), which provides for a reasonable duration of trial. The European Court of

[1] Simona Grossi, *A Comparative Analysis between Italian Civil Proceedings and American Civil Proceedings before Federal Courts*, 20 IND. INT'L & COMP. L. REV. 213, 280: 230 (2010) (noting that "settlement procedure still remains a 'dead' instrument that is rarely used by the parties . . . Both the lack of a settlement culture and the lack of any real duty of the judge to try to settle the case between the parties, at the beginning or throughout the proceedings, make the Italian proceedings inefficient"); *see also* Pablo Cortes, *A Comparative Review of Offers to Settle: Would an Emerging Settlement Culture Pave the Way for Their Adoption in Continental Europe?* 32 CIV. JUST. Q. 42 (2013) (stating that most continental law countries have not incorporated settlement into court procedures and citing lower litigation costs on the continent as an impetus for litigation).

[2] Elisabetta Silvestri, *ADR Italian style: Panacea or Anathema?*, in C. H. VAN RHEE ET AL., CIVIL JUSTICE BETWEEN EFFICIENCY AND QUALITY: FROM IUS COMMUNE TO THE CEPE, (2008), 249, 250 ("In a country where political parties disagree virtually on everything, there was an extraordinary convergence on the usefulness of ADR mechanisms to relieve the courts' caseloads. With a view to reaching this goal, the focus of the political debate centered on how to develop effective out-of-court ADR procedures and encourage their use. Not much thought was really given to the advantages or to the disadvantages of ADR methods; their allure as a cheap and relatively easy way out of the crisis affecting adjudication was too tempting.")

[3] Jacqueline M. Nolan-Haley, *Is Europe Headed Down the Primrose Path with Mandatory Mediation,* 37 J. INT'L L. COM. REG 981, 983 (2011); Paola Lucarelli, *Il Paradosso dell'Obbligatorietà del Tentativo fra Limiti e Virtù della Scelta Normativa, in* MEDIAZIONE DEI CONFLITTI. UNA SCELTA CONDIVISA (Paola Lucarelli, ed., 2019).

Justice condemned Italy several times for violating principles of due process due to the length of trials.[4]

The external pressure and backlog led to the introduction of ADR-based reforms. Yet, before describing these changes, some background on the ADR movement in Europe is needed.

ADR gained a foothold in Europe in the late 1980s, around a decade after the 1976 Pound Conference promoting ADR in the United States, and close in time to the spread of ADR to Australia, Canada, and New Zealand.[5] The EU published a Mediation Directive in 2008 following a series of decisions encouraging mediation to deal with backlog and simplify transnational disputes.[6] The goals of EU directives are binding, though the means of realizing them are left to the states.[7]

Going even further than the EU Mediation Directive in the effort to curb its case backlog, Italy legislated a Mediation Directive in 2010, *mandating* mediation for certain types of conflict before filing a case in court. Due to public uproar, and consternation on the part of Italy's Bar Association, the directive was challenged in the Court of Cassations (Italy's High Court) and consequently struck down.[8] A revised

[4] For instance, in 2004, the court found in the case of *Apicella v. Italy* that the compensation provided by Italy for undue length of proceedings was "derisory." In 1999, the Grand Chamber of the Court found in the cases of *Ferrari, A.P., Di Mauro and Bottazi v. Italy* that the systemic delays in the Italian judicial system constituted an administrative practice that was incompatible with the Convention.

[5] NADJA MARIE ALEXANDER, INTERNATIONAL AND COMPARATIVE MEDIATION: LEGAL PERSPECTIVES, 42 (2009).

[6] Directive 2008/52/EC, of the European Parliament and of the Council of 21 May 2008 on Certain Aspects of Mediation in Civil and Commercial Matters, 1 2, 2008 O.J. (L 136). *See* Nolan-Haley, *supra* note 3 at 982–83 ("Over the last two decades, the European Union (EU) has intentionally promoted mediation and other forms of ADR to advance access to justice goals, and it has done so with a high degree of intensity. The European Union has funded mediation and ADR projects in both commercial and public justice areas; issued several consultation papers, ADR directives, and resolutions; conducted public consultations on the use of ADR and online dispute resolution (ODR); and promulgated a code of conduct for mediators.").

[7] Article 249 of the Treaty of Rome, which authorizes the issuance of directives, states that "[a] Directive shall be binding, as to the result to be achieved, upon each Member State to which it is addressed, but shall leave to the national authorities the choice of form and methods." Nolan-Haley, *supra* note 3 at 991–92 ("Directives are one of the most common types of legislative acts in the European Union. They are issued, in part, to harmonize the entrance of new Member States into the Union.")

[8] Giovanni Matteucci, *Mandatory Mediation, the Italian Experience*, REVISTA ELETRÔNICA DE DIREITO PROCESSUAL 16, 189–210:206 (2015) ("Italian judges . . . considered [and still consider] mediation as the 'Child of a Lesser God'").

2013 Mediation Directive narrowed the types of cases for which mediation was mandatory (around 10% of civil cases), declared that only one introductory meeting was compulsory, ensured that lawyers must be present during the mediation attempt, and shortened the time limit on the mediation attempt from four months to three.

Reforms pertaining to judicial function were introduced through the Mediation Directive and changes to the Civil Procedure Code (CPC): Judges, who adjudicated the large majority of cases (in contrast to their counterparts in common law systems), were given specific settlement-promoting authorities. They could demand that parties, rather than just their legal representatives, appear for a *conciliation hearing* (Article 183*bis* CPC) – civil hearings in the Florence first-instance court were usually attended by lawyers, without the parties – during which the judge could encourage conciliation between the parties.[9] At any point during legal proceedings, until the end of the evidentiary phase, judges could offer a *conciliation proposal* (which the sides could reject, as stated in Article 183 CPC). In addition, they could demand that the parties attempt mediation, issuing a *mediation order* according to the Mediation Directive; or send them to a *court-appointed technical expert*, who, in addition to having the authority to give an expert opinion on an issue arising in the case, could conciliate between the parties (Article 696 CPC).

While these highly specific authorities differ from the usually expansive authority to settle cases given to US judges throughout their long history of settling cases, as set out in the general settlement authority given to judges in Rule 16 and practiced even earlier,[10] they represent a departure from the generally accepted adjudicative role of judges in Italy. Judges in Italy had the authority to conciliate cases beforehand, yet it was rarely used. Early judicial assessment of the case prior to these new articles was even grounds for recusal, and thus the revised CPC specifically stated that judges would not be recused for such practice.[11]

[9] Formerly, for decades, legislation formally required the judge to try to conciliate the parties, yet this legislation was an abject failure and was not implemented: See explanation to Art. 183 CPC at www.brocardi.it/codice-di-procedura-civile/libro-secondo/titolo-i/capo-ii/sezione-ii/art183.html?q=183+cpc&area=codici.

[10] For background and wording of Rule 16, see Cheryl L. Roberto, *Limits of Judicial Authority in Pretrial Settlement under Rule 16 of the Federal Rules of Civil Procedure*, 2 OHIO ST. J. DISP. RESOL. 311 (1987).

[11] Article 185 *bis* CPC states: “The conciliation proposal cannot constitute grounds for recusal or abstention of the judge.”

The specificity of the judicial authorities provided in the reform reflect a serious effort by legislators to change the judicial culture. Yet the question remained: Would judges in fact implement these changes, transplants from US legal culture, which were placed at their discretion?

2.1.2 *From Black-Letter Transplant to Practice*

Setting out to the Florence first-instance court (*tribunale*) to see how these changes were implemented, if at all, researchers of this study performed fifty-five court observations, eight interviews with judges, and a statistical analysis of court dockets. The Florence Court is situated in a main metropolitan area, and was one of a few courts in Italy[12] that introduced a program to implement the reforms for judicial referral to mediation. The court collaborated with Florence University to facilitate the diagnosis of cases for court-referred mediation, and this model is currently being replicated in other courts as well. The Florence court thus provides a window to study ways in which Italian judges may combine their traditional adjudicative role with the new settlement-promoting authorities that seemed to scholars to be foreign to the legal culture.

The research at the Florence Court was both qualitative and quantitative. Courtroom observations and interviews of judges were conducted during October–December 2018. We received special permission to conduct trial observations, and thus observed fifty-five civil trials. (Trials are conducted in judges' chambers and are not open to the public.) We also conducted interviews with eight (out of eighty-five) judges. The research did not include the "justices of the peace" (parallel to small claims courts). The quantitative analysis of cases was conducted by examining a random sample of case documents from 2013 to 2016.

We found that judges issued mediation "orders" primarily when the legal representatives gave their consent, unless the parties had not fulfilled their obligation by law to first attempt mediation in certain types of cases. The relatively informal setting fit well with this stance – hearings in civil matters are mostly private, with the judge sitting behind a desk in her office with the two lawyers sitting on the other side of the desk, and relations between judges and lawyers were for the most part collegial (most often parties were not present).

For instance, in a case regarding corporate responsibility, the lawyers of four parties sought to conciliate with the help of a judicial conciliation

[12] Such as courts in Milan, Rome, and Bari.

proposal. The judge stated his preference for mediation and said that the fact that another proceeding between the parties was taking place in another court strengthened his position. However, he deferred his decision to consider the lawyers' requests, explaining to the observer after they had exited that the lawyers' willingness to mediate was important and decisive for the mediation's success.

In another case, which involved a former romantic relationship that had also been a working relationship, the judge deferred to the lawyers' opinion while expressing her opinion regarding mediation. The claimant was suing for payment for her work while the defendant argued that they had not signed a proper contract and thus was willing to grant only half of the sum. All three present (the judge and lawyers) were women.

JUDGE:	Why have you not conciliated this case yet? I have given you all the time... It is impossible that you cannot find an agreement here, is it perhaps a matter of your obstinant attorneys? [The lawyers seemed annoyed by the judge's words – this indeed deviated from the usually observed collegial stance. They moved forward on their chairs and started speaking at the same time.]
CLAIMANT'S LAWYER:	It is not easy to communicate with the other side, your honor... However, we still believe that our legal position is strong, thus we would appreciate more cooperation from the defandant.
DEFENDANT'S LAWYER:	It is not the time to argue about our legal positions, colleague. The judge has asked us to find an agreement, but your client does not want to renounce to any of her claims... [They started arguing between themselves about legal questions. After listening for a few minutes, the judge interrupted the conversation.]
JUDGE:	Stop, attorneys, please. I do not want to listen to these questions right now, as I have reserved them for the next stage of the trial. Instead, I would like to know if you sincerely believe that the sides might reach an agreement. Is there anything I can do to help you? Because I thought that, perhaps, a mediation order would be appropriate in this case... It would allow the sides to communicate again. What do you say in this regard?
DEFENDANT'S LAWYER:	Your honor, I would suggest continuing with the negotiation ... There is a strong conflict between the sides, and I am afraid that productive communication between them will take much time.

CLAIMANT'S LAWYER: On behalf of my client, I say that I would prefer to end these months of negotiation with a satisfying agreement, rather than start a new procedure now. Thus, my request is to fix another hearing in two months. I am sure that our clients will be more willing to cooperate.

DEFENDANT'S LAWYER: I support the claimant attorney's request, your honor. [The judge seems weary. While she looks for a time to fix another hearing, she sighs noisily.]

JUDGE: I will give you a very last deferment and, please, do not disappoint me.

The judicial diagnosis of cases for mediation, as in the example presented above, is supported behind the scenes by trained interns, who analyze cases for suitability for mediation and provide recommendations to judges along certain parameters. Judges peruse the files along with the interns' recommendation and choose how to manage the case. By law, judges must specify their reasoning for referring a case to mediation in a mediation order. One judge told us: "Every judge must edit the mediation order written by the researcher . . . We edit it according to what emerges from the hearing." By showing the benefits of mediation in certain cases, this system can create a positive view of mediation when offered to litigants

This practice differs greatly from the practice of judges in some countries where the incentives to settle are great (see *infra* Sections 2.2 and 2.3): Judges may pressure the parties to attempt mediation by emphasizing the *negative aspects* of legal proceedings (expressing legal aversion) rather than the positive aspects of mediation, thus proverbially cutting off the (judicial) branch on which they sit. During the court observations in the Florence Court, however, judges tended to point out to the parties (usually the lawyers) why the cases seemed appropriate for mediation when offering it to them rather than emphasizing the negative aspects of the court system. As one interviewed judge told us, "I always make clear to the parties who are present at the hearing that I am about to order the mediation and that I deem it a useful instrument and the reasons for the mediation." One judge expressed a concern that otherwise the mediation order could be seen as a pretext to clear the table, and indeed, there are probably instances when this occurs.[13] Our observations found that judges in Florence gave specific, grounded

[13] Commission Giustizia II, Resconto Stenografico, Mar. 20, 2021 (Italy governmental commission protocol, in which one of the participants stated that this was the experience of some of the parties reaching court).

reasons for preferring mediation in a certain case and did not coerce the parties to use mediation unless the parties did not conduct mediation in the areas in which it is mandatory.

In the analysis of court documents, we found that, despite initial skepticism regarding judges' cooperation in the implementation of reforms,[14] judges were making use of the tools and encouraging sides to settle in 39.3 percent of the cases reaching them.[15] Cases in which judges used settlement tools were more likely to settle. However, our court observations and interviews with judges uncovered that *even while using these tools, judicial conduct did not deviate much from its traditional nature.* For instance, in line with the inquisitorial origins of the Italian legal system, which place great emphasis on judicial truth-seeking, judges would not issue a conciliation proposal without first determining the liability of each party. Usually this occurred after receiving an expert opinion; in other cases liability was assumed by law (strict liability as determined in certain cases).

The conciliation hearing, to which the judge orders the parties to be present for a conciliation attempt, was hardly used. Actually conciliating a case would require a departure from the diagnosing or adjudicating role – in other words, the sharp separation between the judicial role and mediation. The one case that we observed and others that were reported in an interview demonstrated that judges may have trouble using this tool, even reverting to legal aversion. In the observed case, one judge exerted much pressure on a party, emphasizing costs and time of litigation, until the party agreed to settle.

The judge might also refer the side to a court expert with conciliation authority when technical issues were unclear. This option was usually used as a warning to nudge the lawyers to reach an agreement or attempt mediation, and was actually implemented in 3.5 percent of the cases.[16]

In sum, while a settlement culture has made inroads in a primarily adjudicative culture, the separation between the adjudicative role and mediation was for the most part maintained in the Florence first-instance court. Judicial conciliation proposals took place for the most part after liability was discerned, and were very close to the practice of adjudication

[14] For a review of the social and professional reaction to the reforms, *see* Matteucci, *supra* note 8.

[15] Paola Lucarelli et al., *Fitting the Forum to the Fuss While Seeking the Truth*, 36(2) OHIO ST. J. DISP. RESOL. 213 (2020).

[16] *Id.*

or prediction (until recently, prediction was considered as grounds for recusal[17]). When a mediation attempt seemed appropriate, judges would not try to mediate themselves but rather recommended referral to a mediation agency and, if they received consent, issued a mediation order. The convening of a conciliation meeting – in which the judge would have a conciliating role – was a rare occurrence. Thus, for the most part, the judicial role could be characterized as diagnosing the most appropriate path of the case and providing a recommendation upon this diagnosis[18] while seeking the truth (i.e., legal liability).

Is this the balance that has been struck or just the beginning of a process? Recent legislation has allowed mediation training for judges and emphasized the importance of dialogue in mediation, perhaps taking Italy a step further in promoting a mediation culture. In addition, the case types for which mediation is mandatory have been expanded to include real estate and taxation benefits for parties who mediate their cases have been increased.[19] It seems that Italy may be going through piecemeal change to more strongly incorporate mediation into the judicial role and the legal system in general. However, it may continue to maintain relative separation between mediation and the judicial role – a separation that may, in fact, reinforce a positive perspective on each form of dispute resolution as providing a sound solution depending on the circumstances of the case.

2.2 Israel: High Noon of Judicial Settlement Practices

2.2.1 Efficiency-Based Reforms

Whereas in Florence we found a separation between the role of the judge and the role of the mediator – with judges applying expertise in diagnosing cases to siphon cases to mediation, a conciliation proposal, a conciliation hearing, or a court expert – in the Tel Aviv first-instance ("Ha'Shalom") court we found that the pretrial judge often takes an

17 Grossi, *supra* note 1.

18 Frank E. A. Sander & Stephen B. Goldberg, *Fitting the Forum to the Fuss: A User-Friendly Guide to Selecting an ADR Procedure*, 10 NEGOT. J. 49 (1994).

19 See Gianfranco Gilardi, *Introduction. The Civil Justice Reform: From the Legislative Decree 1662/S/XVIII to the Delegated Law of 26 Novemebr 2021*, 206 Gazettta Ufficiale Della Republica Italiana (Nov. 29, 2021) www.questionegiustizia.it/rivista/articolo/introduzione-dal-ddl-1662-s-xviii-alla-legge-26-novembre-2021-n-206 (accessed Jan. 31, 2022).

active role to settle cases. The transplanted concepts in Israel were not a reaction to extreme backlog as in Italy (though there was some backlog) or a financial crisis as in England and Wales (*infra* Section 2.4). Rather, they were part of a general pursuit of efficiency, in tandem with that of the US legal system, the prestige of which made it the prime exporter of legal constructs worldwide in the twentieth century.[20]

The prime forum for judicial settlement in Israel, as in the United States, is the pretrial (a stage that does not exist in Italy). Pretrial as a unique stage between the filing of a claim and trial has existed in Israel formally since 1963 and has evolved and been modeled along the lines of the US pretrial.[21] The logic behind this stage is that the judge can prepare the case effectively for trial so that it runs smoothly and efficiently by ensuring that all documents have been submitted, clarifying the contended issues that will be explored during trial, and checking whether the claim should be disqualified by law. As in the United States, the large majority of cases reaching pretrial settle at this stage.[22]

The formal basis for judicial settlement activity in the civil sphere in Israel appears in regulation introduced in 1996,[23] specifying that one of the possible goals of pretrial is to probe the possibility of settlement between the parties. The model adopted was influenced by the US legal system, which gave the judge settlement-making authority during pretrial, an authority that was used with growing legitimacy and prevalence since the 1970s and was formally encouraged in 1983 with the modification of Federal Rule 16.[24] Similarly, during the 1990s, following a pointed

[20] Maximo Langer, *From Legal Transplants to Legal Translations: The Globalization of Plea Bargaining and the Americanization Thesis in Criminal Procedure*, 45 HARV. INT'L L.J. 1 (2004); Ugo Mattei, *A Theory of Imperial Law: A Study on U.S. Hegemony and the Latin Resistance*, 10 IND. J. GLOBAL LEGAL STUD. 383 (2003).

[21] *E.g.*, 288/89 *Cohen v. Oshiyot Insurance Co. Ltd.* (43) 434 (1989) (where Supreme Court Justice Barak references several US academic sources to describe the nature of pretrial).

[22] ERC-JCR findings, to be published.

[23] With the amendment of art. 140 of the Israeli Civil Procedure Rules.

[24] *See* Marc Galanter, *A Settlement Judge, not a Trial Judge: Judicial Mediation in the United States*, 12 J.L. & SOC'Y 1,2 (1985) ("The adoption of the Federal Rules of Civil Procedure in 1938 made the pre-trial conference a feature of litigation in the federal courts of the United States. Some proponents viewed the new reformed procedure as a vehicle for judicial arrangement of settlements. The prevailing view among leading spokesmen for the federal judiciary was insistence that the function of the pre-trial conference was to prepare cases for trial; settlement was seen as a desirable 'by-product' of the pre-trial conference. By the 1960s the preparation for trial rhetoric had faded away and there was heightened emphasis on judicial promotion of settlements. By the 1970s whatever reticence remained among federal judges was barely perceptible. There was a forthright

debate that included legal scholars, lawyers, and judges, the amendments to Israel's Civil Procedure Regulations (Articles 140–145) established the broad discretion of judges during pretrial. The Courts Act as amended authorizes the judge to promote settlement: The judge could refer parties to arbitration or mediation (Articles 79b, 79c), and – in a unique move on the part of the Israeli legislator – decide the case during pretrial with the consent of the parties (without the evidentiary phase; Article 79a). Additionally, the obligation to create a full court transcript was waived for the pretrial stage: Judges are permitted to conduct off-the-record discussions with the consent of the parties and thus to include in the transcript only the main issues discussed during the hearing (Israeli Court Order, Rule 68a). In most courts, the pretrial judge is the same judge who decides the case if it continues to trial, thus adding to the weight of the judge's comments during pretrial.

Judges' efficiency in disposing of cases is tracked in an electronic system implemented by the court administration (called *Net Hamishpat*), thus providing an incentive for judges to dispose of cases at the earliest stage possible. Reform to the Civil Procedure Regulations, which was enacted in January 2021, has kept the active nature of the judge during pretrial but has sought to shorten this stage, which in the past could spread over numerous hearings (up to seven in our sample), thus upending the aim of this stage to make proceedings more efficient.[25]

It is interesting to note that while Israel has adopted many aspects of the American pretrial, pretrial judicial case management tools are

and ardent embrace of active participation in settlement negotiations. This was based on a warm endorsement of settlement as preferable to adjudication not only on the ground of administrative convenience but because it produced superior results."). The original Rule 16 contained no mention of settlement. *See* David Shapiro, *Federal Rule 16: A Look at the Theory and Practice of Rulemaking,* 137 U. PA. L. REV. 1969, 1980–81 (1989) (summarizing the 1938 committee's deliberations over Rule 16). *See* Charles E. Clark, *Objectives of Pre-Trial Procedure,* 17 OHIO ST. L.J. 163, 166–67(1956)(warning of potential adverse effects on pretrial of judicial involvement that forced settlements); Judith Resnik, *Changing Practices, Changing Rules: Judicial and Congressional Rulemaking on Civil Juries, Civil Justice, and Civil Judging,* 49 ALA. L. REV. 133, 163–65 (1998) (on the debate over Rule 16 and the assertion that settlement was specifically excluded from Rule 16). In 1983, with a view toward lightening the caseload, settlement was explicitly added as a possible pretrial conference topic. See Robert G. Bone, *To Encourage Settlement: Rule 68, Offers of Judgment, and the History of the Federal Rules of Civil Procedure,* 102 NW. U. L. REV. 1561 (2008).

25 Israel Civil Procedure Rules (2018), which came into effect in 2021.

sometimes described as inquisitorial in both the United States[26] and Israel, as they entail an active judicial stance. As described by the Israeli Supreme Court, "The pretrial judge must take the reins ... the pretrial phase is inquisitorial, in contrast to the other two stages [filing and trial], which are adversarial."[27]

In 2001, fast-track proceedings – modeled on fast-track proceedings in England and Wales following the Woolf Report[28] – were introduced for claims up to a certain sum (at first the sum was set for 50,000 NIS but was updated from time to time and today stands at 75,000 NIS). Rigid time limits are set for filing of documents, proceedings, and the reaching of a verdict. Parties must adhere to wide discovery requirements at the filing stage, one pretrial conference is permitted, and the trial is set to end within one day using written affidavits of witnesses rather than direct examination. Judges have the discretion to change the status of cases from accelerated to regular proceedings, and vice versa, depending on the complexity of the case.

In 2002, institutional case management was also fortified with the establishment of a Case Management Department (MANAT in Hebrew) in the Israeli court system. This department is operated by the secretary of the court and performs a variety of activities, among them classification of cases, directing cases to judges according to their specialties, and directing cases to ADR processes. Today, this role has been accorded to a designated court secretary according to the revised Civil Procedure Regulations.

These two strategies – case management (whether judicial or institutional) and abbreviated proceedings – were introduced to, on the one hand, promote settlement, and on the other, provide accelerated adjudication.

Recently, with the reform to the Civil Procedure Regulations, a preliminary direct negotiation exchange has been made mandatory, and the objective of civil procedure has been modified to include proportionality These changes hearken to English civil procedure reform, as will be described in Section 2.3, and may signify a move from substantive justice

[26] See also Judith Resnik, *Managerial Judges*, 96 HARV. L. REV. 374 (1982) (criticizing the inquisitorial nature of the pretrial). It is important to make a distinction, however, between the goal of active judicial management, which is often settlement, and the traditional goal of inquisitorial judicial intervention: uncovering the truth.

[27] Justice Amit in CA 4810/15 *Interior Ministry vs. ICM Investments*.

[28] Ehud Brosh, *Cutting Corners or Enhancing Efficiency? Simplified Procedures and the Israeli Quest to Speed up Justice*, 8(4) ERASMUS L. REV. 185, 186–87 (2015). For information on the Woolf Report, see *infra* Section C.

to proportionate justice. In addition, after filing, a free pre-mediation meeting to assess the possibility for mediation has been made mandatory for a greater part of the claims.

2.2.2 *Into the Field: The Indelible Mark of Transplants on Judicial Practice*

The settlement-promoting authorities given to judges have resulted in active judicial management of cases and the centrality of the pretrial in disposing of cases. Our observations of pretrial hearings in the Tel Aviv first-instance court (i.e., excluding small claims) uncovered a wide range of judicial practices to encourage settlement.

The judicial practices seemed to have much influence on the parties, especially since the judge presiding over the pretrial is the same judge who presides over the case if it continues to trial. Parties thus know that waiting out the pretrial and going to trial with a different judge is not a possibility. Moreover, parties that do not follow a judge's preference for settlement may worry that the judge may view them in a less than positive light during trial.

The case that follows, which demonstrates some judicial settlement tactics, involved a claim against a shipping company, which had not reported damage to a ship on time, and as a result, the delivered product was not marketable. The claimants had not filed their case immediately.

JUDGE: Enough, close this case. I suggest that you show generosity and reach a compromise. From the nature of things, if this reaches trial, it can go either way, and I suggest you reach an understanding between yourselves. [Turning to a claimant:] Consider this eagerly. Understand, it's in your interest to speak with them. There are many problems here, and the time that has passed damages your case – it will be difficult for you.

CLAIMANTS' LAWYER: I'd like to discuss the case off the protocol because the gap between the sides is not great. We've come here so that your honor will help us come closer. My clients are determined not to go under half of the damages that were caused them, and will not go under 130,000 under any circumstances. The other side proposed 95,000.

JUDGE: And where does this figure come from, 95,000?

DEFENDANT'S LAWYER: We calculated only one type of damage.

JUDGE: I have my own directions of thought as well. Since the other side does not even have a letter from the Health

Ministry, I'm also trying to reach a sum, I was thinking of half-half which is 115,000, but [speaking to the defendant's lawyer] I'd like to help you come closer – would 110,000 work? Or 100,000? How much would your client agree to add [the client was not in the room]?

DEFENDANT'S LAWYER: I was thinking together with the claimants' lawyer of going halfway.

JUDGE: So 110,000 it is then. Let's put that in writing – perhaps that will cause your clients to leave their burrowed stances [dictates the decision in the name of the lawyers as well]. Friends – as you know very well, this case should be closed, don't try to litigate it in court.

As in the above instance and many others, judicial settlement practices may include directly stating an expectation for settlement, portraying the dangers of trial, pointing out the strengths or weaknesses of a case, speaking directly to the party involved, taking the hearing on and off the record to allow free discussion, and splitting the difference. Judges may also ask the lawyers to assess the probability of reaching the desired sum and thus include the risk in the sum to narrow the differences between the parties. In addition, they may predict the outcome of a case. It is rare for the judge to carry out mediation in the original sense – that is, addressing the underlying needs of the parties and creating a dialogue. Since parties to the next cases are present in the courtroom, judges' practices have a carryover effect on other disputes.[29]

In addition, judges make use of their authority to refer sides to ADR (79b and 79c of the Courts Act) and to decide cases by compromise during the pretrial phase with the consent of the parties (79a of the Courts Act).[30] The latter unique quasi-arbitrational tool –

[29] Ayelet Sela, Nourit Zimerman & Michal Alberstein, *Judges as Gatekeepers and the Dismaying Shadow of the Law: Courtroom Observations of Judicial Settlement Practices*, 24 HARV. NEGOT. L. REV. 83 (2018).

[30] §79A of the Israeli Courts Law enables litigants to authorize the judge to rule on a matter partly or fully "by way of compromise." While the law provides no definition for this form of ruling, the "law in action" appears to be that this authority is used to provide a final outcome without a reasoned decision, to render a judicial decision that does not necessarily result from direct application of the law, or to create a judicially perceived fair settlement between the parties. In one observation, the judge referred to a ruling according to §79A in contractual terms, as "a tri-party agreement between the defendant, the plaintiff and the court." Nearly all judges emphasize that a judgment by way of compromise is final, does not pronounce the reasoning behind the decision, and can rarely be appealed. For a discussion of this section and a parallel use of judicial arbitration

which is closest to adjudication among the tools used by judges in pretrial – is sometimes offered to the parties after the judge has probed the possibility of settlement between them using other settlement-promoting tools.

ADR tools *in the courtroom* consist mainly of narrow practices that are far removed from the ideal of mediation (which would ideally involve expressing empathy and addressing the underlying needs of the parties). They often involve a statement on the nonbinary nature of conflict. For example, one judge commented to a resilient party: "We cannot accept the perception of either party that it is the only one who is hurt and has a just cause." Another commented that the expectation of each side to find catharsis through judicial acknowledgment in a verdict is unrealistic and futile.

The judicial stance in pretrial seems to be a central factor in stemming the tide of case. The study's statistical analysis, which was conducted in the years before the 2021 enactment of the revision to the Civil Procedure Rules (stated above), uncovered that 47.9% of cases lodged in the Tel Aviv first-instance court reached pretrial, while only 8.3% proceeded to trial, and 4% received a verdict at trial.

While the transplant of US constructs has had a major effect on Israeli court proceedings and the nature of the judicial role, it has resulted in a somewhat different translation. As mentioned in Section I, US judges (or magistrates) may meet with the parties separately in their chambers, and thus negotiate the case much like a mediator, taking offers from one party to another until reaching an agreed offer. This is not possible in Israel, where proceedings are public and both parties are present at all times, along with parties to other cases waiting their turn in court. This requirement is tempered by placing parties on and off the protocol (with their agreement) to allow a freer interaction while trying to settle the case. The parties are present throughout the discussion of the case, but the protocol may not include parts of the discussion on appeal. In sum, while Israel has transplanted US concepts and practices, it has done so while putting limits on judicial negotiation and keeping it in the public eye – though compromising on its inclusion in protocols.

in the United States, *see* Yuval Sinai & Michal Alberstein. *Court Arbitration by Compromise: Rethinking Delaware's State Sponsored Arbitration Case*, CARDOZO PUB. L. POL'Y & ETHICS J. 13 (2014): 739.

2.3 England: Twilight Hour of Trial?

2.3.1 Getting Out of Trial, Managing the Margins

During the past three decades, the civil justice system of England and Wales has been overhauled to cut costs, transitioning to a legal system in which litigation is formally defined as a "last resort"[31] and settlement without court involvement is the preferred form of dispute resolution. Refusing a settlement offer or offer to mediate can result in heavy post-trial cost sanctions (even if the party succeeds in trial).[32] Pre-action protocols have been introduced to regulate party actions before the filing of the claim to promote settlement,[33] thus placing the focus of conflict on the pre-filing stage and frontloading legal costs.[34] Thus, costs are not averted for litigants, undermining one of the original intentions of the reforms, which was to provide a path of dispute resolution that did not involve high litigation costs and thus would increase access to justice.

Costs to the government, nevertheless, have indeed been slashed. The number of filed claims has considerably declined due, probably, to the high cost of litigation coupled with the cost sanctions and pre-action protocols introduced in the reforms.[35] Of claims that are filed, 84% are

[31] UK MINISTRY OF JUSTICE, The Practice Direction for Pre-Action Conduct and Protocols, Section 1.8. ("Litigation should be a last resort. . .the parties should consider whether negotiation or some other form of ADR might enable them to settle their dispute without commencing proceedings."). In England, alternatives to civil trial include arbitration, early neutral evaluation by a judge, and numerous ombudsmen schemes.

[32] Neil Andrews, *Fundamental Principles of Civil Procedure: Order Out of Chaos, in* CIVIL LITIGATION IN A GLOBALISING WORLD 19–38 (Kramer and van Rhee, eds., 2012).

[33] UK Civil Procedure Rules (CPR), 1998. Since 1998, pre-action protocols for a wide variety of legal issues have been introduced (e.g., for debt claims, travel package claims, disease and injury claims, construction and engineering disputes).

[34] The first pre-action protocols were introduced as a result of the Woolf Reforms; see LORD WOOLF, ACCESS TO JUSTICE: INTERIM REPORT TO THE LORD CHANCELLOR ON CIVIL JUSTICE SYSTEM IN ENGLAND AND WALES 4 (1995). For reports on the effect of the reforms, *see* TAMARA GORIELY, RICHARD MOORHEAD & PAMELA ABRAMS, MORE CIVIL JUSTICE? THE IMPACT OF THE WOOLF REFORMS ON PRE-ACTION BEHAVIOUR RESEARCH STUDY 43, UK JUSTICE MINISTRY REPORT (2002); JOHN PEYSNER & MARY SENEVIRATNE, THE MANAGEMENT OF CIVIL CASES – THE COURTS AND POST-WOOLF LANDSCAPE, UK DEP. FOR CONSTITUTIONAL AFFAIRS REPORT (2005).

[35] Peysner, *id.*, citing data from the Constitutional Affairs Statistical Branch (in 1998, the year before the reforms, 2,245,324 cases were filed annually; five years after the reforms 1,571,976 cases were filed); *see also* Robert Dingwall & Emilie Cloatre, *Vanishing Trials? An English Perspective*, 1 (2006). In recent years, the steady decline has leveled off (or bottomed out); *see* Linda Mulcahy and Wendy Teeder, *Are Litigants, Trials and Precedents Vanishing After All?* MOD. L. REV. (2021).

A Settlement

Under the Civil Procedure Rules parties should make every effort to settle their case before the hearing. This could be by discussion or negotiation (such as a roundtable meeting or settlement conference) or by a more formal process such as mediation. The court will want to know what steps have been taken. Settling the case early can save costs, including court hearing fees.

For legal representatives only

I confirm that I have explained to my client the need to try to settle; the options available; and the possibility of costs sanctions if they refuse to try to settle. ☐

For all

Your answers to these questions may be considered by the court when it deals with the questions of costs: see Civil Procedure Rules Part 44.3 (4).

1. Given that the rules require you to try to settle the claim before the hearing, do you want to attempt to settle at this stage? ☐ **Yes** ☐ **No**

2. If Yes, do you want a one month stay? ☐ **Yes** ☐ **No**

3. If you answered 'No' to question 1, please state below the reasons why you consider it inappropriate to try to settle the claim at this stage.

Figure 2.1 First section of Money Claims Allocation Questionnaire, UK Ministry of Justice.

undefended.[36] If a claim is defended, the parties must fill out an Allocation Questionnaire, which aptly demonstrates the institutional preference for settlement. The first section deals with settlement promotion (Figure 2.1).

Indeed, in line with this institutional preference, more than half of the courts in England and Wales closed between 2010 and 2019 (and more closures are planned).[37] The proportion of judges to population has plummeted, and is very low in comparison to that of most other European countries: 3.1 judges per 100,000 inhabitants, according to a 2020 report by the European Commission for the Efficiency of Justice. In comparison, in the Commission's 2008 report, analyzing data from 2006 – when there were fewer pre-action protocols in England and Wales – the ratio was more than twice as high, 7:100,000 (of course the emphasized stage of the legal system may not be the only factor affecting the figures).[38]

[36] For statistics on civil cases, *see* UK Ministry of Justice website, at www.gov.uk/government/collections/civil-justice-statistics-quarterly (last accessed Jan. 6, 2023).

[37] The Law Society, *Court Closures* (Mar. 10, 2022), at www.lawsociety.org.uk/campaigns/court-reform/whats-changing/court-closures

[38] European Commission for the Efficiency of Justice (CEPEJ), European Judicial Systems Evaluation Report, 2020 Evaluation Cycle (2018 data), Part 2, Country Profiles, 96 (2020); European Commission for the Efficiency of Justice (CEPEJ), European Judicial Systems

Judges are expected to expedite the few cases that do reach them through active case management in conferences in the pretrial stage (cost and case management conferences), whose aim is to control the costs of litigation and define the time schedule for the case. As Simon Roberts, a legal anthropologist, eloquently stated, "[t]he Case Management Conference, a meeting presided over by a District Judge at which defended claims are guided forwards to settlement – or exceptionally trial – has come to replace trial and judgment as the central public activity of the court,"[39] and "[t]he articulated priorities of government, and of the courts themselves, have shifted dramatically. Sponsorship of settlement is now explicitly identified as the courts' primary responsibility, with supervision of trial and the delivery of judgment becoming residual. . ."[40] Even this activity, however, is to be conducted in writing or by phone when practicable.[41]

The duty of the court to actively manage cases to ensure effective cost allocation appears in Section 1.4 of the Civil Procedure Rules (CPR). The definition of active management includes: ". . .(f) helping the parties settle the whole or part of the case." Yet, as demonstrated in our fieldwork (described in the next section), despite this clause, these conferences are primarily focused on bringing down costs and setting the schedule of the case, often indirectly assisting settlement efforts; judges do not settle the case themselves (unlike US or Israeli pretrial judges, and more rarely Italian judges in conciliation hearings).

Despite the substantial differences, the introduction of this stage in April 1999 may have been influenced by its extensive use by then in the United States – though it is interesting to note that in the case of England, as progenitor of the common law, transplants from the United States, such as the pretrial, can be influenced by English roots.[42]

Evaluation Report, 2008 Evaluation Cycle (2006 data). There are no such reports predating the Woolf reform that led to pre-action protocols. For comparison: In Italy, in 2006, the ratio was 11:100,000, similar to its 2018 figure. Israel is not listed in the 2008 report.

39 SIMON ROBERTS, A COURT IN THE CITY, 5 (2013).

40 Simon Roberts, *'Listing Concentrates the Mind': The English Civil Court as an Arena for Structured Negotiation*, 29 (3) OXFORD J. LEGAL STUD. 457, 458 (2009).

41 Practice Direction 3.16(2) of the Civil Procedure Rules.

42 Pretrial in the United States may have been influenced by the English practice of summons for directions. The pretrial as a stage to better prepare cases for trial has existed in the United States since the 1930s. R. E. Holland, *Pre-Trial Conferences in Canada*, 7 ADVOC. Q. 416 (1987). In England the common practice before civil trial was a summons for directions, a perfunctory stage in which the court summoned directions for trial; *see*

Thus the term "diffusion" may provide a broader view that takes into consideration a longer timeline.[43] However, the last century, sometimes called the "American century," has yielded distinctly American constructs,[44] such as the ADR movement and its promotion by the legal system,[45] which can be analyzed as transplants in themselves.

The shift to litigation as a last resort was indeed to be made possible through an era of negotiation and ADR.[46] Mediation began to make its mark in England in the 1990s, following the establishment of the commercial mediation provider Centre for Effective Dispute Resolution (CEDR) in London and in line with the 1990 Courts and Legal Services Act, which introduced procedural changes to encourage early settlement in civil disputes.[47]

Institutionalized mediation in London is targeted toward an efficient, speedy resolution of the case – much like adjudication or any other activity of the court.[48] It is often evaluative positional bargaining[49] – that is, mediators point out the weaknesses of each party's legal case – limited in time, and is often conducted without dialogue between the parties. Roberts describes mediators shuttling between rooms (parties were not seated together) to negotiate a compromise.[50] In addition,

Edson R. Sunderland, *Theory and Practice of Pre-Trial Procedure*, 36 MICH. L. REV. 215 (1937).

43 William Twining, *Diffusion of Law: A Global Perspective*, 36 J. LEGAL PLURALISM & UNOFFICIAL L. 1 (2004).

44 Mattei, *supra* note 20 at 390 (2003) ("By the early part of the last century, a century significantly labeled 'the American century', U.S. law had already received from Europe, and digested in a genuinely original way, the fundamental components of its legal structure.")

45 Nolan-Haley, *supra* note 3. Alexander *supra* note 5.

46 Practice Directions, *supra* note 34.

47 Hazel Genn, *Civil Mediation: A Measured Approach?* 32(2) J. SOC, WELFARE & FAM. L. 195, 197 (2010). Mattei, *supra* note 20 (including ADR as a US export meant to empower global corporate governance).

48 Sue Prince, *"Fine Words Butter No Parsnips": Can the Principle of Open Justice Survive the Introduction of an Online Court?* 38(1) CIV. JUST. Q. 111 (2019).

49 Nadja Alexander, *The Mediation Meta-Model: The Realities of Mediation Practice*, 12(6) ADR BULLETIN 126–31, 126 (2011) (presenting a spectrum of mediation practices, with positional bargaining on the one end, interest-based negotiation in the center and dialogue-based discourse on the other side: "Interest-based negotiation and positional bargaining are both negotiation discourses and therefore outcome-oriented in nature; by contrast, the focus of dialogue is relational development and perspective sharing, rather than settlement or resolution.")

50 Roberts *supra* note 39; Prince, *supra* note 48.

parties may enter mediation merely as a necessary step to avoid cost shifting.[51]

Mediation in London seems to have little semblance to the ideal or traditional conceptualization of mediation yet even in its truncated form it does still have benefits. According to a study on voluntary mediation in London courts, "Overall, reaction to mediation was positive, with users and representatives displaying confidence in mediators and their neutrality. Parties valued the informality of the process, the skill of the mediator, and the opportunity to be fully involved in the settlement of the dispute. The most common features disliked were that the mediation was rushed, failure to settle, facilities, or poor skills on the part of the mediator."[52]

While an effort to evaluate which cases are appropriate for adjudication is lacking (other than urgent cases or cases in which it can be shown that following pre-action protocol would unduly compromise the case), a 2017 government report evaluating mediation processes has stated that the benefits of mediation hinge upon a realistic prospect of access to trial:[53]

> We are conscious that the primary concern of the system of civil justice must be genuine access to the Court. Not only does ADR not supplant the court process but ADR provision only works as an adjunct to an efficient system of adjudicative justice. To put it crudely, Defendants do not make fair or realistic offers of settlement if there is no real prospect of the Claimant being able to get the matter before a court for judgment. ADR is not a substitute system but a complementary one. Mediation and conciliation work best "in the shadow of the law."

As mentioned earlier, the shift to negotiation and ADR in England has been explained by scholars as resulting from cuts to civil justice. Describing the background in further detail will allow for a deeper

[51] HAZEL GENN, P. FENN, M. MASON, A. LANE, N. BECHAI, L. GRAY & D. VENCAPPA, TWISTING ARMS: COURT REFERRED AND COURT LINKED MEDIATION UNDER JUDICIAL PRESSURE. MINISTRY OF JUSTICE RESEARCH SERIES 1/07 (London 2007) (stating that demand for the voluntary ADR scheme at Central London increased significantly following the case of *Dunnett v. Railtrack* in 2002, which confirmed the power of the courts to deny a successful party legal costs following an unreasonable refusal to mediate, and that the rush to mediate was mitigated after the *Halsey* judgment in 2004, which offered a nuanced interpretation of "unreasonable." Since then, there have been further conflicting judicial decisions on the matter).

[52] *Id.* at iv.

[53] UK CIVIL JUSTICE COUNCIL, ADR AND CIVIL JUSTICE INTERIM REPORT (2017).

understanding of the findings presented in the next section. Thus, we will take a pause for some history.

Legal aid was first introduced in 1949. Originally, legal aid was almost universal, with 80% of British people eligible. The combination of cuts to legal aid since the 1980s and high litigation costs in England and Wales has left much of the population without redress.[54]

Following the cuts to legal aid, Lord Justice Woolf was commissioned to review the civil justice system, resulting in a report that centered on the problem of high costs as a barrier to the legal system, as litigation costs could be many times higher than the value of the case. "We have become the laughingstock of the world" he wrote, and laid out his solution, which resulted in an overhaul of civil justice in England and Wales, placing its emphasis on the pre-filing stage (through pre-action protocols) and judicial case management before trial. Following criticism that costs had been frontloaded rather than reduced (thought outcomes such as modifying the adversarial culture were noted),[55] the Woolf Reforms were followed by another review of the legal system by Lord Justice Jackson.[56] Justice Jackson devised a cost regime that incentivized settlement (increasing the risk of parties that did not accept a settlement offer or invitation to mediation) while strengthening certain claimants (particularly in personal injury claims) by minimizing their cost risk ("No win, no fee"). *Additional emphasis was placed on judges' critical role in bringing down litigation costs – the words "at proportionate cost"*

[54] Asher Flynn & Jacqueline Hodgson, *Access to Justice and Legal Aid Cuts: A Mismatch of Concepts in the Contemporary Australian and British Legal Landscapes*. In A. Flynn & J. Hodgson (Eds.) ACCESS TO JUSTICE AND LEGAL AID 1–22 (2020); John Sorabji, *Austerity's Effect on English Civil Justice*, 1 ERASMUS LAW REV. (2015).

[55] Goriely et al., *supra* note 34 (Conducting a qualitative study including lawyers, insurers, and claims managers, they discovered that while the Woolf reforms had positive consequences such as providing clearer litigation structures and improvement in the level of cooperation and settlement, the reforms had not resolved the problem of costs. Costs had, in fact increased, most likely due to frontloading.). These findings were replicated by Peysner et al., *supra* note 34 at 2 in 2005 (stating that although the overall sentiment was that the culture of litigation had changed for the better, this was not translated into reduced expenses or of delay. In addition, although the settlement rate had increased as a consequence of the Woolf reforms, the majority of cases settled in the pre-filing stage not as a consequence of ADR being incorporated into the court process.).

[56] See LORD JACKSON, REVIEW OF CIVIL LITIGATION COSTS (2009). The Jackson Review was conducted because the senior judiciary was concerned at the disproportionate litigation costs, despite the implementation (and the perceived success) of the Woolf reforms. The report concluded that the costs system should be based on legal expenses that reflect the nature/complexity of the case.

were added to the CPR's overriding objective, which now read: "to deal with cases justly and at proportionate cost."[57] *This seems to have made an significant mark on the judicial role, as will be seen below in our court observations.* From reportedly minimal intervention of judges in case management conferences after the Woolf reforms,[58] it seems, according to our observations, that judges have stepped up efforts to control litigation costs and are intervening actively in planning the course of the case to ensure its time-effectiveness. In doing so, they often state their obligation to ensure proportionate cost according to the CPR. Notably, judges receive training to conduct these conference effectively, further showing the promise of judicial training, as in Italy.

Yet, as has been commented upon by representatives of the legal system, and as the numbers demonstrate in our court observations, legal costs are still high. As Lord Justice Briggs, commissioned to conduct a subsequent review of the justice system, stated, "[T]he single most pervasive and indeed shocking weakness of our civil courts is that they fail to provide reasonable access to justice for the ordinary individuals."[59] The fact that litigation is inaccessible to a large part of the population has been the basis for propositions of mandatory mediation – since that is the only realistically open avenue.[60] Briggs suggested taking resolution of disputes online to allow ordinary people to resolve their conflicts, a suggestion that is being heavily invested in by the legal system (as of this writing, the Online Court is being developed through pilots, new regulations, and a recently appointed online supervising committee).[61] The idea is that the disputants will be guided on their dispute through automatic processing and, if needed, will be referred to online facilitators; if that is

57 CPR, Part 1.1.

58 Peysner et al., *supra* note 34.

59 LORD JUSTICE BRIGGS, CIVIL COURTS STRUCTURE REVIEW: FINAL REPORT, 28 (2016).

60 Masood Ahmed & Dorcas Quek Anderson, *Expanding the Scope of Dispute Resolution and Access to Justice,* 1 CIV. JUST. Q. 1,8 (2019)(quoting a statement by Justice Neuberger to that effect).

61 CIVIL JUSTICE COUNCIL ONLINE DISPUTE RESOLUTION ADVISORY GROUP, ONLINE DISPUTE RESOLUTION (2015) (promoting an online solution to enhance dispute resolution in the United Kingdom. Among its proposals, the Group recommends "online facilitation to support dispute containment; and online evaluation to support dispute avoidance."). Its proposals were adopted by Lord Justice Briggs in his review of the justice system that aimed to overhaul the structure of the civil justice system. *See* Briggs *supra* note 59; The Judicial Review and Courts Act 2022 (Commencement No. 3) Regulations 2023; UK Government (June 12, 2023) *New Online Procedure Rule Committee Launched* www.gov.uk/government/news/new-online-procedure-rule-committee-launched.

insufficient, they will be able to bring their before a judge (either online or in person).[62]

In sum, the diminished number of claims in England and Wales raises important questions. Are disputes indeed settled early or are they discarded due to high pre-action costs and cuts to legal aid? Indeed, with no real prospect of trial, settlement may be on the decline and could be "vanishing" as well. Due to the privatization of disputes,[63] we cannot know. The continued preoccupation with bringing down costs to enable access to justice and the phenomenon of unrepresented parties that began after the cut in legal aid suggest that redress may be in need.[64]

2.3.2 *Into a Shrunken Field*

Going into the field in London was a different experience than in the other two legal systems. Case management conferences, when they occur, often occur by phone. Trial is a rare event. The head of litigation at a law firm with well over 100 lawyers and legal professionals told us that the law firm takes about one case to trial a year.

While litigation is rare, the threat of litigation and mediation is a part of negotiations, with an invitation to mediation incorporated into the letter exchange (with a reminder that refusal could result in cost penalties). Mediation can be expensive when lawyers are involved. In our observations of case and cost management hearings at the London County Court (a first-instance court), the cost for mediation with lawyers was regularly cited as around £10,000. Regarding the form of mediation, a senior mediator at one of the two major mediation firms in London echoed Roberts' accounts cited above, saying: "The parties are in the

62 Joshua Rozenberg, *The Online Court: Will IT Work?* (2020) at https://long-reads.?thelegaleducationfoundation?.org/ (last accessed Feb. 1, 2022).

63 HAZEL GENN, JUDGING CIVIL JUSTICE (2008).

64 Richard Moorhead, *The Passive Arbiter: Litigants in Person and the Challenge to Neutrality*, 16 SOC. & LEGAL STUD. 405 (2007); Rosemary Hunter, Anne Barlow, Janet Smithson & Jan Ewing, *Access to What? LASPO and Mediation* in Asher Flynn & Jacqueline Hodgson, eds. ACCESS TO JUSTICE AND LEGAL AID (arguing that the removal of legal aid funding for the majority of private family law disputes in England and Wales, and the expectation that all such matters will now be resolved through mediation, reflects a moral as well as an economic ideology. Drawing on their extensive qualitative empirical research, they conclude that mediation – the only option available to those with limited means – is not appropriate for all cases, and in the cases where it is unsuccessful, there is no alternative procedure available to the parties.)

same room for a brief opening, then the mediator does shuttling between the parties."

While the legal system takes the view of litigation as a "last resort," one judge speaking on a panel took a more nuanced approach:

> It is important that a judge promote settlement when it is the right thing to do for both sides ... There are instances in which it is better for the sides and necessarily more useful ... At the same time, judicial experience allows to know when you should not end the case with a settlement agreement. Directing behaviors, perhaps creating norms, are another consideration – such as empowering a disempowered litigant that dared to take legal action. In such cases perhaps it is the duty of the legal system to empower him and to encourage others like them to use the legal system in the future ...You must ask: Are there disempowered sides and is there a concern that turning to the path of compromise will only duplicate the weakness with which they arrive to the legal process...

In the case and cost management conferences, however, it was apparent that the judges greatly preferred settlement, perhaps due to the nature of their roles to ensure proportionate costs and to encourage parties to agree on costs, and the fact that it is not a trial setting in which the merits are explored. In London, litigants waited their turn outside the courtroom in a designated room, allowing lawyers to discuss the case and settle on case management or the case itself.[65] We witnessed two such cases in which the lawyers entered the courtroom with an agreement that they had reached outside, to the satisfaction of the judge. In one instance, when lawyers told the judge they had reached a settlement of the case, he responded:

> I offer congratulations. No one can be more pleased than me. It's always better that the parties reach a settlement themselves. Do you want a Tomlin order [a form for a confidential written settlement]? I don't want to rush you into that ... if the parties reach a settlement, I never rush. Take all the time that you need and, when you have a minute, make it signed... Proportionality is on your side. I congratulate the parties!

The judges, who had received training in cost management, often took a hands-on approach to costs.[66] They took an active stance to minimize the use of experts and thus reduce litigation costs. For example, in a claim

[65] In contrast to the case in Israel, where parties wait their turn in the courtroom. The cases that they see can have a carryover effect, in which they realize that settlement is the main course of the day in the eyes of the judge.

[66] Peysner et al., *supra* note 34.

regarding damages due to pipe leakage, the barristers disagreed about the need for an expert to determine the cause for leakage. The judge thought that perhaps it was premature to decide on the need for an expert on corrosion: "If it turns out that the building servicing person can decide on the matter of the corrosion, why did both sides need an expert?" He then left the room to allow the barristers to discuss this matter. When he returned, he asked: "Did you manage to agree or should I come back in a bit?" The barrister answered: "My learned friend was just about to crunch the numbers." They agreed on the costs of the expert phase – £17,292.50. The judge then addressed the parties' disagreement on disclosure costs. The lawyer for the defendant said: "The claimant is saying that it is a document light case, but that is not correct." The judge responded: "Let me hear the other side." After hearing the claimant's lawyer, the judge said: "Forty-five hours is too much." The last point of contention between the parties was the cost of mediation. The judge said: "Counsels will not spend seven hours but more like five hours, and I suggest getting down from 38 hours to 30 hours. I approve 15,000 pounds."

In a case with a different judge, the plaintiff was a woman who slipped on debris in the stairwell of her apartment building, injuring her ankle. Interestingly, the judge, in ensuring proportionality, made a realistic evaluation of the claim itself. The interaction contained many of the recurring motifs – citing proportionality and the CPR, limiting expert use, reducing legal costs, encouraging the parties to agree but deciding for them when needed – yet most cases that we observed did not involve a realistic evaluation of the sum of the claim and were more technical in nature.

JUDGE:	We saved 45 minutes for this. Is there any agreement regarding costs?
LAWYER:	Two aspects are agreed (discusses sums) ... The parties have made attempts, but the rest remains not agreed.
JUDGE (AFTER STATING THAT HE HAS READ THE AFFIDAVITS):	Why do we need liability experts? According to CPR 35, I have to make a decision whether an expert is going to help the court. It's a factual matter. I don't see how a liability expert can help. So, we are not having liability experts.

Then the judge turned to the question of proportionality. He stated his duty to ensure proportionality according to law and asks the lawyers to address that issue. The costs lawyer (a new profession arising from the reforms) sat with a very big calculator in front of him.

JUDGE:	This is a QC [Queens Counsel – a senior lawyer] case.
LAWYER:	The budget has been prepared based on the assumption that this is a QC case.
JUDGE:	If you have junior counsel, how much does it come to?
LAWYER (CALCULATING A NEW SUM):	62,861 costs coming forward.
JUDGE:	Address the proportionality please.
LAWYER:	There are issues of liability, losses. If we assume that this goes to a trial, this sum is proportionate.
JUDGE:	You already spent 25,000 for pre-action. This is a fairly straightforward case, isn't it?
LAWYER:	There are a lot of medical records.

Then the judge referred to the sums that the plaintiff was actually asking for in her lawsuit (not the costs):

JUDGE:	We have all heard of the Alexander technique, I don't think you are going to persuade a judge that 35,000 for future Alexander treatments is necessary.
DEFENDANT'S LAWYER:	The sums asked for in the lawsuit are realistically too high, therefore, asking for 91,000 in expenses is not proportionate to the damages that may be decided upon at the end – 60,000 is a sensible figure.

After some more conversation regarding the sums, the judge dictates a decision to the parties.[67] He states that a junior lawyer rather than a senior lawyer should represent the case, with the senior lawyer a phone's call away. In addition, the value of the claim itself should in fact be lower, affecting proportionality of litigation costs:

> **JUDGE:** My sense is that she is an active lady and has done what she can to alleviate the damage. But the bulk of the claim relates to other damages … and some remarkable 35,000 for future Alexander massages … I sympathize with the defendants' claim that the sum asked for is too high and that if [the claimant] wins her lawsuit, she will not get its entirety. My function today is to deal with costs. CPR

[67] There is no court reporter, the judge just speaks out the decision and the lawyers write it down; hearings are recorded, but judges often ask lawyers to send them summaries, so perhaps transcripts are not sent to them unless they ask for them.

> 43 (2) states that only proportionate costs will be allowed. CPR 44 (3)(5) defines what proportionate costs are. It is an unfortunate accident, but it is not complicated. It is straightforward, bread and butter for personal injury lawyers. So far 24,000 has been spent. Claimants have spent time and money that is excessive and disproportionate. The issues can be litigated within 40–60 thousand pounds.

Our court observations show that as judges determine the costs of each phase (expert reports, legal fees), they are not hesitant to tell the sides that a certain cost is too high or not proportional to the issue at hand. The judge may ask the parties to reach an agreement on a lower sum, offering to leave the chamber while they do so. The parties may reach an agreement, and if not, the judge may decide on the cost. Judges might ask if the parties had attempted mediation but not tie this option to the concrete cases (unlike judges in Italy, who must explain to parties why a case is suitable for mediation when issuing a mediation order).[68]

In sum, unlike the diagnosing role of judges in Florence, or the settlement-making role of pretrial judges in Tel Aviv, the judges in the London County Court limited themselves to clarifying the scheduling and sequence of the trial (should it occur) and determining the costs. They did not attempt to go into the substance of the issues in dispute, though they are authorized to do so by law, or to find ways to reach a settlement of the case between the parties (aside from judges in family courts). As one judge said on a panel, "I am not a court of mediation – a court of mediation is a contradiction in terms." Lawyers with whom we spoke also said that settling the case was not part of a judge's role, though one lawyer noted, "I have heard it exists but I've never seen it."

2.4 Criminal Justice

Though the general emphasis of the study was on judicial settlement practices in civil justice, we have also addressed the transformation of the criminal justice system into a multidoor arena, and noticed equivalent trends of institutionalization of abbreviated proceedings and consent-based dispositions. These changes correspond with the civil justice trends in each legal system. In Italy, transplants related to settlement (plea bargaining) or other abbreviated proceedings have been introduced while

[68] Judges in England and Wales have been documented as saying something to the effect of "this case cries out for mediation" in extreme cases. Simon Roberts, *supra* note 40 at 467.

preserving a main role for adjudication and maintaining the separation between adjudication and settlement practices. In Israel, transplants have resulted in a central role in pretrial – the criminal pretrial judge intervenes during arraignment hearing days (*moked*), mostly in a managerial manner, to encourage the parties to reach a plea bargain using a variety of narrow settlement strategies.[69] In England and Wales, the legal system incentivizes guilty pleas at the first possible opportunity (the earlier the plea, the greater the sentence reduction), leaving the judge with a relatively minor role in facilitating pleas and adjudicating cases. Judges usually do not incorporate ADR into their practice, and the institutional preference for settlement is grounded mainly in efficiency (despite the transplant of some restorative practices to deal with a minority of cases). Our study uncovered the multidoor criminal justice nature of legal systems today, which follows the original civil idea of a multidoor courthouse as presented by Frank Sander, the founder of the ADR movement, and has explored the different meaning of it for judges' work in the civil and criminal setting.

2.4.1 Italy: Tension between Adversarial and Inquisitorial Criminal Procedure

Italy's criminal justice system tried to ingest, and digest, large swathes of US-inspired adversarial constructs near the end of the twentieth century.[70] Its traditional inquisitorial stance had placed great emphasis on the investigative phase before trial. This stage was conducted either by prosecutors (themselves judges in the inquisitorial system, receiving the same training[71]) or instruction judges, entrusted with carrying out an

[69] Sari Luz Kanner, Dana Rosen, Yosef Zohar & Michal Alberstein, *Managerial Judicial Conflict Resolution (JCR) of Plea Bargaining: Shadows of Law and Conflict Resolution*, 22 NEW CRIM. L. REV. 494 (2019).

[70] William T. Pizzi & Mariangela Montagna, *The Battle to Establish an Adversarial Trial System in Italy*, 25 MICH. J. INT'L L. 429, 430 (2004); Giulio Illuminati, *The Frustrated Turn to Adversarial Procedure in Italy (Italian Criminal Procedure Code of 1988)* WASH. UNIV. GLOBAL STUD. L. REV. 4 (2005).

[71] See European Union website: "In Italy, the role of public prosecutor is played by career magistrates, who exercise their functions under the supervision of the chief of their bureau. This operates as a kind of hierarchy that applies only to the public prosecutors' offices." https://e-justice.europa.eu/content_judicial_systems_in_member_states-16-it-maximizeMS-en.do?member=1. See also information on the School of the Judiciary in Italy, training judges and prosecutors: www.ejtn.eu/About/EJTN-Affiliates/Members/Italy/

objective investigation to uncover the innocence or guilt of the suspect. Only if the prosecutor or instruction judge decided there was enough evidence to continue to trial could the trial be referred to the trial judge, who would receive the investigative file, which had an aura of neutrality.[72] Concerns were raised regarding the length of the investigative phase and the aura of neutrality that might prevent defendants from receiving a fair chance in court.[73]

In 1988, with a view to the US adversarial system,[74] which was perceived as protecting the rights of defendants,[75] and due to criticism of the long duration of the investigative phase – which could take years, and was criticized from a human rights perspective by the European Union, the United Nations, and Amnesty International[76] – the Code of Criminal Procedure was revised in Italy. This reform aimed to change the criminal justice system to an adversarial one along the lines of the American legal system.[77] Among other measures, it prohibited the trial judge from having access to the investigative file: Evidence was to be presented during the trial in adversarial fashion. The judge was to receive but a few pertinent details (such as the criminal history of the defendant).[78]

According to various scholars, this legislative change did not have the desired effect due to its blunt departure from the prevailing legal culture.[79] In 1992, many of the provisions of the reforms were struck down

72 Illuminati, *supra* note 70.

73 *Id.*

74 The United States was perceived as having hegemonic stature in the second half of the twentieth century. *See* Mattei, *supra* note 20 at 394.

75 Langer, *supra* note 20 at 24 ("Many commentators have said that while in the adversarial system the defendant is a subject of rights, in the inquisitorial system he is an object of investigation. This was probably true for a long time, but after World War II – and even earlier in some jurisdictions – most inquisitorial countries began considering the defendant as a subject of rights, both at the rule level – constitutions, human rights treaties, criminal procedure codes – and at the law in action level. Thus, in most continental law jurisdictions today, the defendant is presumed innocent, has a right against compelled self-incrimination, a right to assistance of counsel, etc."); Thea A. Cohen, *Self-incrimination and Separation of Powers*, 100 GEO. L.J. 895 (2012) (analyzing the Self-Incrimination Clause).

76 Similar to the case in civil justice, the European Court of Human Rights condemned Italy's criminal trial lengths and pressed it to increase efficiency and cut the lengthy trial process, in addition to criticism from the United Nations and Amnesty International. *See* Pizzi & Montagna, *supra* note 70 at 437.

77 Illuminati, *supra* note 70.

78 *Id.*

79 *Id.* at 573 ("The fault of the 1988 codification was that it had not been adequately prepared in cultural terms. The bar and judiciary were not fully involved in the reform.

by the Court of Cassations as unconstitutional (which did so again after another attempt by Parliament in 1997).[80] Only after amending the Constitution and legislating Law n. 63/2001, which restored most of the provisions struck down by the Constitutional Court in 1992, was Parliament finally able to entrench the adversarial system in the Italian criminal justice system. Yet, as in most adversarial systems, there was a need for "crutches."

The main drawback of the adversarial system was the length of the full trial.[81] If the judge does not have the investigative file, all of the evidence must be presented, with examination and cross-examination, during trial. It soon became apparent that the time saved through a shorter investigative phase was short-lived. Adversarial systems around the world have dealt with the drawback of lengthy trials through plea bargains, which dramatically shorten proceedings, often leaving the judge limited opportunity for intervention.[82] This adversarial crutch – used

This is especially true for the judiciary, where the deepest changes were imposed. Italian judges were accustomed to having an almost unlimited power to introduce evidence, to having full knowledge of the investigative dossier and the freedom to use any document from that dossier for the decision. Judges conceived of their role as one of seeking the truth, where they were supposed to search in all possible ways and with all the permitted means in order to accomplish their duty. Judges were accustomed to being the active protagonists of the trial; the focus now shifted to the parties' initiatives and arguments. The first criticisms to the new Code were, not surprisingly, made by prosecutors and judges concerned over a perceived loss of efficiency. But it is apparent that the real disappointment was grounded in a belief that the newly introduced accusatorial context was useless. That is to say, the same – if not better – results could have been reached more expeditiously under the old procedures.").

80 *Id.* at 576 (suggesting that the Italian Constitutional Court was making decisions that went against the Parliament's changes based on the ideological belief that truth at trial was being compromised).

81 Albert W. Alschuler, *Implementing the Criminal Defendant's Right to Trial: Alternatives to the Plea Bargaining System*, 50 U. CHI. L. REV. 931, 971–72 (1983) (writing over 30 years ago, when trials were simpler than they are now, Alschuler states: "[T]he American jury trial now has become so complex that our society usually refuses to provide it. Reluctant to reconsider our expensive trial procedures, we press most defendants to forgo even the more expeditious form of [bench] trial that defendants once were freely afforded as a matter of right."); Susan R. Klein et al., *Waiving the Criminal Justice System: An Empirical and Constitutional Analysis*, 52 AM. CRIM. L. REV. 73, 76 (2015) ("As we transformed from an adversary process where guilt was determined by trial to an administrative process where guilt and penalties are determined by negotiation, many prosecutors began demanding waiver of all constitutional criminal procedure rights, not just the trial and investigative-related ones.").

82 See Laurie L. Levenson, *Peeking Behind the Plea Bargaining Process: Missouri v. Frye and Lafler v. Cooper*, 46 LOY. L.A. L. REV. 457, 459–60 (2013) (explaining that plea bargaining is "a system that is tolerated because, without it, our criminal justice system would be

extensively in common law countries (disposing the large majority of criminal cases) – may run counter to inquisitorial culture, which is based on the centrality of the judge and the seeking of an objective truth.[83] In addition, it runs counter to another important principle of inquisitorial culture – the limited value of the admission of guilt in establishing liability.[84] A guilty plea is not sufficient to establish guilt in inquisitorial systems, but rather is a piece of evidence that is taken into account while uncovering the truth. Thus, while the plea bargaining concept was taken up – sparingly – in Italy (and other inquisitorial countries), it was changed. The bargain between prosecution and defense pertains only to the punishment without a plea (defendants agree only to the punishment and cannot incriminate themselves through pleas).

Another crutch – this time with inquisitorial facets – involves the defendant's request for a summary trial in exchange for a reduced sentence if the defendant is proven guilty. If the prosecution agrees and the judge views the case as appropriate for this type of disposition, the judge adjudicates the case based on the investigative file alone – reverting to the previous inquisitorial-fashion trial, in which the judge has access to the investigative file. The defendant forgoes the evidentiary phase.[85]

Omission of the evidentiary phase is only one way to abbreviate trials. The investigative phase preceding trial – shortened in the reforms – can be done away with altogether in certain cases, as can the pretrial: when the prosecutor decides there is enough clear evidence against the accused

so overwhelmed that it would collapse"); Kyle McCleery, *Guilty Pleas and Plea Bargaining at the Ad Hoc Tribunals: Lessons from Civil Law Systems*, 14 J. INT'L CRIM. JUST. 1099, 1110 (2016) ("American prosecutors have the power to determine whether or not to lay charges, what charges to lay, whether to withdraw charges and the sentence to be sought in the event of a conviction. This discretion is largely unchecked by the judiciary, which will typically intervene only in cases of gross misconduct.").

83 *Cf.* Christopher Slobogin, *Plea Bargaining and the Substantive and Procedural Goals of Criminal Justice: From Retribution and Adversarialism to Preventative Justice and Hybrid-Inquisitorialism*, 57 WM. & MARY L. REV. 1505, 1518 (2016) ("Where the parties control the adjudicatory input, waivers that truncate or eliminate the trial process are not only justified, they become an entitlement, regardless of the validity of the state's or the defendant's case."); Lucarelli et al., *supra* note 43.

84 McCleery, *supra* note 82 at 1112 ("Whereas common law/adversarial systems view admission of guilt as a mechanism for relieving the court of the burden of deciding which party prevailed at trial, inquisitorial systems tend to see admissions only as evidence that can assist the court in establishing the truth. However, in no way does this relieve the court of its duty to establish a complete account of what occurred.").

85 Pizzi & Montagna, *supra* note 70.

(*immediate trial,* which can also be requested by the accused) or when there is a strong *prima facie* case, such as a person arrested during the act of the crime or an accused who has confessed (*direct trial,* which skips over the pretrial decision to go to trial and often the investigative phase).

For minor offenses punishable by fines or up to three months in prison, the prosecutor can request a penal decree consisting of a reduced fine (reduced up to 50% of the minimum required law) to the defendant without trial. The defendant can oppose the penal decree. Going further are measures for decriminalization and non-punishment, such as the *messa alla prova*, allowing for suspension of trial with probation.[86]

While the reforms from 2003 to this day have not resulted in a reduced backlog of criminal cases, according to the Italian Ministry of Justice statistics,[87] this is expected to change with reform to the statute of limitations, which had continued to run during the criminal case, thus creating disincentives to settle. Preference for abbreviated trial may increase with the cancellation of statute of limitations in Italy, which has prevented defendants from using abbreviated proceedings in the hope that delay tactics could work to their benefit to cancel the trial altogether.[88]

At present, the full trial is still on the plate. The judicial conflict resolution role of the Italian judges in the criminal arena – which is relevant to the 16 percent of cases terminated through agreement between the prosecution and defendant – is mainly passive. The use of plea bargaining and abbreviated forms of trial is estimated at around a third of cases.[89]

[86] Oriana Binik, *Testing for Adults in the Milan Area: Analysis of the Application of an Innovative Measure in the Italian Sanctioning Landscape*, ITALIAN REV. CRIMINOLOGY 16 (2018).

[87] See statistics for 2003–2021 at Italian Ministry of Justice website: www.giustizia.it/giustizia/it/mg_1_14_1.page?contentId=SST1288006&previsiousPage=mg_1_14 (accessed Jan. 20, 2022).

[88] Beatrice Coscas-Williams & Michal Alberstein, *A Patchwork of Doors: Accelerated Proceedings in Continental Criminal Justice Systems*, 22 NEW CRIM. L. REV. 585 (2019).

[89] Maximo Langer, *Plea Bargaining, Conviction without Trial, and the Global Administratization of Criminal Convictions*, 4 ANN. REV. CRIMINOLOGY I.1, I.21; *see also* Golan Luzon, *Judicial Conflict Resolution in Plea Bargaining as the Golden Mean between the Adversarial and Inquisitorial Legal Systems*, 20 CARDOZO J. CONFLICT RESOL. 597 (2019).

2.4.2 *Israel: Judicial Plea for Pleas*

While used sporadically for centuries in different parts of the world,[90] plea bargains were not accepted as a mainstream method for disposing of cases until the 1970s in the United States. Since then, plea bargaining has spread globally as a common practice,[91] becoming the primary mode of case disposition in the criminal justice systems of England and Wales, Israel, and, to a much lesser extent, Italy.[92]

In Israel, judicial settlement powers in the criminal sphere have developed in practice in courts, with the main goal of facilitating plea bargains. Like many common law countries following the example of American criminal procedure,[93] Israel makes extensive use of plea bargains – in over 60 percent of criminal cases – to lessen the load on courts.[94] Plea bargains became accepted practiced through recognition by the Supreme Court in the 1970s[95] and have yet to be formalized in law, despite an attempt in 2010 by legislators to do so. Proactive judicial practices to promote plea bargains have developed in courts since the 1990s,[96] and – aside from judicial criminal mediation to facilitate plea bargains – later received recognition in law, as described below.

One central tool for encouraging plea bargains between the prosecution and defendant is the criminal pretrial,[97] which had long been in

90 Albert W. Alschuler, *Plea Bargaining and Its History*, 79(1) COLUM. REV. 1 (1979).
91 Langer, *supra* note 20.
92 Langer, *supra* note 89 (16% of criminal cases are disposed through plea bargains in Italy).
93 In the United States, the most recent data on the topic indicates that the plea bargain has become the most dominant form of conviction, with more than 95% of convicted defendants pleading guilty; BUREAU OF JUSTICE STATISTICS, U.S. DEPT. OF JUSTICE, FEDERAL JUSTICE STATISTICS 2014, COMPENDUIM OF FEDERAL JUSTICE STATISTICS (MAR. 2017). www.bjs.gov/content/pub/pdf/fjs14st.pdf; Langer, *supra* note 89 at 378–79 ("Four decades ago, scholars characterized plea bargaining as a uniquely American phenomenon (Langbein & Weinreb 1978, Langbein 1979a). Although at the time there were commentators who questioned how uniquely American plea bargaining truly was (Baldwin & McConville 1979, Goldstein & Marcus 1977), there is no question that in many jurisdictions a trial was a requirement to issue criminal convictions for all offenses or at least for all non-petty offenses.").
94 ANNUAL REPORT OF THE STATE ATTORNEY'S OFFICE, ISRAEL DEP'T OF JUSTICE, 30, (2017) (62.3%) www.justice.gov.il/Units/StateAttorney/Documents/data-report-2017.pdf
95 The Israeli Supreme Court case *Bahmoutzki v. State of Israel* (1972) 26(i) *P.D.* 543 was the first thorough decision about the legitimacy of plea bargaining and its requirements
96 1958/98 *State of Israel vs. John Doe.*
97 The criminal pretrial was set in Article 17.1 of the U.S. Federal Rules of Criminal Procedure in the 1960s. ARTICLE 17.1 FEDERAL RULES OF CRIMINAL PROCEDURE COMMITTEE NOTES – 2002 AMENDMENT. The language of Rule 17.1 has been amended as part of the general restyling of the Criminal Rules to make them more easily

effect in the United States and bears many similarities to the American model. It developed in Israel in judicial practice in the 1990s, around the same time that judges presiding over civil cases received wide-ranging pretrial settlement powers by law. The criminal pretrial and the judicial settlement powers accompanying it were introduced on the initiative of first- and second-instance courts, and approved by the Supreme Court. In 2006, this practice was formalized in law in Article 143a of the Criminal Procedure Law. According to the law, a criminal pretrial may be conducted to clarify the defendant's position on the charges, to narrow disagreement on legal or factual issues, to obviate the need for the evidentiary phase, and to end the case during pretrial.[98] Unlike the civil pretrial, the judge presiding over this phase *does not* continue to sit on the case if it continues to trial; pretrial transcripts are not transferred to the trial judge. The numbers speak to the effectiveness of the criminal pretrial, with 87 percent of plea bargains made before reaching the trial phase.[99]

To further encourage plea bargaining, another judicial practice has developed in recent years: judicial mediation between the prosecution and the defendant.[100] In this setting, the pretrial judge or, if a trial has begun, a specially-appointed judge (who does not preside on the case), tries to facilitate settlement between the prosecution and the defendant with the aim of reducing judicial bench time (thus this practice is

understood and to make style and terminology consistent throughout the rules. These changes are intended to be stylistic only, with some exceptions: Current Rule 17.1 prohibits the court from holding a pretrial conference where the defendant is not represented by counsel. It is unclear whether this would bar such a conference when the defendant invokes the constitutional right to self-representation. *See Faretta v. California*, 422 U.S. 806 (1975). The amended version makes clear that a pretrial conference may be held in these circumstances. Moreover, the Committee believed that pretrial conferences might be particularly useful in those cases where the defendant is proceeding *pro se*. On its own, or on a party's motion, the court may hold one or more pretrial conferences to promote a fair and expeditious trial. When a conference ends, the court must prepare and file a memorandum of any matters agreed to during the conference. The government may not use any statement made during the conference by the defendant or the defendant's attorney unless it is in writing and is signed by the defendant and the defendant's attorney.

98 As in the United States, the law conditions the pretrial on the legal representation of the defendant. The condition is not adhered to in practice when defendants choose not to be represented (though public lawyers can be accessed without a fee).

99 ISRAEL ATTORNEY GENERAL ANNUAL REPORT, 45 (2018).

100 Michal Alberstein & Nourit Zimerman, *Constructive Plea Bargaining: Towards Judicial Conflict Resolution*, 32 OHIO ST. J. DISP. RESOL. 279 (2017).

considered especially suitable for cases that are expected to be protracted).[101] The judge presiding on the case is not involved in the mediation and is not permitted to see transcripts of the meeting(s). Judges are very active during these mediations, taking on an inquisitorial stance and a negotiating role,[102] although unlike in inquisitorial procedures in continental jurisdictions, victims do not have a right to participate in these procedures.[103]

Observations of criminal arraignment hearings and pretrials in the Tel Aviv first-instance court uncovered active judicial interventions to encourage plea bargains, and a tendency to prolong the preliminary phase and enable more hearings until an agreement between the parties could be reached.[104]

When judges intervene, they employ a variety of judicial practices to facilitate plea bargains, which are often accompanied by pressure on the prosecution to settle (as is the case in civil pretrials). Judges in criminal pretrial use the following tactics that were also found in civil pretrials: (1) facilitation of litigotiation, (2) prediction of the legal outcome, (3) portrayal of the trial in a negative light, (4) using lawyer–client relations to promote agreement, and (5) using ADR techniques.[105]

A technique that was used in criminal pretrials and cannot be used in civil pretrials was the overriding of the prosecutor's opinion by referring to a senior prosecutor (ordering the prosecutor to go outside and consult by phone with a senior prosecutor, or ordering a senior prosecutor be present in the next pretrial hearing regarding the case). Another interesting finding in criminal pretrials is the reference by judges to former plea bargains in similar cases. Thus the judges' predictive practices were not based only on judicial decisions in relevant cases but also included former plea bargains. The fact that judges have the final word on whether

101 Ami Kobo, *Criminal Mediation*, 24 HAMISHPAT (2018) (Hebrew).

102 Michal Alberstein & Béatrice Coscas-Williams, *La médiation pénale en Israël*, Les cahiers de la justice # 2018/3 (French).

103 HCJ 8417/13 *John Doe v. State of Israel*, Justice Hendel.

104 Sari Luz Kanner, Dana Rosen, Yosef Zohar & Michal Alberstein, *Managerial Judicial Conflict Resolution (JCR) of Plea Bargaining: Shadows of Law and Conflict Resolution*, 22 NEW CRIM. L. REV. 494 (2019); Hadar Dancig-Rosenberg & Tali Gal, *"The Fast and the Furious": An Empirical Study on Arraignment Hearings at Lower Courts in Israel*, 33 BAR-ILAN LAW REVIEW (2021).

105 For a comparison with judicial practices to bring about plea bargains in the United States, *see* Nancy J. King & Ronald F. Wright, *The Invisible Revolution in Plea Bargaining: Managerial Judging and Judicial Participation in Negotiations*, 95 TEX. L. REV. 325, 331–34 (2016); Alschuler, *supra* note 90.

the case could move to trial was also mentioned by one judge when a defendant's lawyer commented that there was no choice but to go to trial. While judges are given freedom to settle cases in almost any manner that they please, they often choose narrow settlement practices, such as casting trial in a negative light (costs, time).

Observations of judicial criminal mediation showed a huge disparity of judicial approaches: from a truly mediation-oriented approach that seeks to address the emotions and needs of the parties, construct a letter of apology and to take a larger view of the issue at hand to a heavy-handed, acerbic approach and refusal from the start to speak with the defendant, only with the lawyer. *The large majority of mediations were between these poles, with the judge taking an evaluative approach, pointing out the weaknesses in the case (of the prosecution, the defendant, or both), and attempting to bring the parties closer to an agreement.* The meeting would take place with the prosecutor and legal representative of the defendant, sometimes in the presence of the defendant. Yet the victim or a representative of the victim was not a part of the process. When needed, the judge would ask one of the parties to exit the room and speak to the other party separately. The benefits of a relatively free-flowing conversation in which the adversarial mode is reduced and a real discussion can take place have been commented upon.[106] While such mediations have the potential to involve the victim, they rarely do.

A broadening of the role of the judge takes place in community courts, in which the needs and rehabilitation potential of defendants who have committed minor offenses are more greatly emphasized. The Israeli community court model was inspired by the Red Hook Community Justice Center, a community court that was created in Brooklyn, New York. Some adaptations were made to the original model to meet the social, religious, and structural needs of the Israeli population.[107] Judges in community courts manage a team of experts whose aim is to rehabilitate defendants who have pleaded guilty to minor offenses. The victim, as in the original model, is usually not a part of the process. Since 2014, six community courts have been established in Israel, handling approximately 100 cases each per year, a slight percentage of the total criminal cases in Israel.[108]

[106] Kobo, *supra* note 101.

[107] Hadar Dancig-Rosenberg, Jeffrey Fagan & Victoria Malkin, *Theorizing Community Justice through Community Courts*, 30 FORDHAM URB. L.J. 897, 954 (2003).

[108] ISRAEL JUSTICE MINISTRY, COMMUNITY COURT ANNUAL REPORT (2020).

The focus on the offender and the primarily managing role of the judge are far from the ideal of a broad judicial conflict resolution role. Nevertheless, the community courts are the apex of judicial conflict resolution activities in the criminal justice system, for they take a relatively deep look into the needs of the defendant and take the community into account in finding ways for rehabilitation. However, this judicial role is limited to very few cases, specifically only relatively minor offenses in which the defendant has admitted guilt.

2.4.3 England and Wales: Incentivizing Pleas

While legal aid is available for defendants in criminal cases, the same economic concerns that have motivated legal reform in civil cases are relevant to reform in criminal justice, along with a concern regarding growing rates of crime and its effect on the handling of cases. The strategy to economize criminal justice has been similar to that of the civil realm: an emphasis on processes preceding trial with the aim of early disposition of cases, along with active judicial case management for cases that are not resolved. Thus a large variety of out-of-court processes (waiving trial) have been developed for relatively minor offenses (including cautions, conditional cautions, fixed penalty notices and more).[109]

Pretrial procedure requires the prosecution and the defendant to communicate on the case and elucidate the points of agreement and differences between the parties.[110] In general, the legal system encourages defendants to plead guilty *at the earliest possible moment*: the earlier the admission, the greater the sentence discount. Judges have been poised to assist in this endeavor by predicting at a "Goodyear hearing" what the sentence would be considering the charges if it went to trial. The predicted sentence is shortened by one-third if the defendant pleads guilty,

[109] Nicky Padfield, *Judicial Rehabilitation? A View from England*, 3(1) EUR. J. PROBATION 36 (2011) (noting the vast use of fixed penalty notices for many high-volume offenses and noting criticism of the police and prosecution for a broad interpretation of the type of offenses that can be included and disposing offenses that include violence in this manner); Richard Young, *Street Policing after PACE: The Drift to Summary Justice*, in REGULATING POLICING: THE POLICE AND CRIMINAL JUSTICE ACT 1984 PAST, PRESENT, AND FUTURE 149 (Ed Cape & Richard Young eds., 2008).

[110] Criminal Procedure Rules (2015), Pre-trial procedure, Rule 3.3 (The duty of the parties). This rule requires parties to communicate with each other to find whether the defendant is likely to plead guilty or not guilty; what is agreed and what is likely to be disputed; what information or other material is required by one party of another, and why; and what is to be done, by whom, and when.

and the defendant continuing to trial is binding upon the sitting judge as the maximum penalty.[111]

The adversarial nature of trial is tempered by broad pretrial discovery requirements and a foretelling of the defense's case to prevent "ambush defense" tactics: "Rather than resting the burden of proof squarely on the prosecution, the accused is co-opted into participating in the construction of the case against her and promoting the wider system goal of efficiency-in some instances, with the penalty of adverse inference for non-compliance."[112]

Cases that proceed to trial are actively managed by the judge, and a long chapter in the Criminal Procedure Rules is dedicated to this effort. The judge can interfere in the cross-examination of a witness, interrogate the witness, exclude evidence or witnesses, and demand appropriate time forecasts and limits from the attorneys for any part of the criminal trial. This interrogating, managing, and evidence-screening role is reminiscent of that of an inquisitorial judge.[113] In addition, the weakening of the defense is reminiscent of the traditional inquisitorial criminal regime, which based judicial decisions mainly on the prosecution file, with the trial itself considered a symbolic and largely futile effort of the defense to change the judge's bias.

While the changes to the adversarial system have often been accompanied by the disclaimer that this does not mean that the system is becoming inquisitorial (just less adversarial), and scholars have noted that the move toward managerialism does not equal a move toward inquisitorialism, some voices in the English legal system have already noted that judges are becoming more inquisitorial.[114] The accumulated

[111] *See* Golan *supra* note 88.

[112] Anthony Edwards, *Do the Defence Matter*, 14 INT'L J. EVIDENCE & PROOF 119 (2010) (arguing that foretelling the defense gives an unfair advantage to the prosecution and compromises cross-examination of prosecution witnesses, who know in advance what the issues are, and can thus prepare themselves for questions that will be asked). Jacqueline S. Hodgson, *The Future of Adversarial Criminal Justice in 21st Century Britain,* 35 NCJ INT'L L. & COM. REG. (2009): 319, 331 ("[C]riminal justice reforms have sought to dissuade the accused from exercising her right to trial, but have also attempted to shift the weight of the proceedings and of case disposition to the pre-trial investigation.").

[113] J. A. Jolowicz, *Adversarial and Inquisitorial Models of Civil Procedure,* 52 INT'L & COMP. L.Q. 281 (2003).

[114] *Id.;* Justice Lightman, *The Civil Justice System and Legal Profession-The Challenges Ahead* (2003) 22 C.J.Q. 235; Resnik, *supra* note 22 (describing US judges' active stance during pretrial also makes this comparison).

impact of the reforms on the judicial role seems to suggest that this is true.

With the simplification of criminal procedure also encouraged by the European Union,[115] active judicial case management in criminal cases has been promulgated in legislation in criminal justice as well. Plea bargains have been an accepted form of disposing claims for decades, as in many common law systems, following acceptance in the United States. A full trial or the hearing of oral evidence are the exception, while guilty pleas and alternative forms of case disposal are the rule.[116] Data is lacking for the first-instance (magistrates) courts,[117] which try minor offenses. In the Crown Courts, guilty pleas on all counts were entered in 63 percent of criminal cases in 2018, and a further 33 percent consisted of pleas that were partial (guilty pleas on some of the counts) or not guilty pleas.[118] As the latter category makes it difficult to estimate the percentage of guilty pleas, the 2016 figure of 88.2 percent of cases sentenced by the Crown Court involving a guilty plea gives a more accurate picture.[119] Guilty pleas are greatly encouraged by the legal system through sentence reductions that hinge on the timeliness of the plea.[120] Problem-solving

[115] COUNCIL OF EUROPE, RECOMMENDATION NO R (87) 18 OF THE COMMITTEE OF MINISTERS TO MEMBER STATES CONCERNING THE SIMPLIFICATION OF CRIMINAL JUSTICE (1987).

[116] Hodgson, *supra* note 112.

[117] Surprisingly, despite the widely held estimate that the vast majority of criminal trials are disposed through plea bargains, no figures on plea bargains are presented in UK criminal justice reports. *See* Carol A. Brook , Bruno Fiannaca, David Harvey & Paul Marcus, *A Comparative Look at Plea Bargaining in Australia, Canada, England, New Zealand, and the United States*, 57 WM. & MARY L. REV. 1147 (2016).

[118] UK CRIMINAL COURT STATISTICS QUARTERLY JULY–SEPTEMBER 2018, Table C3 at www.gov.uk/government/statistics/criminal-court-statistics-quarterly-july-to-september-2018

[119] UK CRIMINAL JUSTICE STATISTICS QUARTERLY 2016 (FINAL) (2017) (72,474 guilty pleas out of 82,118 cases sentenced by the Crown Court) at chrome-extension://oemmndcbldboiebfnladdacbdfmadadm /https://assets.publishing.service.gov.uk/government/uploads/system/uploads/attachment_data/file/614414/criminal-justice-statistics-quarterly-december-2016.pdf; *Cf.* Alschuler, supra note 90 at 1 (In the United States, as early as the 1970s, "roughly ninety percent of the criminal defendants convicted in state and federal courts plead guilty rather than exercise their right to stand trial before a court or jury. Behind this statistic lies the practice of plea bargaining, in which prosecutors and trial judges offer defendants concessions in exchange for their pleas.").

[120] Criminal Justice Act 2003, Section 144 Reduction in sentences for guilty pleas: (1) In determining what sentence to pass on an offender who has pleaded guilty to an offence in proceedings before that or another court, a court must take into account – (a)the stage in the proceedings for the offence at which the offender indicated his intention to plead guilty and (b)the circumstances in which this indication was given.

courts, where judges might have a more substantial role, account for only 3.5 percent of criminal cases in England and Wales in recent years.[121]

2.5 Two Central Factors Influencing the Trajectory of Adversarial-Inquisitorial Melds

In theory, the judicial role could have been broadened through an infusion of consensual values. However, as shown in Chapter 2, it has, in effect, been sequestered in England and Wales through disincentives to litigate and constricted in Israel due to the centrality of the abbreviated role of the pretrial judge. In Italy, the centrality of the judicial role has thus far been maintained alongside a diagnostic judicial role regarding mediation.

These differences raise a central question for comparative scholars, who take interest in the effect of transplants on receiving legal cultures. As shown, settlement-related transplants originating mainly in the United States have swept across these legal systems (and many others). What was different in each legal system that led to a unique implementation that is generally replicated in civil and criminal justice? And can the disparate modes of implementation be predicted?

The broad differences in implementing the transplants seem to reinforce the concept of transplants as irritants,[122] which produce far-reaching change through a largely unpredictable ripple effect. However, we show that the transformation of transplants in receiving cultures may not be entirely unforeseeable or random. Whether the differences are merely temporal, rooted in a specific context, or reversible is a question that is explored in this book. The role of legal culture, the tension between ideals and efficiency considerations, and insights relating to the impetus for such transplants are also discussed.

See Maximo Langer *supra* note 89 at 388 (citing studies that show that in the UK "almost all defendants that plead guilty receive a discount of one third or less, that these discounts largely comply with the sentencing discounts established by English law"). On Section 144 of the Criminal Justice Act, and the direction of the criminal justice system in general, *see* Hodgson, *supra* note 112.

121 See UK JUSTICE MINISTRY, CRIMINAL STATISTICS REPORT (2015).

122 Gunther Teubner, *Legal Irritants: Good Faith in British Law or How Unifying Law Ends Up in New Divergences*, 61 MOD. L. REV. 11 (1998) (suggesting that transplants produce change in legal systems not through smooth reception of the borrowed concepts but rather through the reaction of the receiving legal culture to them, which creates numerous effects along a multitude of legal factors in the system).

We propose two elements that can contribute to the understanding of the different transformations that occurred in each legal system: (1) adversarial roots or lack thereof and (2) the impetus for the transplants in the context of the tension between the aspiration to high ideals of justice on the one hand and the search for efficiency on the other.

Adversarial legal systems, which place an emphasis on the agency of the parties, have long included a significant settlement component. Well before the institutional promotion of settlement and the vanishing trial phenomenon, settlement was a common mode for disposing of disputes in these legal systems. The traditional perception of the judge was of a passive umpire, while the parties that reached trial were responsible for actively making their case. In a setting that places emphasis on the parties, it is perhaps more natural to take dispute resolution to the parties, even to the point of nearly privatizing civil justice as in England and Wales. This can be conceived as traveling along an already existing continuum of party agency, nearly reaching its farthest point. A similar hypothesis has been raised in regard to the administratization of criminal justice in adversarial systems: Legal systems with adversarial roots may have a higher tendency to dispose of criminal cases through managerial means, such as plea bargains, than do legal systems with inquisitorial roots.[123]

In contrast, legal systems with inquisitorial roots (i.e., continental law systems), have traditionally placed an emphasis on the active role of the judge and the application of formal legislative rules to implement social norms. In these systems, adjudication has been the primary mode of disposing of cases, and the option of settlement has been relatively disregarded. While this is changing, the historical milieu shapes the subsequent transplants. Thus, in Italy, settlement reform is itself is introduced in a formalistic fashion (with judges required to explain their

[123] Langer, *supra* note 89 at 401 ("[T]here could be a relationship between accepting and using plea bargaining (and other trial-avoiding conviction mechanisms) and the predominance of a party-driven conception of the criminal process in a given jurisdiction, as these mechanisms afford the parties a large say in the adjudication of the case. Legal actors educated and socialized in common law adversarial systems would thus consider the use of guilty pleas, plea bargaining, and other trial-avoiding conviction mechanisms as a natural phenomenon (Langer 2004). By this hypothesis, one would expect that, everything else being equal, the more important the adversarial ideology or structures of interpretation and meaning in a given jurisdiction, the larger the rate of administratization of criminal convictions.").

reasons for referring cases to mediation in writing), and the effect for the time being is moderate.

However, adversarial roots do not account for the differences described in this study within legal families. The model adopted in England and Wales is strikingly different from that which was adopted in the United States, which saves a central settlement role for pretrial judges, akin to the role of pretrial judges in Israel. Since the United States is the origin of many of the discussed transplants, this deserves a close look, and brings us to the next contributing factor that can explain some of these differences: the impetus for the transplants within the context of ideals and reality.

The tension between ideals and the pragmatic need for reducing caseloads (efficiency) accompanied the adoption of ADR from the outset in the US legal systems. The transplant of ADR and other settlement-related reform has produced different manifestations of this original tension in other legal systems.

As has been mentioned by scholars, ADR largely lost its founding values in the United Stsates when it expanded from the corridors of academia into the legal system.[124] As an idealist movement, ADR suggested an alternative to achieving legal justice through adjudication, which is the search for external rationality in human interaction.[125] Efficiency was not as the main motivation for the proponents of ADR; high caseloads, rather, were an opportunity to promulgate consensual dispute engagement and, for many, to offer an alternative to what they viewed as dysfunctional and narrow justice, also expressed by realist and critical legal studies movements.[126]

Yet this vision did not converge with that of the US legal system. The impetus for adopting ADR was the reduction of caseloads (efficiency) while the benefits of dialogue were a side effect.[127] The implementation of ADR into the legal system, whether through various court-connected

[124] Carrie Menkel-Meadow, *Pursuing Settlement in an Adversary Culture: A Tale of Innovation Co-opted or the Law of ADR*, 19 FLA. ST. U. L. REV. 1 (1991); Lela Love & Ellen Waldman, *The Hopes and Fears of All the Years: 30 Years Behind and the Road Ahead for the Widespread Use of Mediation*, 31 OHIO ST. J. DISP. RESOL. 123 (2016).

[125] This is one possible definition based on Lon L. Fuller & Kenneth I. Winston, *The Forms and Limits of Adjudication*, 92(2) HARV. L. REV. 353 (1978).

[126] Michal Alberstein, *Fast Justice vs. Sublime Justice: An Anatomy of the Relations between Practice and Theory in Conflict Resolution*, 9 ALEI MISHPAT 85(2011)(Hebrew); Menkel-Meadow *supra* note 124.

[127] Menkel Meadow, *id.*

ADR schemes or in-court ADR led by judges, took on the nature of the underlying impetus – efficiency. ADR in practice in the United States has become increasingly devoid of consensual values, and caucusing often takes the place of dialogue.[128] In many cases, ADR is not different from bargaining between lawyers, and this may account for the fact that ADR seems often underused.[129]

This same type of analysis can be made of transplants across legal systems. Is the impetus for adopting the original concept (in the United States) and the transplanted concept (in the importing legal system) the same? The impetus for efficiency in England and Wales was *even more powerful* than in the United States due to deep cuts in civil justice and thus the cancellation of legal aid except for the very poor. The exorbitant cost of litigation, without legal aid, left "the ordinary litigant" (neither very rich nor very poor) without recourse to courts, and the continuing cuts to civil justice led to an aversion to any caseload at all. The drive for efficiency was not a result of high caseloads but rather due to an aversion to any form of caseload, since most citizens couldn't afford it, and the justice system was looking to cut costs in any way possible. Thus the legal system embraced settlement and ADR – incentivizing them through cost sanctions and pre-action protocols to resolve differences between them rather than file a claim in court. The strong emphasis on efficiency has resulted in both a fall from the adjudicative ideal of "justice on the merits at all cost" (the implementation of social norms through judicial decisions) and a fall from mediation's ideal – due to the prevalent use of caucusing. The declarative call of the Woolf reform for "access to justice" addressed the "vanishing litigant" through encouraging them to use out-of-court settlement and ADR.

In promoting a settlement culture, the impetus for efficiency in Israel was also significant, yet it was part of a general pursuit of ways to reduce caseloads, not as part of a crisis situation. In an interesting way, inquisitorial tools are used in Israel both in the criminal and the civil setting not to seek for the truth but to actively encourage settlement. This unique mode of transplantation reflects the central role of the judge in Israel,

[128] *Id.*, Roberts *supra* note 39; *see* interview with senior mediator in Section 2.3.

[129] Robert A. Baruch Bush & Joseph P. Folger, *Reclaiming Mediation's Future: Re-focusing on Party Self-Determination*, 16 CARDOZO J. CONFLICT RESOL. 741, 741–742 (2014) ("[M]ediation is presently underutilized almost everywhere . . . the problem lies not with an uninterested community of potential users, but with the failure of mediation providers to deliver a "product" that lives up to its promises and offers something truly new and valuable to its users.").

who is considered an umpire of justice and professionalism. It thus has allowed for some space for the adjudicative ideal: Israel has not blocked the door to court altogether. It is possible to file a claim without pre-action requirements and running a costs risk, though an informational mediation meeting is obligatory for claims above 40,000 NIS. Most cases reaching pretrial settle at that stage, often through intervention of the pretrial judge. The somewhat lower emphasis on efficiency also allows for some expression of the ideal of mediation, as court-connected mediation usually includes dialogue. When ADR was brought to Israel, Frank Sander was invited to advise, and the Supreme Court chief justice Aharon Barak announced the "mediation revolution," referring in a sense to the "constitutional revolution" he announced at the same time in the public arena when basic laws were introduced.[130] A high professional standard of problem solving integrative mediation is used to recruit the mediators for the Israeli pre-mediation mandatory meetings, and supervision and training in the field are conducted by conflict resolution champions.[131] Recently, Israel inserted proportionality into its objective for civil justice,[132] hearkening to this central concept in England and Wales. The continuing pursuit of efficiency will thus probably result in increasing gradual measures.

In Italy, the impetus for efficiency and ADR-related transplants stemmed from a notorious caseload that has caused both external (EU) and internal criticism due to the length of proceedings. The country has thus conducted a sequence of reforms to stem the caseload. While the caseload problem has existed for a long time, and there is no acute need (such as an impending EU sanction or deep budget cut) to clear all cases at once, it is expected that continuing efforts will be made, yet will also result in gradual rather than drastic measures such as those taken in the reform to civil justice in England and Wales. Recently, Italy has allowed for judicial training in mediation, raising the possibility that judges will become more involved in the settlement of cases, perhaps gravitating toward an active judicial settlement role. Italy has also established mediation centers supervised by the Ministry of Justice, yet privately handled and include professional mediators who are not necessarily lawyers. There are also indications of efforts to emphasize the importance of dialogue in mediation.

[130] Michal Alberstein, *The Mediation Revolution in Israel: Current Mapping of Intersections of Conflict Resolution and Law*, THE ISRAEL JOURNAL ON CONFLICT RESOLUTION (2015), (Hebrew).

[131] Israeli Courts Regulations (Mediation), 1993. Revised Aug. 12, 2019.

[132] Civil Procedure Rules 2018 (enacted since 2021).

Table 2.1 *Two elements affecting the implementation of transplants and the judicial role in the three legal systems. The presence of adversarial roots and the strength of the impetus for efficiency may contribute to a trend of disintegration of the judicial role.*

	Roots	Efficiency Impetus	Judicial Role
England and Wales	Adversarial	Extreme	Sequestered
Israel	Mixed	Strong	Constricted (mainly pretrial judge)
Italy	Inquisitorial	Strong	Traditional judicial role, with some alternative roles

A crisis situation calling for extreme measures to increase efficiency might change this gradual move. For instance, when the COVID-19 pandemic ends and courts may be flooded with claims that were not brought forth or were filed yet not dealt with during the pandemic years due to social-distancing measures, ways to stem the tide may accelerate the move toward privatized dispute resolution. For the time being, each reform brings with it a small step toward the current state in England and Wales.

Of course, adversarial culture and impetus are not the only factors delineating the course of legal transplants. Yet this should not hinder us in identifying these influences, which may be no less central than the mode of implementation of transplants by first-instance judges – who were observed in this study to, for the most part, faithfully implement legislation on settlement practices. The strength of adversarial roots and the need for reduction of caseload can be summed up in Table 2.1, which indeed does not encapsulate the full breadth of factors that influence the judicial role but perhaps can provide an insight into two elements that may have come into play.

The transplants of constructs are malleable. As demonstrated, comparing the original impetus of a legal construct (including its underlying formants) to the impetus of its transplantation in another legal culture might help predict the transplant's trajectory. In addition, adversarial roots may portend a more natural tendency to privatize civil justice and promote plea bargaining in criminal justice. While in common law countries a drive toward settlement prevails, Italy has for the time being preserved judicial truth seeking.

3

New Legal Families

3.1 Pre-filing, Pretrial, Trial

The widespread promotion of settlement (whether through ADR programs or incentives to settle) has caused a reordering of legal systems.[1] In explaining the differing legal emphases that have emerged, we took England and Wales, Italy, the United States, and Israel as examples. However, this trend is apparent in legal systems across the globe, whether it is the United States, Vietnam, Armenia, Poland, China, or Holland. The extent of change differs among the legal systems, and is dynamic. It seems that as time passes from the initial introduction of ADR and efficiency-oriented reforms in a legal system, they gather pace to create a more profound change.

In general, it seems that legal systems can be classified into families according to their emphasis – whether it is a pre-filing emphasis such as that in England and Wales, a pretrial emphasis such as that in the United States, or a trial emphasis such as that in Italy. Since legal systems are dynamic and often undergo series of reforms, this legal family taxonomy, likewise, is dynamic: Legal systems move along a continuum between pre-filing, pretrial, and trial (often changing to some degree with each major reform). Thus, one can find legal systems, such as Germany's, which are situated between families.

In Germany, judgments account for disposing 24.7 percent of cases in district courts (claims up to 5,000 euros) and near 30 percent in regional

[1] Nofit Amir & Michal Alberstein, *New Families of Legal Systems in Transition and Implications for AI*, 33 (1) TRANSNAT'L L. & CONTEMP. PROBS., 1 (2024); Marc Galanter, *A World without Trials*, 7 J. DISP. RESOL. 34 (2006) (on which much of this chapter is based); Herbert M. Kritzer, *Disappearing Trials? A Comparative Perspective*, 1 J EMPIRICAL LEGAL STUD. 735 (2004); Ayelet Sela, Nourit Zimerman & Michal Alberstein, *Judges as Gatekeepers and the Dismaying Shadow of the Law: Courtroom Observations of Judicial Settlement Practices*, HARV. NEGOT. L. REV. 24 (2018); Maria J. Glover, *The Federal Rules of Civil Settlement*, NYU L. REV. 87,113 (2012); *see also* William G. Young, *Vanishing Trials, Vanishing Juries, Vanishing Constitution*, 40 SUFFOLK U. L. REV. 67 (2006).

courts (claims over 5,000 euros) – a higher rate than in pretrial systems but relatively low for trial systems.[2] This percentage of judgments does not include default judgments and procedural decisions. This seems to indicate a trial emphasis. However, a mandatory conciliation meeting with a judge (close in nature to pretrial) precedes trial[3] and accounts for 14.5 percent of civil case dispositions in district courts and 26 percent in regional courts.[4] Moreover, the majority of civil cases that are disposed of through trial do so *without an evidentiary hearing*. Thus, while the percentage of judgments is higher than the percentage of judgments in pretrial systems, it seems Germany can be positioned between a trial emphasis and a pretrial emphasis.

Some Eastern European legal systems that have only recently begun officially integrating ADR mechanisms may be studied to find if they have a trial emphasis, which would perhaps be more accentuated than the emphasis of the legal systems of Italy and Germany. According to the European Justice Scoreboard, four out of five countries with the highest ratio of incoming litigious cases to population are from Eastern European

[2] Amir & Alberstein, *id. See also* Michael Berlemann & Robin Christmann, *Determinants of In-Court Settlements: Empirical Evidence from a German Trial Court*, BEITRÄGE ZUR JAHRESTAGUNG DESAUSSCHUSSES FÜR WIRTSCHAFTSSYSTEME UND INSTITUTIONENÖKONOMIK IM VEREIN FÜR SOCIALPOLITIK, 1, 8 (2016) (examining a random sample of 2,360 case records in an intermediate German trial court (Amtsgericht) in Hamburg in 2009: "689 cases in our sample (37 percent) were resolved with a default judgment because one of the two parties failed to appear in court. In 173 cases, the defendant recognized the plaintiff 's claim. The claim was abandoned by the plaintiff in 24 percent of the cases because the suit was unsubstantiated or the parties successfully resolved the dispute without further court action. In a small number of cases (3 percent), the lawsuit aimed at a preliminary injunction. The remaining 860 cases led to court proceedings. In 279 of these cases, the parties eventually established an in-court settlement under the judgés supervision and the dispute was resolved. In the remaining 581 cases (25 percent), the court had to promulgate a first-instance decision.").

[3] Michael Stürner, *Sharing Responsibility: The German Federal Court of Justice and the Civil Appellate System,* Bravo-Hurtado, P., van Rhee, C.H., eds., SUPREME COURTS UNDER PRESSURE, (83) IUS GENTIUM: COMPARATIVE PERSPECTIVES ON LAW AND JUSTICE (2021) (describing the development of a settlement culture in German courts and the emphasis on the first-instance court to dispose of cases through settlement); John Sorabji, *Managing Claims,* 6(1) PEKING UNIV. L. J. 179 (2019).

[4] The German Federal Office of Justice, which compiled statistics in English on this topic in response to our inquiry – on file with authors (response sent by email on Dec 23, 2021). The sources used were Federal Statistical Office, Fachserie 10 Reihe 2.1 "Civil Courts," 2018, 2019, and 2020.

countries.[5] This indication and other indications that these legal systems may have a more traditional trial focus[6] may make them interesting to focus on in further studies.

Many legal principles and practices are transformed when the emphasis of civil justice moves to an earlier stage. For instance, perspectives on access to justice change to include access not only to courts but also – or even primarily – to dispute resolution mechanisms.[7] The role of law differs among the proposed classifications, and even the "shadow of law"[8] in negotiation recedes as the emphasis gravitates to an early stage.[9] Legal culture, too, may affect and be affected by the prevalence of trial.[10] We explored the effects of the different emphases on a range of core principles, showing that, taken together, the move to pretrial and pre-filing emphases may create new legal families that merit classification (see Section 3.2).[11] The core legal aspects that differ among the legal families include access to justice, the function of law, judicial presence, the institutional role of courts, and, overall, the main aim of legal systems.

Thus we propose a new classification into legal families that includes: (1) legal systems that place an emphasis on the pre-filing stage – creating financial disincentives or bureaucratic obstacles to filing cases in court on the one hand and incentives to negotiating cases on the other; (2) legal systems that place an emphasis on the pretrial stage – keeping the option of filing cases open yet discouraging the option of trial through various measures, such as involvement of a judge to help settle the case or court-mandated ADR mechanisms; and (3) legal systems that place an

[5] EUROPEAN COMMISSION, EU JUSTICE SCOREBOARD 7 (2020) (comparing the number of incoming civil and commercial litigious cases in first-instance courts; Romania, Lithuania, Poland, and Czechia.)

[6] *See, e.g.*, Zdenek Kuhn, *Worlds Apart: Western and Central European Judicial Culture at the Onset of the European Enlargement*, 52 AM. J. COMP. L. 531 (2004); Bartosz Karolczyk, *Pretrial as a Part of Judicial Case Management in Poland in Comparative Perspective*, COMP. L. REV. (2013) (describing the lack of pretrial conferences in Poland, making trial the first venue for cases).

[7] *Infra* Section 3.2; *see also* Hadas Cohen & Michal Alberstein, *Multilevel Access to Justice in a World of Vanishing Trials: A Conflict Resolution Perspective*, 47 FORDHAM URB. L.J. 1, 33 (2019).

[8] For the role of the "shadow of the law" during negotiation, *see* R. H. Mnookin & L. Kornhauser, *Bargaining in the Shadow of the Law: The Case of Divorce* 88 YALE L.J. 950 (1979).

[9] *Infra* Section 3.2; *see also* Marc Galanter, *The Vanishing Trial*, 10 DISP. RESOL. MAG. 3 (2004).

[10] *Infra* Section 3.2.

[11] Amir & Alberstein, *supra* note 1.

emphasis on the trial stage, while channeling disputes to other modes of dispute resolution as well.

Looking at legal systems through the prism of emphasized stage allows for fluidity as legal systems transform from one type to another through an ongoing process of legal reform. If one views emphasized stages on a continuum, with a pre-filing emphasis at one pole, a trial emphasis at the other, and a pretrial emphasis in between, there seems to be a general movement of legal systems in the direction of a pretrial and pre-filing emphasis, changing core legal function. For instance, the decision-making process gravitates from judicial decision-making (trial family) to diffused decision-making by the judge and disputants (pre-trial family) to disputant-based decision-making (pre-filing family). If one looks further into the future to legal systems that may be governed by AI, this decision-making process would largely be hidden from the disputants themselves. They might receive an output, but the process of analyzing big data through AI may be considered too complex to enable the understanding of the interaction between factors that lead to a decision.[12]

3.1.1 *Further Classification within the Pretrial Family*

Due to the large variation of possible pretrial mechanisms, legal systems with a pretrial emphasis can be further defined into subcategories according to the types of pretrial mechanisms they offer or require, their scope, and the cost involved. In this way, a continuum of the level of possible judicial involvement within the pretrial stage is constructed: At one extreme are legal systems implementing ADR programs as a primary focus (taking into consideration factors such as the mandatory, binding and costly nature of the programs) while at the other are legal systems whose central pretrial mechanism is a settlement conference (or other similar mechanism) by a magistrate or judge.

For instance, the Southern District of New York has an automatic referral system that channels certain types of cases to free mediation; types of cases that are referred are often characterized by a cost of litigation that exceeds cost of recovery due to plaintiff caps or otherwise.[13] In parts of Ontario, mediation is mandated for a larger scope of

[12] Andreas Theodorou & Virginia Dignum, *Towards Ethical and Socio-legal Governance in AI*, 2 NATURE MACHINE INTELLIGENCE, 10 (2020).

[13] Interview with Rebecca Price, Director of the Southern District of NY Mediation Program (Sept. 1, 2022).

case types and is paid for by the parties. Thus these parts of Ontario may be considered more limited in terms of judicial settlement involvement than in the Southern District of New York.

The framework of mandatory *arbitration* in Oregon state courts could be considered a still more comprehensive or stringent requirement, since the result is a binding decision – unless appealed by one of the parties within one month (exemptions from mandatory arbitration can be requested).[14] Arbitration, paid for by the parties, is mandatory for filed civil cases up to $50,000 (as of this writing) where the relief claimed is recovery of money or damages, except for small claims. Only a small minority of civil cases have a value over $50,000, allowing for a regular jury or bench trial.[15]

In distinguishing among legal systems that have a pretrial emphasis, it is important that the "law in the books" (i.e., the local rules of civil procedure) be compared to "law in action." It may be surprising to find that some courts with automatic pretrial conferences may have, in fact, a very small percentage of cases going to them, while courts with an optional "masters" mechanism (a paid decision by a lawyer) have a higher percentage of cases going to pretrial conferences.[16] Thus the distinction would optimally be based both on the rules of civil procedure (law in the books) and the actual flow of cases (law in action).

Judges may decide to take a hands-on approach in cases even when an automatic referral to ADR is in place (during the scheduling and discovery phase, or during motions). Their preference may be affected by their individual caseload or view on scheduling mediation earlier or later in the

[14] *See* Oregon's Uniform Trial Court Rules (UTCR) Section 36.400–36.425 (partly quoted in notes 51 and 53). An expedited civil jury trial is possible for some types of cases instead of mandatory arbitration, yet according to a state report, this alternative is "underutilized" – *see* OREGON JUDICIAL DEPARTMENT, CIVIL JUSTICE IMPROVEMENTS TASK FORCE REPORT TO THE CHIEF JUSTICE 12, 26 (JUNE 20, 2018).

[15] *See* Oregon's Uniform Trial Court Rules (UTCR) Section 36.400–36.425: "Mandatory arbitration programs. (1) A mandatory arbitration program is established in each circuit court . . . (3) Each circuit court shall require arbitration under ORS 36.400 to 36.425 in matters involving $50,000 or less) . . ."; *see also* State of Oregon Website on arbitration at www.courts.oregon.gov/courts/tillamook/programs-services/Pages/Arbitration.aspx; and State of Oregon Website on Small Claims www.courts.oregon.gov/courts/multnomah/go/Pages/smallclaims.aspx.

[16] U.S. COURTS JUDICIAL BUSINESS REPORT, Table C-4A (2019). *See, e.g.*, figures for the Northern Oklahoma district, which has an automatic pretrial conference. However, data may not be accurate due to possible different reporting discrepancies between districts. Pretrial conference figures may seem low for this reason (Interview with Donna Stientstra, Senior Researcher at the Federal Judicial Center (Aug. 17, 2022).

process.[17] Court observations and interviews would optimally be further used to uncover such judicial practices to estimate the level and nature of judicial involvement within the pretrial stage.

3.2 Core Principles That Differ According to Family

The changes in the emphasis of legal systems have implications that change basic notions of law. The pre-filing, pretrial, and trial emphases each create a different legal family, in which core legal principles carry divergent meanings. Table 3.1 summarizes some central legal functions and concepts as they are expressed in legal systems according to their emphasized stage. These are further explained in this section as far as the scope of this article allows.

3.2.1 Main Aim of Civil Justice System

More than two decades ago, Simon Roberts, speaking of England and Wales, noted "a growing recognition of 'settlement' as an approved, privileged objective of civil justice."[18] In his opinion, the main departure of the Civil Procedure Rules (CPR), which were introduced following the Woolf Reforms, from the previous regime of civil justice was the institutional recognition of settlement as an aim, even a preferred aim. This approach greatly differed from the previous *laissez faire* approach that did not interfere with the work of lawyers in negotiating a settlement. The legal system moved to encourage settlement through a variety of pre-action obligations and incentives and declared litigation a "last resort."[19]

Subsequently, due to unremittingly high litigation costs in England and Wales and further reforms,[20] a few words were inserted into the overriding objective of the CPR: "(1) . . . enabling the court to deal with cases justly *and at proportionate cost* [emphasis added – N.A.]." While the concept of proportionality (meaning the sum being claimed must be

[17] Interview with Rebecca Price, *supra* note 13.

[18] Simon Roberts, *Settlement as Civil Justice*, 63 MOD. L. REV. 739, 739 (2000).

[19] *Id. See also* Masood Ahmed, *Bridging the Gap between Alternative Dispute Resolution and Robust Adverse Costs Orders*, 66 N. IR. LEGAL Q. 71, 71 (2015) ("One of the defining features of the Woolf reforms was its attempt to shift the focus in civil litigation away from the traditional adversarial cultre of resolving disputes to one which was centered on a philosophy of party cooperation and, more significantly, on settlement. As Lord Woolf made clear in his 1996 Final Report, 'the philosophy of litigation should be primarily to encourage early settlement of disputes.'").

[20] LORD JACKSON, REVIEW OF CIVIL LITIGATION COSTS, 234, 346 (2009).

Table 3.1 *Three legal families*

	Pre-Filing Family	*Pretrial Family*	*Trial Family*
Main aim of civil justice system	Settlement without court intervention	Settlement, partly facilitated by a judge and/or court administration	Judicially led application of rules
Function of law in resolving disputes	Role of law is obscure	Shadow of the pretrial judge, who combines law with settlement considerations	Judicially led application of law; corresponding shadow of law in negotiations
Judicial presence (first-instance courts)	Rare	Central in bringing about settlement	Central in implementing the law
Decision-making	Left to the parties	Diffused (parties and judge)	Mainly the judge
Access to justice	ADR-oriented	Pretrial and ADR-oriented	Trial and ADR
Institutional function of courts	Low	Medium	Medium

proportionate to the legal costs expended to attain it) had previously been emphasized during the Woolf Reforms, it had not been formally stated in the CPR. Since high legal costs remained a problem following the Woolf Reforms, the concept was inserted explicitly into the overriding objective. As documented in court observations in the London County Court, judges take their mission to ensure proportionate costs seriously, reflecting the emphasis on this concept, which is also instilled through judicial training. Judges often refer to their obligation to ensure proportionality during Case and Cost Management hearings, even referring to this obligation several times during a hearing.[21]

[21] Nofit Amir & Michal Alberstein, *From Transplant to Disintegration? A Comparative Study of the Judicial Role*, 37(4) OHIO ST. J. DISP. RESOL. 555 (2022).

The added goal of proportionality inserted into the formal aim of the CPR could be interpreted as giving priority to high-value claims (as the costs claimed might be more likely to exceed litigation costs), yet high-value claims, too, are preferably settled regardless of their precedential value as demonstrated by the variety of disincentives to litigation. In other words, the public aim of norm-setting and implementation seems to have receded into the background.

The aim of justice along with proportionality as stated in the overriding objective is limited to court action ("justly by the courts"). Thus, in fact, the "overriding" objective of the CPR misses some of the CPR's own rules affecting parties mainly outside of court. CPR Rule 36, which, through an extensive list of clauses, regulates parties' settlement offers by providing cost sanctions if the parties continue to trial and the award is equal to or smaller than the award offered in settlement, is most relevant outside of courts, where settlement offers are made. Striving toward justice seems difficult to measure when accompanied by lack of oversight, and thus the objective of civil justice is largely focused on settlement.[22]

In pretrial-focused legal systems, in contrast, access to the (pretrial) judge is relatively facile. Yet the main aim of the legal system remains on settlement – facilitated by the court by efficient administration of cases, a mandatory court program, and/or pretrial judge. The pretrial judge encourages parties to dispose of the case – at times by giving a legal prediction of the outcome or pointing out the merits of a case. This is not necessarily a neutral application of the law, since the aim of the pretrial judge is to settle the case (see *infra* Section 3.2.2). In other words, the focus of legal justice is mainly on reaching settlement with the involvement of the judge who applies both the law and settlement practices for this purpose. As stated in *Neary v. Regents of the University of California*,

> The primary purpose of the public judiciary is 'to afford a forum for the settlement of litigable matters between disputing parties. We do not resolve abstract legal issues, even when requested to do so. We resolve real disputes between real people. This function does not undermine our integrity or demean our function. By providing a forum for the peaceful

22 Nancy A. Welsh, *Magistrate Judges, Settlement, and Procedural Justice*, 16 NEV. L.J. 983 (2016); Judith Resnik, *Managerial Judges*, 96 HARV. L. REV. 374 (1982). Perhaps the planned Online Court, which may introduce oversight of the pre-filing phase, is a step in altering this equation.

> resolution of citizens' disputes, we provide a cornerstone for ordered liberty in a democratic society.[23]

The goal of civil justice in trial systems is to implement the law (whether through rules or precedent). The incorporation of ADR and other settlement promotion mechanisms in systems with a trial emphasis has not gone so far as to unsettle that main aim, which is considered essential in the attempt to achieve fairness, preserve order, and develop public norms.[24]

Yet trial systems that are beset by backlog, such as Italy's, need to deal with the paradox that "too much trial" also creates access to justice problems due to delay. Thus the objective of Italy's last legislative decision on reforms (on November 2021), as inserted into the title of the legal decree, was "*increasing the efficiency of civil trials, reviewing alternative dispute resolution mechanisms and taking urgent measures for rationalizing the procedures regarding rights of individuals and families as well as enforcement procedures.*"[25] The decree aims to reduce the duration of trials by at least 40%, as one of the objectives agreed with the EU in order to access the resources of the National Recovery and Resilience Plan.[26] Despite the title of the reforms, they do not lunge to an efficiency extreme but rather take previous reforms some steps forward, as explained in Chapter 2. However, the objective of efficiency, interpreted as reducing

[23] *Neary v. Regents of the Univ. of Cal.*, 10 Cal. Rptr. 2d 859, 864, 865 (Cal. 1992), cited in Deborah R. Hensler, *Our Courts, Ourselves: How the Alternative Dispute Resolution Movement Is Re-Shaping Our Legal System*, 108 PENN ST. L. REV. 165, 193–94 (2003) (adding at footnote 111: "In dissent, Justice Kennard responded: More than just a dispute resolution service, the judiciary is an integral part of our government. Working in the context of actual disputes, courts interpret and enforce the policies adopted by the legislative process, striving always to give those policies coherence and vitality. Thus, when a trial court renders judgment in a particular case, it is not just deciding who wins and who loses, who pays and who recovers. Rather, the ultimate purpose of a judgment is to administer the laws of this state, and thereby to do substantial justice.").

[24] Guido Calabresi, *Two Functions of Formalism: In Memory of Guido Tedeschi*, UNIV. CHI. L. REV. 67.2 (2000): 479–88.

[25] Legal Decree No. 206/2021 (Nov. 26, 2021), which is called *"Delegation to the Government for the efficiency of the civil process and for the revision of the discipline of the alternative resolution tools of disputes and urgent measures to rationalize proceedings regarding the rights of individuals and families as well as in matters of forced execution", published in the* GAZZATTA UFFICIALE DELLA REPUBBLICA ITALIANA (Dec. 9, 2021)*; see* Gianfranco Gilardi, *Introduction. The Civil Justice Reform: From the Legislative Decree 1662/S/XVIII to the Delegated Law of 26 Novemebr 2021*, 206 Gazettta Ufficiale Della Republica Italiana (Nov. 29, 2021).

[26] *Id.*

the duration or dependency on trial, demonstrates how the legal system is moving along the continuum toward a pretrial//pre-filing focus and in the process perhaps modifying the aim of civil justice.

3.2.2 The Function of Law in Resolving Disputes

Legal rules and precedent (the latter most relevant in common law countries) have traditionally created a body of norms that is implemented in court and forms a "shadow" in negotiation.[27] In negotiation theory, this shadow is related to the "best alternative to a negotiated agreement" and "worst alternative to a negotiated agreement," both of which influence negotiations.[28] In legal systems with a trial emphasis, the parties weigh the expected trial outcomes and factor them into negotiations along with other considerations, such as costs, emotional turmoil, and time.[29]

When the emphasis of the legal system moves to *pretrial*, the function of legal rules becomes less direct. Pretrial judges and magistrates may use the law to persuade parties to settle (1) through prediction of the legal outcome, (2) by pointing out the weaknesses of each case, and (3) by factoring in the law as a consideration in judicial settlement offers or the rarer practice of judicial arbitration.[30] Since in many cases pretrial is "all

[27] Catrina Denvir & Amanda Darshini Selvarajah, *Safeguarding Access to Justice in the Age of the Online Court*, 85(1) MOD. L. REV. 25, 26 (2022) ("the outcomes that emanate from the formal justice system, when coupled with the 'coercive power of the state', play a key role in establishing the normative expectations that govern the behaviour and negotiations that occur in the informal dispute resolution setting. The court's role as arbiter and enforcer of legal outcomes operates to give substance to individual and collective rights. Whilst courts may remain peripheral to the experience of civil justice for many individuals, their operation and existence is of fundamental importance for individual civil justice outcomes and for society at large."); Mnookin & Kornhauser, *supra* note 8; Hazel Genn, *What Is Civil Justice For? Reform, ADR, and Access to Justice* 24 YALE J.L. & HUMAN. 397 (2012).

[28] ROGER FISHER & WILLIAM URY, GETTING TO YES (1981)(introducing the concept of the best alternative to a negotiated agreement, or BATNA); Francisco Andrade et al., *Using BATNAs and WATNAs in Online Dispute Resolution, JSAI International Symposium on Artificial Intelligence* (2009).

[29] Mnookin & Kornhauser, *supra* note 8 (introducing the concept of the shadow of the law, "the outcome that the law will impose if no agreement is reached gives each parent certain bargaining chips – an endowment of sorts").

[30] Yuval Sinai & Michal Alberstein, *Court Arbitration by Compromise: Rethinking Delaware's State Sponsored Arbitration Case*, 13 CARDOZO PUB. L. POL'Y & ETHICS J. 739 (2015); for general settlement practices of pretrial judges, *see* Ellen E. Deason, *Beyond Managerial Judges: Appropriate Roles in Settlement*, 78 OHIO ST. L.J. 73 (2017); Amir &

there is"[31] (i.e., very few cases continue to trial), the judge's first impression forms the shadow of the law. This impression is based, among others, on written documents, prediction, and heuristics. The judge and the lawyers know that a first impression can change with the presentation of evidence in trial, but since the probability of trial is low, parties assess the outlook of the pretrial judge and factor it into negotiations to reach a settlement. In court observations, pretrial judges themselves may refer to previous settlements that they have encouraged[32] – in other words, they use the same tactic to influence negotiations, referring to themselves.

The application of law by the pretrial judge is often not straightforward, since it can be affected by the desired end result – settlement. For instance, to an overconfident party, the judge may point out weaknesses for the purpose of settlement rather than give an overall assessment of the case.[33] This settlement-promoting stance is part of the shadow of the pretrial hearing. Lawyers negotiating a settlement, even if they have not reached the pretrial stage, may comment that the judge will offer a compromise, which would probably go along this other line.[34]

In other words, the best alternative to a negotiated agreement has changed. For claimants, the best alternative to negotiations preceding pretrial is not the receipt of full compensation for claimed damages but rather the most one would receive in a settlement following an optimal first impression by a pretrial judge. If a party wants to create a shadow of law or that is more focused on legal rules and precedent, the prospects of continuing to trial (rather than stopping at pretrial) must be presented as credible.[35]

Legal systems with an emphasis on the pretrial stage that mandates ADR mechanisms (e.g., mediation, some form of arbitration, or early neutral evaluation by an attorney) create a more complex shadow of law.

Alberstein, *supra* note 21; Marc Galanter, *A Settlement Judge, Not a Trial Judge: Judicial Mediation in the U.S.*, 12 J. L. & SOC'Y 1 (1985).

[31] Judith Resnik, *Mediating Preferences: Litigant Preferences for Process and Judicial Preferences for Settlement*, J. DISP. RESOL., 155, 157 (2002) ("For most cases, the pretrial process is all there is.").

[32] Amir & Alberstein, *supra* note 21.

[33] *Id.*

[34] John Lande, *The Role of Law in Legal Disputes* (2021). University of Missouri School of Law Legal Studies Research Paper No. 2021-14 (describing "ordinary legal negotiation" (OLN) or "norm-based negotiation." Using this approach, lawyers try to reach a reasonable agreement based on shared norms, which typically are the expected court outcomes or typical agreements in similar cases.).

[35] *Id.*

This shadow of law includes the law that would be applied in the ADR mechanism as well as the law applied by the judge during motions or pretrial conferences at any time before, during, or after the use of the ADR mechanism. The probability that the case will move forward in court after use of the ADR mechanism also affects the shadow of trial: Courts that place more obstacles or greater disincentives to moving on to court proceedings after failure of ADR thus limit the shadow of law as applied in court.

The emphasis on the pre-filing stage alters the significance of law even further, especially in pre-filing systems that have extensive pre-filing requirements (which preclude court involvement). The low prospects of trial, low prospects of institutional involvement, and relatively small number of judicial decisions translate into an eroded role for legal rules and the shadow of law. The realistic best or worst alternative to a negotiated agreement that one party can present to another (or to itself) can be unrelated to any form of judicial involvement – that is, an assessment during pretrial or a verdict at trial. It might be expected that in this setting, reference to other settlements would take the place of legal precedents. Yet while settlements are referred to,[36] the process and causes for reaching the final outcome are not public or documented in a way that would allow for a realistic comparison.[37] Nevertheless, some "soft law" may emerge through authority-based mediation that deals with precedential polycentric complex cases, and will be discussed in Chapter 8, which deals with the future of mediation.

The overall result is that bargaining can occur largely free from the shadow of the law, or even the shadow of other settlement agreements. This can be compared to whole areas of law largely resolved through arbitration in the United States, where mandatory arbitration clauses in a variety of contracts, including consumer and employment agreements, are enforced.[38] In addition, large swathes of insurance claims are resolved

[36] Amir & Alberstein, *supra* note 21.

[37] Resnik, *supra* note 22.

[38] Cynthia Estlund, *The Black Hole of Mandatory Arbitration*, 96 N. C. L. REV. 679, 684 (2018) (stating that these is evidence that mandatory arbitration "effectively enables employers to nullify employee rights and to insulate themselves from the liabilities that back up crucial public policies"); Jill I. Gross, *Bargaining in the (Murky) Shadow of Arbitration*, 24 HARV. NEGOT. L. REV. 185, 189 (2019) ("If the law is indeed under-developed, or even frozen in industries where virtually all account agreements include an arbitration clause (such as securities and app-based ride-sharing), parties trying to settle

through "settlement mills,"[39] where business models rather than legal considerations take the fore and in which set sums undercut serious claims in favor of satisfying the large bulk of small, and even spurious, claims.[40] While government reports in England and Wales have recognized that court decisions are in many cases vital for the success of ADR – that is, the shadow of law facilitates private ordering[41] – the legal system has not yet created credible options for litigating cases. However, the Online Court that is in preparation may provide a partial remedy by introducing supervision into the pre-filing phase and possibly lowering pre-litigation costs.[42]

Another change in the function of law when the focus is on pretrial or pre-filing regards the role of precedent. Depending on the rareness of trial, the reservoir of precedents and types of cases that can be litigated may decrease to the point that the shadow of law may be non-apparent. Thus, even if parties want to negotiate in the shadow of the law, it may be difficult to do so.

3.2.3 *Judicial Presence*

In trial-focused legal systems, disputants file cases in court without substantial pre-filing obligations and can expect their cases to be adjudicated. In other words, the judge maintains a central adjudicative role and presence. In Italy, a country whose legal system has incorporated ADR yet still contains a trial emphasis, the role of the first-instance judge consists mainly of adjudication and subordinately of diagnosing cases for mediation (the extent of the latter function varies among judges and courts).[43] In certain cases, the judge might try to persuade the lawyers that the case is appropriate for mediation yet, at least in observations conducted in the Florence first-instance court, will usually not try to

disputes arising out of those account agreements are negotiating in the shadow of murky legal norms and a "black hole" of arbitration outcomes.").

39 Nora Freeman Engstrom, *The Diminished Trial*, 86 FORDHAM L. REV. 2131 (2018).

40 *Id.*

41 UK CIVIL JUSTICE COUNCIL, ADR AND CIVIL JUSTICE INTERIM REPORT (2017).

42 Masood Ahmed & Claire Pennells, *Online Courts Take the Stage*, 7746 NEW L.J. (2017; for concerns regarding digital proficiency of disputants, *see* Denvir & Selvarajah, *supra* note 27.

43 Paola Lucarelli, Nofit Amir, Hadas Cohen, Dana Rosen & Michal Alberstein, *Fitting the Forum to the Fuss While Seeking the Truth: Lessons from Judicial Reforms in Italy*, 36 OHIO ST. J. DISP. RESOL. 213 (2020).

force it upon them.[44] Judges are present in a large proportion of filed cases, adjudicate many of them, and use judicial settlement tools in limited fashion.[45]

In pretrial-focused legal systems, disputants also file cases in court without substantial pre-filing obligations. Yet adjudication is largely replaced by judicial bench time[46] to dispose of the case in the pretrial stage. Judges have a central role in leading to the settlement of cases through a variety of techniques in pretrial[47] and adjudicating a smaller portion of them. A unique landscape for judicial discretion emerges for these settlement judges, as will be elaborated in Chapter 7. In some pretrial jurisdictions, where judges are allowed to conduct negotiations *ex parte* in judicial chambers, the judicial presence may not always be public.[48]

In contrast to the two families of legal systems described above, which involve significant judicial presence, the pre-filing family does not position the judge at a central junction to help resolve disputes. Due to extensive pre-filing obligations that incur costs and require time and effort, judicial presence is rare. The judicial role may consist mainly of behind-the-scenes, largely automatic functions such as allocation of filed cases to track and default judgments.[49] In a small minority of cases, judges may perform case management and adjudicative roles.

The 2020 European Commission for the Efficiency of Justice (CEPEJ) Evaluation Report (evaluating 2018 data) may provide an indication, however anecdotal, of the centrality of judges in the different families. According to the report, there are 11.6 professional judges in Italy per

[44] *Id.*

[45] *Id.*, Nofit Amir & Michal Alberstein, *Designing Responsive Legal Systems: A Comparative Study*, 22 PEPP. DISP. RESOL. L.J. 263 (2022). In some cases, parties must attend an introductory mediation meeting before the first hearing in court, yet this is true only for a minority of cases.

[46] Ayelet Sela & Limor Gabay-Egozi, *Judicial Procedural Involvement (JPI): A Metric for Judges' Role in Civil Litigation, Settlement, and Access to Justice*, 47(3) J. L. & SOC'Y 468 (2020).

[47] Amir & Alberstein, *supra* note 21; Deason, *supra* note 30; Berlemann & Christmann, *supra* note 2; Nadja Marie Alexander et al., *Mediation in Germany: The Long and Winding Road*, GLOBAL TRENDS IN MEDIATION (2003).

[48] Resnik, *supra* note 22; Leslie W. Abramson, *The Judicial Ethics of Ex Parte and Other Communications*, 37 HOUS. L. REV. 1343 (2000).

[49] PENNY DARBYSHIRE, SITTING IN JUDGMENT: THE WORKING LIVES OF JUDGES (2012).

100,000 inhabitants.[50] In Israel, there are 8.2 judges per 100,000 inhabitants.[51] In England and Wales, the ratio of judges to population is low: 3.1 judges per 100,000 inhabitants. In comparison, in its 2008 report, analyzing data from 2006 in England and Wales, when there were fewer pre-action protocols, the ratio was more than twice as high, 7:100,000.[52] In Italy, in 2006, the ratio was 11:100,000, similar to the 2018 figure (Israel is not listed in the 2008 report). Of course the emphasized stage of the legal system may not be the only factor affecting the figures.[53]

Relatedly, decision-making in civil cases is led by the judge in the trial family. In the pretrial family, it is diffused between the pretrial judge/magistrate and disputants, sometimes with the involvement of other court-mandated mechanisms. In the pre-filing family, decision-making in civil cases is generally left to the disputants. This may mean that the pre-filing family is more bounded by market forces: Assuming that litigants are usually unequal (e.g., repeat players such as companies or governments vs. individuals), the lack of court supervision may result in more disparities and may require monitoring by institutions other than the courts.

3.2.4 Access to Justice

The concept of access to justice has evolved over the years from mere access to courts to a range of other issues, including ADR and legal aid.[54] In the context of this article, the way ADR is integrated into the definition of access to justice changes with emphasized stage. If ADR were merely additive, access to justice would entail free access to trial as well as to ADR. However, access to dispute resolution often competes with access to trial, especially when dispute resolution mechanisms are mandatory or highly incentivized by legal systems.

[50] European Commission for the Efficiency of Justice (CEPEJ), European Judicial Systems Evaluation Report, 2020 Evaluation Cycle (2018 data), Part 2, Country Profiles, 50 (2020).

[51] *Id.*, at 102.

[52] *Id.* at 96 (2020); European Commission for the Efficiency of Justice (CEPEJ), European Judicial Systems Evaluation Report, 2008 Evaluation Cycle (2006 data). There are no such reports pre-dating the Woolf reform that led to pre-action protocols.

[53] TAMARA GORIELY, RICHARD MOORHEAD & PAMELA ABRAMS, MORE CIVIL JUSTICE? THE IMPACT OF THE WOOLF REFORMS ON PRE-ACTION BEHAVIOUR RESEARCH STUDY 43, UK JUSTICE MINISTRY REPORT (2002); JOHN PEYSNER & MARY SENEVIRATNE, THE MANAGEMENT OF CIVIL CASES – THE COURTS AND POST-WOOLF LANDSCAPE, UK DEP. FOR CONSTITUTIONAL AFFAIRS REPORT (2005).

[54] Richard Moorhead, *Conditional Fee Agreements, Legal Aid and Access to Justice*, 33 U. BRIT. COLUM. L. REV. 471 (2000); Cohen & Alberstein, *supra* note 7.

In the trial family, access to justice still often equates to access to trial, with dispute resolution introduced as an additional option – or, as in Italy, a quasi-mandatory option for a small proportion of civil disputes ("quasi," since the obligation only entails one free introductory mediation meeting, yet participation in it must be substantial). However, the easy filing of cases and unobstructed route to trial can contribute to case backlog, which in itself may hinder access to trial.

In the pretrial family, access to court is maintained, but less so access to trial. Other options – access to a pretrial judge, to court-connected mediation, and other ADR options – are more readily available, and only a minority of cases proceed to trial. In contrast, in the pre-filing family, dispute resolution mechanisms are the central form of justice to which parties have access. Parties expend costs to fulfill pre-filing obligations and risk cost sanctions if they do not accept a settlement offer or offer to mediate,[55] making access to courts difficult.

In other words, the interaction between access to trial and access to ADR differs in the different families: from (1) a mainly additive ADR component; to (2) a component that, together with abbreviated mechanisms such as pretrial, competes and may take the place of trial (as the latter is disincentivized); to (3) a dominant component of access to justice that, along with negotiation, largely takes the place of trial and pretrial.

The emphasized stage may have an effect not only on the interaction between trial and ADR options but also on the *nature of* ADR. The promotion of ADR by legal systems often "co-opts" ADR, infusing it with the legal systems' efficiency concerns and subordinating, and even doing away with, the goals of dialogue or solutions to contend with underlying issues.[56] Mediation in the United States and England and Wales often consists of a shuttling between the parties sitting in different rooms, with

[55] See Chapter 2, Section 2.3; *see* UK Civil Procedure Rules, Part 36 ("Offers to settle") (If a claimant declines an offer to settle and receives the same or lower amount through judgment, "the court must, unless it considers it unjust to do so, order that the defendant is entitled to – (a) costs (including any recoverable pre-action costs) from the date on which the relevant period expired; and (b) interest on those costs.").

[56] Carrie Menkel-Meadow, *Pursuing Settlement in an Adversary Culture: A Tale of Innovation Co-Opted or The Law of ADR,* 19 FLA. ST. U. L. REV. 1 (1991); Patrick G. Coy & Timothy Hedeen, *A Stage Model of Social Movement Co-optation: Community Mediation in the U.S.*, 46(3) THE SOCIOLOGICAL. Q., 405 (2005); SIMON ROBERTS, A COURT IN THE CITY (2013); Hazel Genn, P. Fenn, M. Mason, A. Lane, N. Bechai, L. Gray & D. Vencappa, *Twisting Arms: Court Referred and Court Linked Mediation under Judicial Pressure*. MINISTRY OF JUSTICE RESEARCH SERIES (2007).

various bargaining proposals.[57] The most stalwart warriors of mediation have lamented the loss of its founding principles as well as the loss of disputant choice.[58] In Italy, where the option of trial is still valid, a genuine broad perspective of mediation is enabled, and judges acknowledge the different form of justice that litigants can pursue when seeking this forum or mandated to use it.[59]

Access to justice is of course affected not only by the emphasized stage but also by litigation costs,[60] which may in turn cause legal systems to choose a pre-filing or pretrial emphasis.[61] The Woolf Reforms and subsequent reforms in England and Wales, which led to a pre-filing emphasis, are a case in point. The Woolf Reforms – compiled into a report titled "Access to Justice" – were introduced on the heels of numerous cuts to legal aid, which left most of the population without recourse to courts due to high legal costs. By obligating parties to negotiate before filing a case and incentivizing them to use dispute resolution mechanisms, on the one hand, and providing judges with cases management tools to control the cost of litigation in the cases that did reach them, on the other, it was hoped that parties might find redress.

[57] ROBERTS, *id.* Carrie Menkel Meadow, *When Should I Be in the Middle? I've Looked at Life from Both Sides Now* in (Howard Gadlin & Nancy A. Welsh, eds.) EVOLUTION OF A FIELD: PERSONAL HISTORIES IN CONFLICT RESOLUTION, 421, 437 (2020) ("Another concern is the growing practice, in private mediation, for more evaluative, no-joint-session, shuttle-diplomacy forms of mediation. Major litigation, commercial, employment, and divorce mediation have now become professionalized, organized, and institutionalized as well as commercialized, so that in my home town of Los Angeles, the norm is now closer to dispute management by a mediator who shuttles back and forth between the parties, "selling" solutions or settlements, without any or much quality face-to-face time.").

[58] Menkel-Meadow, *id.* (stating that ADR was supposed to be an additional choice to trial and not a substitute for it. Menkel-Meadow was one of the founders of the ADR movement.).

[59] Lucarelli, P. et al., *supra* note 43.

[60] Asher Flynn & Jacqueline Hodgson, *Access to Justice and Legal Aid Cuts: A Mismatch of Concepts in the Contemporary Australian and British Legal Landscapes*, in (Asher Flynn & Jacqueline Hodgson. eds.) ACCESS TO JUSTICE AND LEGAL AID: COMPARATIVE PERSPECTIVES ON UNMET LEGAL NEED 6 (2017); RABEEA ASSY, INJUSTICE IN PERSON (2015); Anna E. Carpenter, *Active Judging and Access to Justice*, 93 NOTRE DAME L. REV. 647 (2017) (noting the proliferation of *pro se* litigants in US state civil courts).

[61] *See*, e.g., Carlo Vittorio Giabardo, *Should Alternative Dispute Resolution Mechanisms Be Mandatory: Rethinking Access to Court and Civil Adjudication in an Age of Austerity*, 44 EXETER L. REV. 25 (2017) (stating that due to high litigation costs and an age of austerity, mediation can provide access to justice).

While the reforms seem to have encouraged a negotiation culture, one of the outcomes of the pre-filing obligations was a frontloading of legal costs.[62] Thus trial avoidance occurs not only due to the disincentives to trial (such as possible cost sanctions for rejecting a settlement or mediation offer) but also due to the original impetus of the reform – litigation costs. High litigation costs, which are more prevalent in common law countries,[63] may be one reason for the general preference of these countries for pre-filing and pretrial emphases. It may be a chicken-and-egg scenario: When trial is costly and thus undesirable, legal systems may, intentionally or unintentionally, put mechanisms into place that in effect further deter parties from pursuing this channel.

3.2.5 The Institutional Function of Courts

It is a well-documented feature of the litigation landscape that filing a case in court can jumpstart negotiations.[64] This is part of the courts' "institutional function," which is manifest in cases where "no significant discretionary judicial activity takes place and only the court's institutional power and authority are in operation."[65]

The ability to file a claim without pre-filing obligations is often the most effective, timely, and inexpensive way for individuals (especially consumers) to garner the attention of otherwise unresponsive companies

[62] GORIELY ET AL., *supra* note 53. PEYSNER & SENEVIRATNE, *supra* note 53.

[63] Pablo Cortes, *A Comparative Review of Offers to Settle: Would an Emerging Settlement Culture Pave the Way for Their Adoption in Continental Europe?* 32(1) CIV. JUST. Q. 42–67 (2013).

[64] *See, e.g.*, Lande, *supra* note 34 (stating that demonstrating willingness to litigate is important for collaborative negotiations); Berlemann & Christmann, *supra* note 2 at 8 (studying courts in Germany, they found that of a random sample of 2,360 case records, "[t]he claim was abandoned by the plaintiff in 24 percent of the cases because the suit was unsubstantiated or the parties successfully resolved the dispute without further court action." In addition, 173 other cases were resolved because the defendant "recognized the claim."); Fiona Rotstein & Kimberlee Weatherall, *Filing and Settlement of Patent Disputes in the Federal Court, 1995-2005*, Intellectual Property Research Institute of Australia Working Paper No. 17.06, 13 (2006) (analyzing filed patent cases, they note that a high proportion of cases that settle early may partly due to "cases in which the issue of proceedings is a strategy used by a party to indicate their seriousness or to move negotiations forward"); Sela & Limor Gabay-Egozi, *supra* note 46 at 473; relatedly, Christina L. Boyd & David A. Hoffman, *Litigating toward Settlement*, 29 J. L. ECON. & ORG. 898, 900 (2013) ("the mere filing of a motion in a case hastens settlement").

[65] Sela & Limor Gabay-Egozi, *supra* note 46 at 473.

and organizations.[66] As noted in Chapter 2, a substantial portion of filed cases involve no court action (i.e., they are withdrawn or abandoned); presumably settlement accounts for a significant part of such cases.[67] The need for a filing option to incentivize responses to claims, whether through negotiation or submission of defense pleadings, is demonstrated in the case below:[68]

> Bielski alleges that, after the scammer drained his account, he turned to Coinbase for help. He encountered a customer-service nightmare ... Bielski initiated a "live chat" with a Coinbase representative, which turned out to be a mere bot that provided canned responses. Bielski then called the specific customer service "hotline" specified in his user agreement as where to get help for a compromised account. He was once again unable to speak with a human. Bielski then wrote two letters to Coinbase at its San Francisco office pleading for help. It was not until this lawsuit that Coinbase deigned to respond, albeit again with only automated inquiries.

This case demonstrates that an emphasis on pre-filing, which in effect, significantly postpones the filing of a case, does not always promote settlement – the opposite may be true when unresponsive parties are involved. In the pursuit of a legal system that is affordable, blocking free access to courts might be self-defeating. On the other hand, free access to courts can lead to nuisance suits.[69]

In pretrial and trial families, the court's institutional role in resolving disputes is functional but in different ways. In pretrial systems, in which the probable outcome is a court-promoted settlement (e.g., through judicial prediction, judicial negotiation), there is a strong incentive to settle the case, since it will probably settle anyway. Since it is almost a given that claimants will not receive the full sum they may be entitled to in a court-promoted settlement, negotiations may be conducted under that assumption. In the trial family, the backdrop to negotiations is a judicial verdict that may fully vindicate the claimant. This can induce the defendant to settle on a reasonable sum or to even give claimants the full

[66] Notably, consumer ombudsmen schemes do not usually have binding authority, and thus unresponsive companies may not heed demands to communicate.

[67] *See also* Lucarelli et al., *supra* note 43; Sela & Limor Gabay-Egozi, *supra* note 46.

[68] *Bielski v. Coinbase* (N.D. Cal. Apr. 8, 2022) https://casetext.com/case/bielski-v-coinbase-inc

[69] Ways to deal with nuisance claims and prevent them from being filed have been discussed in the literature; *see, e.g.*, David Rosenberg & Steven Shavell, *A Solution to the Problem of Nuisance Suits: The Option to Have the Court Bar Settlement.* 26.1 INT. REV. L. & ECON. 42–51 (2006).

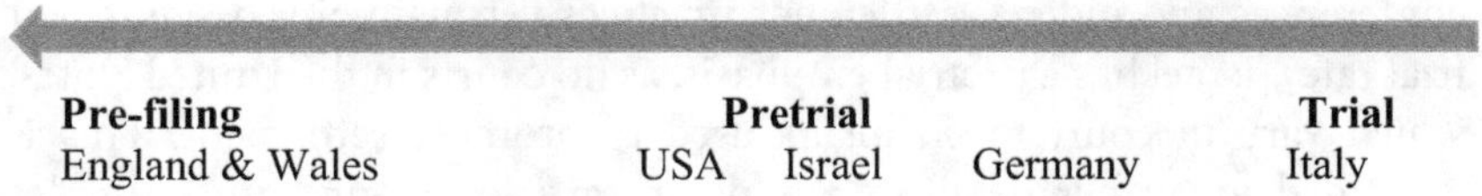

Figure 3.1 Legal systems placed on a continuum.

sum to which they are entitled (however, it also promotes trial and perhaps encourages the defendant to delay to avoid a verdict).

This function of courts to incentivize settlement is marginal in the pre-filing family if it includes extensive pre-filing obligations. The often complex, regulated path to filing a claim may lead parties to abandon their claims or settle for a small amount. In Part III of this book, we discuss the benefits of looking at legal systems through the prism of the individual disputant rather than repeat players such as corporations and public bodies, and thus creating human-centered legal design.[70] Perhaps in the filing of claims, a distinction in favor of individual litigants could be made in legal systems that have pre-filing requirements.[71]

Courts also incentivize normative behavior – that is, the knowledge that the law can be enforced through trial has a role in preventing undesirable behavior, and in preventing disputes. Thus if the option to access courts and trial is unrealistic, this may affect social behavior. Of course, a legal culture of cooperation is also a socially desired norm, but perhaps a realistic option of trial is needed for its promotion. In Chapter 7, we will discuss the possible future horizon of judicial conflict resolution in its ideal integrative form, and will offer a perspective of courts that encourage dispute resolution and conflict prevention as their main goal.

3.3 The Continuum

Legal systems can be visualized on a continuum according to an emphasized stage (Figure 3.1).

While this is not a precise representation, it generally reflects the emphases of the described legal systems. As explained in the previous chapters, Italy retains a trial emphasis while Germany has more of a pretrial emphasis (as it implements mandatory judicial conciliation

70 Amir & Alberstein, *supra* note 45.

71 *Id.*

conferences and judicial settlement practices yet maintains a significant trial rate). Israel has a pretrial emphasis, as do courts in the United States, which vary in court mechanisms used to promote settlement. This is explained in further detail in one of our articles, along with examples from other countries.[72] For instance, if one takes the Southern District of New York as an example, its automatic mediation referral for some types of cases would place it to the left of Israel. Jurisdictions that have a wider scope of mandatory ADR (taking into account the types of cases referred to ADR, the cost of ADR, and whether it is binding in nature), such as areas in Ontario, Canada, can be placed to the left of the Southern District of New York, since the prospects of judicial involvement in settlement are lower.

In England and Wales, pre-action protocols and a cost sanctions mechanism for refusing offers to mediate or settle discourage parties from filing claims in court or pursuing claims after they are filed. In contrast to Oregon state courts, which allow the filing of claims before initiating mandatory arbitration, in England and Wales the mere filing of a claim may be significantly prevented. This pre-filing emphasis seems to draw close to a "no-filing" emphasis, in which disputes are privatized and have little governmental oversight.

Since legal systems often contain combinations of pre-filing, pretrial, and trial components, the continuum could be visualized three-dimensionally with the main emphasis as shown in this chapter and smaller branches with less emphasized components protruding from it for each legal system. Neither is the placing of legal systems on the continuum static – legal systems can and do move along it, and the continuum can portray movement of legal systems following reforms.

3.4 Note on Convergence between Criminal and Civil Justice

Components of the above-described trends found in civil justice may be found in criminal justice as well,[73] and may have far-reaching implications for the function of law, judicial presence, access to justice, and other

[72] Amir & Alberstein, *supra* note 1.

[73] Sari Luz Kanner, Dana Rosen, Yosef Zohar & Michal Alberstein, *Managerial Judicial Conflict Resolution (JCR) of Plea Bargaining: Shadows of Law and Conflict Resolution*, 22 NEW CRIM. L. REV. 494 (2019); Nancy J. King & Ronald F. Wright, *The Invisible Revolution in Plea Bargaining: Managerial Judging and Judicial Participation in Negotiations*, 95 TEX. L. REV. 325, 331–34 (2016).

core principles of justice. Legal systems have introduced mechanisms such as criminal pretrial, plea bargains, or out-of-court disposals (e.g., cautions, penal orders or deferred prosecution), which can significantly replace or abbreviate trial.[74]

The mix of alternatives and their preponderance, as well as the role of the judge in relation to them, varies among legal systems. In the United States, Israel, and Germany – which have a pretrial or close-to-pretrial emphasis in civil justice – the judge may take a hands-on approach to reaching plea bargains. In the United States and Israel, where prosecutors and defendants regularly reach plea bargains, judges may implement a variety of judicial settlement practices to encourage the prosecution and the defendant to settle, much like they do between parties in civil justice.[75] In Germany, judges directly negotiate with the defendant's counsel to obtain a confession in return for a reduced sentence:[76]

> [T]he presiding judge of the first-instance court that is responsible for deciding a pending criminal prosecution engages in a negotiation with the defense counsel who represents the defendant. Their negotiation envisions an exchange, a bargain. In return for the judge's agreement to reduce significantly the punishment that would result if the court were to find the defendant guilty after a full trial on the evidence, the defendant will confess the charge against him. The court then convicts the defendant, relying heavily upon the confession, which greatly shortens the trial and simplifies the work of the court.

In contrast, in England and Wales, both with a pre-filing emphasis, judges have active case management roles during the trial itself[77] but generally do not take part in negotiations.[78] The greater part of criminal

[74] Susan R. Klein et al., *Waiving the Criminal Justice System: An Empirical and Constitutional Analysis*, 52 AM. CRIM. L. REV. 73, 76 (2015); Jacqueline S. Hodgson, *The Future of Adversarial Criminal Justice in 21st Century Britain*, 35 NCJ INT'L L. & COM. REG. (2009); Nicky Padfield, *Judicial Rehabilitation? A View from England*, 3 (1) EUR. J. OF PROBATION 36 (2011) (noting the vast use of fixed penalty notices).

[75] King & Wright, *supra* note 73; Kanner et al., *supra* note 73. Amir & Alberstein, *supra* note 21; Ami Kobo, *Criminal Mediation*, 24 HAMISHPAT (2018) (Hebrew).

[76] John H. Langbein, *The Turn to Confession Bargaining in German Criminal Procedure: Causes and Comparisons with American Plea Bargaining*, 20 AM. J. COMP. L. 1, 1 (2022) (The practice of confession bargaining seems to account for a majority of white collar crimes.).

[77] R. L. Denyer, *The Changing Role of the Judge in the Criminal Process*, 14 INT'L J. EVIDENCE & PROOF 96 (2010).

[78] Amir & Alberstein, *supra* note 21.

cases are disposed through guilty pleas that they must approve but are not usually involved in obtaining. In this, their nonintervention in settlement is reminiscent of their very limited intervention, if any, in settlement in civil cases.

Unlike the previously mentioned legal systems, in which plea bargaining is common (though less so in Germany, which, as mentioned earlier, is situated between a pretrial and trial emphasis), Italy's legal system is still based on trial as the main route for the disposal of criminal cases. Plea bargaining has a relatively small presence.[79] The judge retains an adjudicative function for a large portion of cases, yet at times this function is shortened through a variety of forms of abbreviated criminal trials that are used to accelerate legal proceedings.[80]

Thus, at least in these five countries, it seems that the emphasis in civil justice, especially as it pertains to the judicial role, may reflect components of criminal justice as well regarding the extent of use of plea bargains and the nature of the judicial role. Another aspect that might be interesting to compare is the extent to which out-of-court disposals are used (somewhat comparable to pre-action protocols in civil justice, since their prerogative is to dispose of case before they reach court). Out-of-court disposals can be found in all five legal systems.[81] Further research might examine whether the use of out-of-court disposals and pretrial, as well as the extent of the wider trend of administratization of justice,[82] correlate with the emphasized stage in each legal system.

[79] Riccardo Montana, *Procedural Tradition in the Italian Criminal Justice System: The Semi-adversarial Reform in 1989 and the Inquisitorial Cultural Resistance to Adversarial Principles*, 20(4) INT'L. J. EVID. & PROOF 289 (2016); Amir & Alberstein, *supra* note 1; Maximo Langer, *Plea Bargaining, Conviction without Trial, and the Global Administratization of Criminal Convictions*, 4 ANN. REV. CRIMINOLOGY I.1, I.21 (2021).

[80] *Id.*

[81] Peter Spivack & Sujit Raman, *Regulating the New Regulators: Current Trends in Deferred Prosecution Agreements*, 45 AM. CRIM. L. REV. 159 (2008); Oriana Binik, *Testing for Adults in the Milan Area: Analysis of the Application of an Innovative Measure in the Italian Sanctioning Landscape*, ITALIAN REV. CRIMINOLOGY 16 (2018); Langbein, *supra* note 76; Kobo, *supra* note 75; Padfield, *supra* note 74 (noting the vast use of fixed penalty notices for many high-volume offenses); Richard Young, *Street Policing after PACE: The Drift to Summary Justice*, in REGULATING POLICING: THE POLICE AND CRIMINAL JUSTICE ACT 1984 PAST, PRESENT, AND FUTURE 149 (Ed Cape & Richard Young eds., 2008).

[82] Langer, *supra* note 79.

3.5 Out, Out, Millennia-Old Candle?

Is the progression from a trial emphasis to a prefiling emphasis inevitable? As shown in Chapter 2, Italy represents the dawn of settlement culture: It has just begun its journey to integrate a settlement culture in the legal system, and judges in the Florence Court may present mediation in a soft light, as a beneficial alternative for certain types of cases, while viewing trial in a positive light as well. Israel represents a high noon of judicial settlement activity, with settlement beating down on sometimes reluctant disputants as it is presented by judges many a time as the only good option the former have. In England and Wales, we identify the twilight of the judicial role: The vast majority of cases, both civil and criminal, do not reach a judge, but rather are settled earlier due to disincentives for trial that are high to the point that freedom of choice is questionable.

Will the dawn in Italy naturally progress to high noon, as in Israel? Is the twilight of the judicial role expected thereafter, when costs, efficiency, and technology shift the focus of legal activities outside the courts? Have these important trends in the administration of justice across legal cultures affected the prevailing perspective on legal justice as it is studied in law schools and practiced by lawyers?

These questions go to the heart of the judicial role in all countries: Does it have an important function – is it worth keeping? Should common law countries make an effort to roll back the process of disintegration of the judicial role? What are the implications for other continental law countries that have integrated ADR into their legal systems but at present maintain a relatively high rate of trial? And what can this study teach us about the dynamics of transplants, other than the fact that in the two legal systems described earlier judicial transplants have contributed to the constriction and marginalization of the judicial role?

Despite the differences between the legal systems in implementing a settlement policy, the measures the legal systems have adopted have a common thread – placing increased emphasis on the stage before trial, referral of cases to mediation by the judge, and active judicial management of cases with an eye toward settlement. The continued differences between them might gradually disappear. A powerful impetus for efficiency (as in a period of austerity) might result in a less gradual process to promote settlement, as in England and Wales. The traditional distinguishing features between continental law and common law seem to be less relevant than in the past, reiterating the need for a new typology of legal families, as described in this chapter.

Continental law and common law countries have borrowed legal constructs from each other in large part to increase efficiency and expedite or obviate trials. Italy has borrowed settlement practices that could be perceived as inimical to the inquisitorial tradition (e.g., the centrality of the judge vs. the parties, the emphasis on a judicial search for truth). Yet it has retained some of its original values: Judges still maintain their adjudicative role for a significant portion of cases and generally, according to our observations and interviews, make conciliation proposals only after considering the merits of the case.

Israel and England and Wales borrowed practices from continental law countries, supplementing plea bargains, settlement practices and other adversarial-like shortcuts with *inquisitorial-like* judicial practices that consist of both management and active interrogation in criminal and civil proceedings. The embodiment of both tactics – the inquisitorial penchant for a proactive judiciary and the adversarial penchant for settlement– in the three legal systems is powerful, as it adopts the main tool for reining in litigation from each legal tradition. Notably, the inquisitorial practices were borrowed by these legal cultures for the sake of promoting settlements and less for finding the truth, as in continental jurisdiction. In Israel, a broad spectrum of inquisitorial tools to promote settlement practices has developed in books and in action.

This dual tactic is present to a different extent in each of the legal systems that we studied and can result in a judicial demand for settlement that is hard to deny. The question is whether this is the vision we have for judges in an age of consensual dispositions: judges who are given greater powers for the purpose of pressuring parties to settle. Such a role may not seem significant enough to survive the pressure of digitalization and replacement of the judicial role altogether, a departure from a venerable institution developed more than 4,000 years ago.

Yet the three legal families – pre-filing, pretrial and trial – may not morph into one pre-filing family; the stages do not have to be sequential. England may reopen its gates to litigation; Israel may decide to inject meaningful judicial settlement practices that address the needs of the parties; Italy may decide to stay where it is, with a clearly defined division between adjudication and settlement practices. These would all be conscious decision that buck the current trend of moving along a continuum from trial to pretrial to pre-filing. The typology suggested here is in itself a step to increase the awareness of legal systems to where they seem to be headed, and what they might do to "defy gravity."

There are ways to ensure a meaningful judicial role and protections for individual litigants. All are proactive and require a real effort. The promising part is that, as we have seen in all three legal systems, judicial training can yield real results in practice. Whether the direction is to give judges more cases to adjudicate (through prioritization of case type or otherwise), to infuse meaning into judicial settlement practices, or to reconceptualize legal systems in other ways, the judicial role may still offer meaning in the pursuit of justice – meaning that is consciously formulated by legal systems.

Barring a conscious effort by legal systems to reverse trends, a gradual movement leftward to the pre-filing end of the continuum, coupled with increased technological capabilities, might lead toward judge-less, AI-governed binding decisions on disputes. However, if the Online Court in England and Wales indeed increases access to the court system and to judges, it may demonstrate that trends can be reversed, and perhaps legal systems must reach the pre-filing end of the continuum to bounce back. The following chapters of this book will dive deeper into our data and try to conceptualize the new roles of judges and the courts by combining empirical data with conceptual deliberation and a search for new horizons of legal justice.

PART II

Settlement Practices and Perspectives of Judges

4

Challenges of Studying Judges

While the role of judges has changed dramatically due to the vanishing trial phenomenon, the change has generally slipped under the radar. The extent and nature of the transformation of judicial roles cannot usually be deduced from reading legislation or official public legal records. This stands in stark contrast to the information age, in which a wealth of public information and a forthcoming attitude toward supplying additional information might be hoped for.

We often encountered obstacles to obtaining information from courts. In addition, publicly available information on court files is sparse. Data on case dispositions, judicial interventions, settlement, and the relation between them are lacking even in the countries that often try to make data available, such as the United States. For instance, there is no information on the proportion of cases referred to mediation (even though courts often have in-house mediation programs) and at what stage they are referred. When systematic data on mediation is collected, including success rate, and even when gathered by the court administration, usually no integration and aggregation of it with data on court dockets are conducted. The superficial separation between these two forms of justice is therefore well preserved in data visibility.

As one expert at the US government explained to us when we were inquiring about a possible discrepancy in the publicly available data,

> Here's a favorite quote among the researchers in our division: "The government are very keen on amassing statistics. They collect them, add them, raise them to the *n*th power, take the cube root and prepare wonderful diagrams. But you must never forget that every one of these figures comes in the first instance from the village watchman, who just puts down what he damn pleases."[1]

[1] The official was quoting Josiah Charles Stamp, who was a well known English industrialist and civil servant.

In other words, even when data are collected, many times they are not accurate and reliable. Central governmental agencies that publish data do so after compiling reports from courts around the country (the "village watchmen") – and each court may have its own reporting standards. There is the problem of collecting the right and relevant data, of documenting them in an accurate and accessible way, of making them transparent, and of integrating data with relevant databases while constantly interpreting their meaning.

Going to individual states to find information, we found that relevant state-provided data are sorely lacking. In contrast to our expectation to find most data on case dispositions and judicial activities to be publicly available, in reality we found an empirical gap that has many implications for other efforts to understand contemporary courts and the judiciary.

While lack of reliable data, lack of cooperation of some court systems (the United Kingdom in particular), and sparse data collection by legal systems were all central obstacles to us as researchers, we could not help thinking that they are even more of an obstacle to individual litigants who must assess their best way forward. Considering the fact most of the litigants are repeat players such as banks, insurance companies, or public institutions, which gather data on their cases systematically and litigate strategically based on these data, this problem becomes a serious challenge with which future courts should deal.

In this chapter, we describe the transparency problem and our efforts to persuade courts to divulge information as well the methodological approach that developed in the course of our research to surmount the data challenge. We show the strengths and weaknesses of each research method that we used and the way in which combined research methods have an added value, compensating for weaknesses and uncovering blind spots. By conducting court observations, coding actual court files and analyzing them quantitatively, while interviewing judges and other legal actors, we were able to obtain a rich picture of the trajectory of cases as they move toward settlement.

4.1 The Empirical Challenge of the Judiciary

During the initial stages of gathering court docket and case record data for purposes of quantitative analysis of court-connected settlements and related judicial activity, we discovered that in the countries of research there were significant reliability and coverage problems with regard to electronic docket data. Relevant data are either not available in the official electronic court record, inaccurately recorded, or insufficient for operationalizing key variables of interest, such as mode of disposition. The focus on clearance rate in comparative analytics by units such as the European Commission for the Efficiency of Justice (CEPEJ) revealed very limited information, and no information about the real track of a legal file in court, and on the relationship between judicial activities and case dispositions. Relying mainly on clearance rate enables only limited perspective on the role of judges and the pace of case progress within legal systems, and aggregated data were not provided to us.

We therefore developed a research approach to mitigate these difficulties, and instead of using descriptive statistics of case dockets and learning about settlement by using "big data," we opted to use representative samples in which relevant civil and criminal data were manually coded based on all case documents. This enabled us to provide an accurate representative picture of settlement activities and to generate a predictive model for settlement and plea bargaining.

When access to presiding judges was denied to us, and surveys could not be circulated to them, we approached retired judges for interviews and circulated surveys to lawyers asking about judicial settlement work. We also conducted seminars and academic colloquiums, which judges are allowed to attend. These gatherings, along with judicial trainings we conducted, enabled us to conduct focus groups and gather data through the public participation of judges in academic events. Some of these events were videotaped and can be used for further research on these matters.[2]

The dearth of information has implications for the assessment of the judicial role. Formal requests to access court dockets were usually answered reluctantly and after a long period of waiting and insisting on getting an answer; when permission was provided to access the data, restricting rules made using it difficult, and requests for mitigating conditions were denied. Formal requests to observe judicial proceedings behind closed doors were denied. Petitions to circulate surveys to judges or to interview them while focusing on their perspective on settlement activities were denied with no willingness to allow modifications and approve certain questions or interview format.

In Israel, our petition to access this data was denied by the Chief Justice of the Supreme Court after consulting with the Court

[2] *See* Judicial Conflict Resolution (JCR) Project at http://jcrlab.com/jcr-collaborator-circles

Administration. It took us four years to receive a negative answer to our formal request. In England and Wales, response time was also slow and the answer negative with a few rounds of efforts to answer the suggested limiting conditions and recurring lists of questions to answer. This negative approach came despite our well-established European Research Council scientific support, and in contrast to responses from judges on the ground who were mostly eager to discuss their work and let us observe their activity.

When trying to understand the background to the transparency problem and to capture the cause for the official reluctance of the judiciary to be examined empirically, it may be argued that it reflects a professional mystique of sorts, and conceals a fear of loss of trust. It might also be viewed as an effort to preserve a bespoken professional perspective of law that cannot be fully covered through empirical analysis.

The Court Administration or Supreme Court Justices usually argue that judges provide their opinions in their legal verdicts and therefore should not be interviewed (or use Facebook). This was actually the reasoning provided to us by the Supreme Court of Justice when denying our request to interview presiding justices and judges. In reality, our research shows that judges are writing fewer and fewer verdicts, and, regardless, data are important for any judicial policymaking. We wanted to learn about their perspectives on their new roles in an age of vanishing trials.

We also met another surprising transparency problem. Within the three jurisdictions, there was no integration of the data accumulated by mediation centers despite being readily available. In Italy, mediation centers provided data on the number of cases referred to them, the rate of refusal to continue mediation, and the rate of successful agreements.[3] In Israel, the court administration's coordinator of pre-mediation meetings (*mahut*) issues annual reports on the program's success while providing the same data as the Italian centers.[4] In England and Wales, the mediation agency authorized by the Ministry of Justice to administer

[3] *See, e.g.*, *ADR Center Publications and Video*, ALT. DISP. RESOL. CTR., http://?adrcenter international ?.com/publications/ (providing reports to the European Parliament by ADR Center).

[4] Ayelet Sela, *Attorney's Perspectives of Mediation: An Empirical Analysis of Attorneys' Mediation Referral Practices, Barriers and Potential Agency Problems, and Their Effect on Mediation in Israel* 11 (Apr. 2009) (Master's thesis, Stanford University), at https://law .stanford.edu/publications/attorneys-perspectives-of-mediation-an-empirical-analysis-of-attorneys-mediation-referral-practices-barriers-and-potential-agency-problems-and-their-effect-on-mediation-in-israel/

mediation for the London County Court, the Centre for Effective Dispute Resolution (CEDR), provides audit reports every two years with this information along with mediator and lawyer views of mediation.[5] Despite the centrality of mediation as an alternative to adjudication in all three jurisdictions, mediation outcomes (e.g., anonymized agreements) and an account of the process through which they are achieved are unavailable. Official records in court dockets do not provide information on the use of mediation (save sporadic reports on mediation disposition of files).[6] This would provide a comprehensive picture of mediation's actual potential and the on-the-ground interaction between mediation and the courts. In US federal courts, there is also usually no collection of statistics on mediation, even in court-annexed mediation (for instance, when in the cases mediation occurred). Accordingly, there is no centralized account of mediation statistics in the federal government.

Our efforts to unveil the striking yet barely understood or acknowledged phenomenon of a fundamental transformation of Western legal systems were met with what may be defined as denial and back-to-an-old-fashioned-perspective of law. This is surprising considering the administrative driving force for efficiency, which has transformed legal systems against their grain, changing basic tenets of law. This driving force might be expected to be followed by a systematic assessment of the different factors of change, and true "empirical courage" to examine the unfolding effects of reforms on the ground. Yet this seems to be far from the case. In one of our empirical studies on criminal trends of efficiency, we surprisingly found that changes introduced by committees to increase efficiency in the criminal justice system were not followed by clear criteria for success in achieving their goal, and our own empirical assessment indicated that probable goals of effectiveness have not been met.[7]

5 THE EIGHTH MEDIATION AUDIT (2018), www.cedr.com/wp-content/uploads/2019/10/The_Eighth_Mediation_Audit_2018.pdf. For more mediation reports prepared by the Centre for Effective Dispute Resolution (CEDR) in England and Wales, *see* www.cedr.com/foundation/mediation-audit/

6 *See, e.g.*, Keren Winshall Margal, Talya Yehuda & Aviv Shirtz, Reliability of Case Filing and Disposition Data in Net-Hamishpat Electronic System (2001), https://perma.cc/3A5M-BU5F [IN HEBREW].

7 Sari Luz Kanner, Dana Rosen, Yosef Zohar & Michal Alberstein, *Managerial Judicial Conflict Resolution (JCR) of Plea Bargaining: Shadows of Law and Conflict Resolution*, 22 NEW CRIM. L. REV. 494 (2019).

4.2 Court Docket Analysis of the Judicial Role

The quantitative research design, which was developed after exposing the lack of relevant data, was employed in Israel, England and Wales, and Italy and was adapted to the specific variables and court docket characteristics in each country. Implementation of the research design in each country and, importantly, execution of the sampling, coding, and analysis phases were conducted by local teams with the relevant familiarity, access, and expertise to collect and analyze the data in each country.

In Israel, we found that only 5–10 percent of civil cases in the Tel Aviv first-instance court are decided following a full trial. Correlations between judges' specific mode of intervention and mode of case disposition were uncovered. Judicial procedural involvement (which we termed JPI) was found in 40 percent of cases and the remaining 60 percent did not include JPI and were served solely by the courts' institutional function. Judges have a strong influence on the trajectory of the case and its final settlement, without performing their adjudicative function. The majority of voluntary withdrawals (58%) occur following JPI. Thus, it is plausible that at least some of these withdrawals reflect out-of-court settlements that were not reported to court, especially when the parties were exposed to "bench presence" interactions with the judge during pretrial (21%) and trial (5%) hearings.

The scope and type of JPI in out-of-court settlements and court-approved settlements were found to be different. The significant effect of mode of JPI on settlement and other types of case disposition led to a re-theorizing of access to justice in terms of judicial bench time. In the criminal sphere, we found a similar trend wherein only 7 percent of cases are decided following a full trial. A courtroom-observation study revealed that only 16.8 percent of preliminary criminal hearings included judicial involvement defined as criminal judicial conflict resolution (JCR), and these were mainly managerial in nature. In an empirical study of a representative sample of criminal court dockets, we found that, on paper, most plea bargains are negotiated between the sides while the judge's role is mainly confined to sentencing. In 89 percent of the criminal cases, judges accepted the prosecution's stance on whether or not to impose a punishment. In 40 percent of the cases in which the prosecution requested to impose a punishment, the judges were requested to employ discretion concerning the length of actual or suspended imprisonment, the amount of the fine, sum of restitution, etc.

Italy, a continental law state, seems to have embarked on a moderate vanishing trial phenomenon. In the Florence first-instance court, we found that 43 percent of cases are adjudicated, and that these new judicial practices are being used significantly and correlate with the settlement of cases. Judges refer cases to mediation through mediation orders, and do so according to the nature of the case. They offer conciliation proposals to the parties and, though rarely, convene conciliation hearings. In addition, they may send cases to a court expert that has authority to settle the case. In criminal justice, a variety of abbreviated proceedings have been introduced, and these lower the percentage of cases that are disposed after full trial. The judicial model in Italy seems to be a combination of "fitting the forum to the fuss" and shortened proceedings.[8]

In England and Wales, court statistics reveal the most acute vanishing trial reality, with many disputes prevented from being filed due to pre-action protocols and around 3 percent of civil cases that are nonetheless filed reaching trial. The judge may help introduce clarity to the technical aspects of case (such as costs, issues to be raised in trial and scheduling) through case and cost management sessions. The introduction of cost management sessions, structured allocation of cases, and active management of legal cases have had a fundamental effect on the judicial role. Yet we found that judges do not usually use their authority to directly help the parties settle, though they can do so by law. In addition, their influence is limited due to the small quantity of cases that actually reach them. In criminal justice, the majority of cases are disposed through plea bargaining.

4.3 Qualitative Court Observations of Judicial Activities

Relying on court dockets and quantitative mapping is not enough to understand what judges do in an era of vanishing trials, and therefore we examined courtroom practices in the three research countries to systematically understand the new mode of adjudication that has developed in each place. The hypothesis underlying our inquiry was that the various conflict resolution methods used outside the courtroom as alternatives to

[8] Paola Lucarelli, Nofit Amir, Dana Rosen, Hadas Cohen & Michal Alberstein, *Fitting the Forum to the Fuss While Seeking the Truth: Lessons from Judicial Reforms in Italy*, 36 OHIO ST. J. DISP. RESOL. 213 (2020).

adjudication could have a strong and positive influence, both theoretical and practical, on judicial activities inside the courts.

Based on our quantitative mapping, which enabled us to allocate the most significant stages during the judicial hearing in which judges intervene, we observed and systematically described judicial activities in pretrials and preliminary hearings. Judicial activities may be conceptualized along the lines of generic modes of conflict resolution such as negotiation, mediation, arbitration, and restorative justice. Most of these activities are not officially documented on courts' official records, and therefore our study enabled us to capture the unique styles of judicial intervention in an age of vanishing trials.[9]

After debating within our team how to capture judicial activities we focused on qualitative rich descriptions which we later read in order to extract recurring themes.[10] When building the methodology for court observations we were initially planning to use quantitative schemes based on our qualitative theme gathering, but we finally realized that capturing the interactions within the courtroom always required some context and could not be reduced to a quantitative scale. Integrating both, we found a correlation between judicial intervention and settlement in two legal systems, and a host of recurring judicial practices, such as: direct facilitation of litigotiation (i.e., negotiation during the litigation process), interaction with a view toward the judge-lawyer-client triangle, using costs and procedure to encourage settlement, prediction, quasi-arbitration, negative portrayal of trial and narrow ADR techniques. Levels and nature of judicial interventions varied across legal systems and fields of law.

In contrast to our initial hypothesis about judges conducting distinct generic conflict resolution activities, as conducted outside the court, we found that the conflict resolution process in the shadow of authority has a unique nature. It can be better described as a unique form of

[9] In England and Wales, observations in forty-two civil and twenty-one criminal cases were conducted. In Italy, fifty-one observations were conducted in civil cases and four in criminal cases. In Israel, with the help of clinic students and various research students in seminars and courses given by the primary investigator, we conducted court observations in approximately 1,000 criminal hearings and 1,700 civil hearings. We further observed five authority-based mediation sessions to enrich our understanding of this novel process uncovered during the research process and documented in detail (Amos Gabrieli et al., *Authority-Based Mediation*, 20 CARDOZO J. CONFLICT RESOL. (2018) 1).

[10] See methodology description in Ayelet Sela, Nourit Zimerman & Michal Alberstein, *Judges as Gatekeepers and the Dismaying Shadow of the Law: Courtroom Observations of Judicial Settlement Practices*, 24 HARV. NEGOT. L. REV. 83 (2018).

abbreviated trial, which addresses the tension between legal and conflict considerations. In Israel, observations showed the richest judicial activities and therefore we expanded our study to address hundreds of cases. We have realized that this is a consequence of the pretrial emphasis existing in the Israeli system, as discussed in Chapter 3. (In the United States, where there is also a pretrial emphasis, judges use a variety of tools to settle cases as well.)

In civil cases, we found the most active judicial role, and captured the gatekeeping function of judges that do not allow litigants to pursue the trial while portraying the full legal process in a negative way.[11] In criminal cases, we identified more managerial roles for judges and observed other recurring practices and methods. The shift of the trial to the preliminary hearing was identified in both areas of law and reinforced our insight that contemporary adjudication has declined in some countries, and has sometimes become extinct other than as an abbreviated form of justice with no underlying coherent perspective. We further developed an instrument to capture judicial activities with the help of Atlas.ti software and conducted a quantitative study of judicial practices in civil cases. This inquiry has resulted in new perspectives of judges using unique forms of power and persuasion within the court scene.[12]

4.4 Interviews

Finally, we felt that a study on judges could not be complete without interviewing the judges themselves. The cross-boundary narratives of judges and lawyers about their roles in relation to settlement are pools of data from which we can gain deep insights into different perspectives on the judicial role. Moreover, understanding judges' philosophies and perspectives on the contemporary culture of settlement is crucial, as they are often the legal actors who implement various reforms.

We asked judges about the role of the court, the role of the judge, their perspective on mediation and conflict resolution, their courtroom practices, their perspective on justice and efficiency, the future court, and examined these questions in surveys and interviews of other legal actors, including lawyers and litigants. We further listened to judges in focus

[11] *Id.*

[12] Hadas Cohen & Michal Alberstein, *Power and Persuasion in the Courtroom: The Force of Law and the Settlement Dynamics of Judges*, 6 CARDOZO INT'L & COMPAR. L. REV. 767 (2023).

groups and academic conferences. Many times their perspectives could be gathered from their public speeches. The findings were processed while considering the comparative aspect and the differences between criminal and civil law.

In England and Wales, we conducted around twenty interviews with civil and criminal lawyers and six interviews with key experts such as Lord Justice Woolf, Lord Justice Briggs, Head of CEDR, and leading academics. In Israel, seventeen interviews with judges were conducted, twenty interviews with lawyers (both criminal and civil), and ten interviews with litigants. In Italy, fourteen interviews were conducted with judges, two with lawyers, and four with mediators. Some of the data accumulated for this task was collected during corridor conversations, unofficial courtroom discussions and post-hearing reflections, public speeches of judges, and public colloquiums organized and videotaped for the research.

4.5 Conclusion

The challenges involved in developing an empirical account of the judiciary in this stage of transition are significant. They required us to develop new methodologies or to use self-coded data, since requests for relevant data were often dismissed or answered reluctantly. The data gathered finally enabled the depiction of a realistic picture of the state of the judiciary today.

The integration of findings from interviews, court observations, and statistical analysis of court dockets, and the reflections they offer upon each other, create a multifaceted image of the judicial role. This image includes a host of observed recurring judicial practices, variations between what is written in regulation and actually practiced, and more.

Further systematic inquiry is needed in order to validate the empirical quantitative data we found. The significance of this reality is discussed in other chapters of this book, yet the lack of strong empirical foundations for the public, prospective litigants, and policymakers is a general deficiency that we suggest must be addressed. In the following chapter we will describe the findings from our court observations and interviews with legal actors – central facets of the qualitative data informing this research.

5

Untold Narratives

Stories Judges and Lawyers Tell about the Judicial Role in Settlement

5.1 Introduction to Findings

The stories told by judges and lawyers in interviews give a behind-the-scenes glimpse into the beliefs and dilemmas underlying judicial settlement-promoting decisions in court. Not surprisingly, the views of judges vary greatly and provide multiple points of entry into their world. In several aspects, the narratives of judges seem to clash with the nature of the judicial role as it surfaces in court dockets and courtroom observations, highlighting their unique voices as developed while performing the new roles. Some judges strictly adhered to the law or narrowly promoted settlement, while others used external institutions such as social services or public housing authorities, perceiving themselves as social leaders who take an activist role.

Generational differences are also significant among judges, and we found that new judges were more invested in their settlement role, discussing new notions of "compromise justice" and "social leadership," while more mature judges who have been decades in the system many times maintained the classical perception of the adjudicative role.

In this chapter, we describe findings from our interviews with judges and lawyers. What is their view of the judicial role in the context of settlement? What is their view of ADR? What is their perspective on the interplay between justice and efficiency? Which theories of legal justice do they develop? Findings are described on the background of the comparison between legal cultures.

As expressed in Chapter 2, the Italy is experiencing a "dawn" of judicial settlement culture; Israel (and the United States) can be conceptualized as having a "high noon" judicial settlement culture; England was found to experience the decline of the role of judges – the "twilight hour" of the judicial role – with a great part of cases being disposed of during the pre-filing stage.[1] Judges there may discuss their role in bringing down costs of litigation, but they do not have a significant settlement role due to the fact that the relatively few cases they do see are seen late in the life of the case. Thus most of the impressions in this chapter are based on interviews and observations of Israeli and Italian judges.

Finally, it is important to note that while the views of judges provide an additional piece of the puzzle of the judicial role today, they cannot be taken at face value, and do not stand alone. Rather, they interact with the other methodologies of this research – qualifying them and at the same time being qualified by them.

5.2 The Settlement Scene: Perspectives of Light and Darkness

In one of our preliminary dialogue circles, as we aspired to draw the boundaries of the research and to establish trust among the judiciary, we invited trial court judges to reflect on the role of the judge in an age of settlement. One of the more senior judges among the group related a story she heard from a famous Supreme Court Justice during her judicial training:

> There is a dark city, a dark street, a dark building and a dark apartment. Within it there is a dark room, and inside of it a table with one drawer open and there is a spotlight pointing into this drawer. This spotlight is what you will hold as judges: You will have a very limited access to a very focused legal question, and beyond it, you do not know anything about the context of the conflict – the people and their interests and emotions, the apartment, the building, the city, etc. Always recall your limited perspective in regards to the conflict. As judges, you should always recall your limited role which is to assign legal rights based on the evidence before you and to apply the rule of law.[2]

In response to this restrained perspective on the judicial capacity to perceive the complex picture of the conflict in context, another, younger judge interfered and presented her own perspective:

> I believe that our roles as judges is not to walk in the dark using our legal spotlight. Instead, I would imagine us walking in the field of justice and

[1] Nofit Amir & Michal Alberstein, *From Transplant to Disintegration? A Comparative Study of the Judicial Role*, 37(4) OHIO ST. J. DISP. RESOL. 555 (2022).

[2] This is a free narration based on the told narrative as expressed during the dialogue circle.

aiming to perceive the situation from all directions while aspiring to promote creative solutions based on a broad perspective.

In other encounters with judges during our research we found a generational gap between (1) the judges who remained reserved regarding the conflict resolution prospects of the court, and who reiterated the dangers in mediation and sometimes settlements and (2) usually the younger judges who embraced the practice of settlement and portrayed it as superior to the authoritative decision-making.

One Israeli judge, who later became a Supreme Court Justice, described a difference between "the justice of compromise and formalistic justice." Other judges spoke about the satisfaction and inspiration the peacemaking activity in the courtroom provides for them. They spoke about bringing peace to the courtroom. Many times they described this activity as more difficult and time consuming than using their legal reasoning and deciding a case.

For example, one judge defined his role as resolving conflicts. He said that he is mostly proud "of the verdicts I have not written," and that sometimes he prefers to spend much more time to settle a case, since he believes that deciding it would be bad for parties who have ongoing relationships and sometimes other conflicts. He spoke about the "authority-based therapy" he uses by listening to the parties and letting their voices be heard. His role, he said, was not to "make both parties happy with the solution," but rather to make them unhappy with the settlement and "focus their resentment on me and not each other." Each case, he said, provides its own unique complexity and its specific judge–litigant–lawyer interactions; the scope of intervention, he said, depends on the case, and sometimes it is best to continue straight to the trial. Strict boundaries in terms of timelines and procedures were part of his method.

Another judge developed an articulated perspective of the judge as a social leader and has educated newcoming judges about this role. Their perspectives reflect, in our view, the self-justification of a prevailing settlement culture promoted in the Israeli court system.[3]

The broader perspectives of the judicial role as expressed by younger judges challenge a familiar dichotomy in conflict resolution – the one between legal disputes and social conflicts. When John Burton, one of the founders of the conflict resolution field, declared that *disputes* are

[3] See the description of the differences between judicial activities in three research countries in Chapter 2.

confined to interpretations of documents or normative arguments while *conflicts* involve nonnegotiable human needs, he meant that legal disputes are, many times, just symptoms of broader social conflicts.[4] Such conflicts can be addressed by developing a problem-solving approach aimed at "provention"[5] and by taking an interdisciplinary perspective. Can such an approach be promoted by judges? Aren't they by definition bound by their perspective and unable to capture conflict complexity? It seems like in an age of settlements some judges perceive their ideal role as addressing the social conflict.

However, judges who were mediators before they became judges emphasized the limits of inquiry into the interests of the parties that they can perform in court and the way it may expose opposing parties to hidden information within the adversarial setting. Retired judges whom we interviewed emphasized the difficulty in having no authority when providing their evaluations. One presiding Italian judge declared that her goal is to listen to the parties, understand the true conflict, and, when the legal solution that she mirrors to them does not answer their needs, to reconcile them. This judge said that she would send cases to mediation when emotions are intense, but in many other cases she would explicitly use mediation techniques, while excluding separate meetings with the litigants, which in any case is not a best practice in mediation as well.

The two somewhat contrasting perspectives of settlement in the courtroom (i.e., the broadening of possibilities through judicial settlement vs. the dangers of mixing settlement and the judicial role) recurred in our interviews with judges and lawyers, and are presented here.

5.3 Positive Perspectives of Settlement in the Courtroom

5.3.1 Settlement as Advanced Legal Decision-Making

Some judges in the Tel Aviv court described their role as neutral experts who constantly mirror to the parties their legal situation along the progression of the legal case so that they can make informed risk assessment and thus reach settlement. For most of the judges in Israel, the first and second pretrial hearings enable them to sort out the main

4 JOHN W. BURTON, VIOLENCE EXPLAINED: THE SOURCES OF CONFLICT, VIOLENCE, AND CRIME AND THEIR PREVENTION 94 (1997).

5 JOHN BURTON, CONFLICT: HUMAN NEEDS THEORY (1990) (provention is the prevention of an undesired event by removing its causes).

issues in dispute and obtain an impression of the kind of evidence that the case will depend on.

They can thus reflect the strengths and weaknesses of each side while quantifying risks and translating them into concrete proposals. Sometimes the risks and costs include the drawbacks and the possible emotional implications of hearing testimonies or other negative repercussions of handling the case. Judges keep mirroring the legal situation to the parties usually after each testimony, and they continue to give their legal assessment after all the evidence is heard, after summary arguments, and sometimes just before reading the verdict. This process, which many judges perceive as their main role, depicts the new roles of judges in an age of vanishing trials as providing heuristic transitional decisions along the progress of a legal case through the system. Judges predict their own ruling, and in cases where the pretrial judge is also the presiding judge on the case, this has a strong effect on the parties.

The focus on preliminary assessment sometimes reflects an important contemporary adjustment of the judicial role to conflicts that become more complex and based on big data. Sometimes judges cannot process all the relevant evidence. In complex criminal cases, one of our interviewees explained, the mere retrieval and documentation of all the videos, cellular phone data, and correspondence on social media can take months. Civil cases sometimes include thousands of electronic documents, and sorting out the relevant evidence may be very challenging. Decisions based on preliminary assessment become the probable outcome for such cases. Judges provide predictions based on heuristic assessment of the case, and this mode of evaluation becomes the only possible solution to these cases in order to enable the legal system to survive. Thus, proportionate use of the legal process becomes a new legitimate guideline for access to justice.

In one of the interviews we conducted with a senior criminal attorney, he said that the system focuses on the corridor instead of "the living room," but the latter would collapse after two days if all cases would go to trial. Another approach, expressed by a senior judge who conducts criminal mediation, was that abbreviated proceedings that engage victims and offenders or involve complex evidence are better decided through careful listening, direct conversations with the lay participants, polycentric sensitivity, and holistic management. He presented the new role of judges as a combination of an inquisitorial search for truth combined with therapeutic jurisprudence, and he depicted his approach as a preferred and more professional mode of judging.

When referring to the Italian scene, it is clear that risk assessment takes a different role. In civil proceedings, the accumulation of the written evidence in the file, a stage that in common law is equivalent to the pretrial, signifies the end of the litigation. Italian judges would be expected to provide a written settlement proposal or mediation order (see Chapter 2) before they have all the evidence. At the same time, the reduced emphasis on an oral stage of evidence makes their preference for mediation more substantial, based on the merits of the alternative process (see also the discussion in Section 5.4). In the criminal arena, the shortening of the evidentiary stage before trial (see Chapter 2) simplifies the court proceeding overall yet imposes extra burden on the judge in court, whether when approving pleas or deciding cases in abbreviating proceedings.

5.3.2 Settlement as a Nearly Irresistible Temptation

In our interviews with Israeli judges, as well as in our court observations, we found an interesting phenomenon of resisting the temptation to decide cases by law. A few judges spoke about a dilemma when facing an interesting and complex legal case. On the one hand, judges described the urge to determine the legal norms and to exercise their legal expertise by writing a reasoned verdict. On the other, they described the "waste of time" in pursuing such a goal and the overall drive to settle by all means in order to reduce court dockets and to manage their workload in a balanced way. Some judges not only perceived this role as related to efficiency and to their own ratio of case dispositions but also pointed to their main role as resolving conflicts.

For instance, a judge told us that he presided on a case in which an important precedential normative decision could be made, yet he felt obliged to encourage the parties to settle, and suggested they accept his settlement proposal. When the parties refused to settle, he was happy to write the verdict but thought his first role was to help them resolve the case themselves. This reflection, although brought by an Israeli judge, corresponds with the overriding objective in England and Wales of addressing adjudication as "the last resort." The drive to write verdicts is depicted within this framework as a conflict of interest judges should overcome. When facing the dilemma whether to decide an important case or try to settle it in the current settlement age, the choice will generally be settlement.

Another expression of the effect of the culture of settlement on norm creation was a split between the settlement outcomes and written verdicts. We found a few cases in which judges had begun to write their normative declaration within a verdict, yet in reality the settlement reached by the parties did not correspond with this norm.[6] When the verdict was given, the parties maintained their settlement agreement despite the fact that it did not conform to the norm. Surprisingly, this was the intention of the court. The main function of the court seems to be the pursuit of pragmatic effective solutions, which do not always reflect a solid normative signature.

The emerging narrative is of a pursuit of consent-based dispositions while resisting the temptation to set just precedents and stipulate legal norms. However, there are cases in which settlement is perceived as a tool to create a just result, as described in the next section.

5.3.3 Settlement in the Service of Judicial Activism

When the law does not lead to a just result in the eyes of the judge, settlement can be a means to create justice. "In every judge's lifetime, there will be cases in which the law does not offer the just result," one judge told us, echoing a well-known facet of judicial decision-making. While some judges have traditionally dealt with such cases through a novel interpretation of the law, sometimes this is not easy. As one judge explained,

> In civil cases, a claimant has to prove the case above the probability of 50 percent, in criminal cases, the prosecutor has to prove the case at a 99 percent probability. Sometimes the claimant just does not have enough evidence, though it is clear that it is not a spurious claim and it rests on facts. With settlement, you can give a place to such uncertainties – allowing the claimant to receive part of the damages despite not having enough concrete evidence. A judicial verdict is binary and would not allow the plaintiff to recover any damages. The plaintiff either wins or loses.

Judicial activism in favor of settlement includes the search for "compromise verdicts"[7] – a judicial solution that escapes the binary nature of law. In some legal cases, substantial justice requires a legal solution or a

[6] See CA 5120/16 The *State of Israel vs. Credit Lines Israel*, Financial Services.

[7] For a discussion of compromise verdicts and their jurisprudential foundation, see John E. Coons, *Compromise as Precise Justice*, 68 CAL. L. REV. 250 (1980).

new legal norm that is more precise and accurate[8] to address a specific case. Some judges referred to the search for settlement as enabling to find these more advanced solutions.

One of the judges citing this function of settlement noted a criminal case appealed in the Supreme Court. The justices requested the prosecution settle on a lower prison time so that the defendant, who had already served several years for manslaughter, could be released within a short time period. According to the judge, when the prosecution refused, the justices wrote a verdict in which they changed the factual findings of the lower court so that the defendant could be released. This is an example of an attempt to avoid the law through settlement to achieve what the judges perceived as a just result and can be positively, negatively or somewhere in between. This leads us to the next section which takes a more somber view of judicial settlement practices.

5.4 Negative Perspectives of Settlement in the Courtroom

5.4.1 Perspectives of Lawyers and Litigants in a Settlement Culture

The perspectives lawyers have regarding the intensive judicial settlement culture in Israel were much less idealistic than those expressed by judges. Lawyers in Israel emphasized the pressure judges exercised, and some lawyers perceived their role as resisting the judicial call to settle.

One lawyer described the way he prepares his client to resist a settlement proposal, yet he stated the need to listen to the judges and to acknowledge their interest to close the case. Another lawyer complained about the courts' unwillingness to do their job. Many of the lawyers emphasized the marginal role of the court within the negotiation context between the parties. The lawyers were all active negotiators who aspired to promote settlement even when courts did not intervene. They said they use the court to promote the negotiation, and repeat players used the negotiation to mitigate normative implications of court decisions. One public attorney who represents the state in labor cases indicated that she always creates for herself an unofficial protocol that reflects the nuances and dynamics in the courtroom that would not appear in court's written records.

In reference to judicial activities in the courtroom, lawyers appreciated balanced settlement proposals of judges that were provided in the

8 *Id.*

courtroom. Experienced lawyers claimed that they are not influenced by judicial pressure to settle, yet they indicated the chilling impression it may have on clients.

When asking litigants on their perspective on the judicial effort to promote settlement, some of them expressed disappointment and distrust. One litigant described his experience as being manipulated by the judge to withdraw his claim for justice and his pursuance of a precedent. He said that the court hearing is "an unsuccessful show," since the judge who is supposed to promote justice arrives at the hearing without probing deeply into the legal arguments and tends to convince weak litigants to give up their claims. Other litigants appreciate the problem-solving capacities of judges and acknowledged settlements as the realistic solution to their case, yet most of the litigants felt disappointed by the lack of pursuit of justice and described the judges as volatile and lacking in a genuine search for the truth. The word "show" appeared in quite a few interviews.

The criticism of lawyers and litigants centered on the role of judges in preventing litigants from pursuing trial while having a deep interest in closing as many legal files as possible. The criticism seemed to be echoed sometimes by the judges themselves. Judges in the Tel Aviv court said that they received around ten new cases each week (on top of the many others they are responsible for) and must dispose of at least eight without trial in order to manage their docket effectively. For some of the judges whom we interviewed, the pressure to settle invoked hard feelings, and a few of them retired due to the sense of what they defined as "slavery." The number of cases closed by each judge is tracked and published by the court administration, and some judges were critical of this, saying that it created competition to close cases and affected "the PR and image of judges." Although the chief court administrator claimed that judges could be less inclined to settle and focus on writing verdicts, in reality it seemed like all of the judges felt that they were required to participate in the settlement production machine.[9] In interviews of retired Israeli judges from the labor court we found an even stronger expression of exhaustion, attrition, and despair.[10]

[9] Since in Israel we were not allowed to interview presiding judges, our sample may have been biased.

[10] Aviel Bokovza, *A Study of Judicial Conflict Resolution Activity of Judges in Pre-trial Sessions in Regional Labor Courts* (PhD dissertation, Bar-Ilan University) (2023).

5.4.2 Settlement as Eroding the Public Sphere

Two Supreme Court justices who participated in our dialogue circles emphasized the danger in settlement and have resonated a well-founded call "against settlement" that was brought by Owen Fiss during the 1980s.[11] According to one Justice, in some cases a legal norm should be established, rather than settlement. In other cases, the settlement should reflect a desired public norm or the correct expected legal decision. The compromise, therefore, should reflect the right legal solution and should not be based only on splitting the difference. In particular, disempowered litigants should be encouraged to pursue justice and not forced into settlements that benefit repeat players.

Another justice emphasized the importance of famous Supreme Court precedents such as *Brown v. Board of Education* (abolishing segregation between whites and blacks in public schools) or, in Israel, *Danilovich vs. El-Al* (acknowledging gay partners' labor entitlement as a spouse). Such cases, according to her, should not be settled, and therefore compromise or any other mode of disposition that is not a written verdict is not an ideal.

Although almost all the judges we interviewed, and especially Supreme Court justices, repeated the idea that some cases should be decided and not settled, we could not find consensual criteria to sort out these cases, and all our empirical findings, including a study of the Supreme Court dockets,[12] led us to the conclusion that the pursuit of settlement is the default track for any case, and that no coherent *ex ante* legal criteria can explain the triage that ends in a written verdict. The erosion of the public sphere[13] seems to be inevitable within a settlement culture, and a new market of settlement norms has emerged as part of the vanishing trial phenomenon.

5.4.3 Settlement as an Impetus to File Spurious Claims

One judge noted that in claims regarding faulty construction, lawyers had started a trend of filing spurious claims for numerous clients with the aim of settling (as a way of making money). Noting this trend in their court,

[11] Owen M. Fiss, *Against Settlement*, 93 YALE L.J. 1073 (1984); Tania Sourdin, *Five Reasons Why Judges Should Conduct Settlement Conferences*, 37 MONASH U. L. REV. 145 (2011).

[12] Sari Luz-Kanner, *The Visible Trial* (PhD dissertation, Bar-Ilan University).

[13] David Luban, *Settlements and the Erosion of the Public Realm*, 83 GEO L.J. 2619 (1995).

the judges decided to see such cases through and place cost sanctions on parties who brought forth spurious claims. In this case, judges created disincentives to settlement to prevent the filing of claims. Against the background of the settlement age, this is a unique type of judicial activism – in which judges decide to eschew settlement in favor of adjudication for a certain type of case. In addition, it shows the possibly counterintuitive role of settlement: It can encourage the filing of claims rather than reduce the caseload.

5.4.4 *Judges in Florence: Focusing on Liability and Diagnostics*

The main tools to encourage settlement in Italy are the conciliation proposal (which the parties can decide whether to accept) and the mediation order (the judge is allowed to order the parties to attempt mediation). If judges want to conciliate between the parties – that is, to directly negotiate between them – they can convene a conciliation hearing. However, in the Florence Court this tool was rarely used.

In issuing conciliation proposals, judges first determined the liability of the parties through expert reports or other means. In an interview, one judge explained: "I made my conciliation proposal according to the police report. Indeed, following the police report, I could presume that Tizio[14] was three-quarters liable, and then the compensation had to be estimated according to that liability percentage."[15] Another judge explained: "Banking law disputes are strictly technical, and I usually have a complete overview of the case only after the expert's report. At that moment, I am able to write a conciliation proposal."[16]

Other forms of arriving at liability – presumed liability by law and liability after presentation of evidence – were mentioned as a basis for a conciliation proposal or settlement. An interviewed judge said: "In legal suits under art. 2051 c.c.[10][17] you can presume the liability, so I just had to make the hypothesis about the damages on the basis of the tables. I would say to the parties 'the liability is *x*, the compensation should be *y* . . .'"

14 A generic name used for an unspecified person.
15 Interview with judge (anonymized due to the ethical guidelines of the study), Florence Court, Italy (June 14, 2018).
16 Interview with judge (anonymized due to the ethical guidelines of the study), Florence Court, Italy (Oct. 16, 2018).
17 Art. 2041 C.c. (It.) (denoting liability of a watchperson).

One judge, indeed, lamented that the difference between a conciliation proposal and adjudication seemed nonexistent, and thus the use of proposals, to him, was baffling:[18]

> I haven't yet seen suits where I can presume the liability from the beginning of the trial. Maybe they exist, but it is much more difficult. In a false accounting case, I don't know if the financial report is false or not until I read the expert report, and once I have the expert report, I am ready to write the final judgment. So, how would I make a conciliation proposal if I am able to write the final judgment?

When asked about giving predictions (a common judicial practice in the pretrial family), interviewed judges usually articulated aversion to it. For instance, one judge said:

> Judges should not reveal their final decision . . . it is clear that if the judge lets the parties understand his/her decision, that would be unfair, as the parties' agreement would be based not on the mutual evaluation of their interests, but rather on thinking: "I would lose anyway, hence, better to settle."[19]

This statement reflects the belief of judges that in-court settlement remains close to the rules while mediation – that is, out-of-court settlement – represents a different type of justice, one that addresses the interests of the parties. Indeed, when issuing mediation orders, judges diagnose cases as appropriate for mediation and explain their train of thought in writing in the mediation order. Interns at the Florence Court prescreen cases and alert judges to cases that might be appropriate for mediation before court hearings.

One judge explained: "In mediation the parties have their chance to address the case from a broader point of view . . . Sometimes there is another pending case before a different judge of a different tribunal. Then I tell them that, within mediation, they can deal with the dispute as a whole."

The judges, even if convinced the dispute could be solved through mediation, would not go against the lawyers' opinions. In an interview, a judge explained:

> I am happier to issue the mediation order if they agree . . . The most important thing is the lawyers' approval. They have to share, to approve the mediation order, otherwise . . . I prefer to go on with the trial and

[18] Interview with judge (anonymized due to the ethical guidelines of the study), Florence Court, Italy (June 14, 2018).

[19] Interview with judge (anonymized due to the ethical guidelines of the study), Florence Court, Italy (June 28, 2018).

> maybe make them reflect on the mediation proceeding at a later stage, for instance after the requests for evidence. Sometimes they tell me "I have to talk with my client beforehand" or "I prefer to see the evidence of the other side," and I postpone the mediation order.[20]

In our interviews with judges, the sharp separation between the form of justice meted out in the courtroom and that which could be found in mediation centers was pervasive. In fact, the few complaints we heard about judicial reforms revolved around the link that had been created between ADR and adjudication. One judge thought that ADR and litigation should not be linked (i.e., through a mandatory preliminary session or a mediation order) so that parties could be free to choose whether to argue the case or to conciliate it:

> The problem is the interconnection between the two proceedings. It would be more reasonable to provide two alternative ways. For instance, you can fight – if you go to the court, you go there to argue, and there will be the judge who will state if you're right or wrong and to what extent you're wrong. Otherwise, if you don't want to fight and want to find an agreement, you can follow other ways that maybe could be encouraged by benefits, but those are alternative ways. If we keep them interconnected, I have the feeling that someone will say: "I do not know if they are trying to rub me."[21]

He stated that combining the two methods, in the courtroom as well, seemed to compromise justice, as he felt he might be expected, in a conciliation proposal, to divide a sum between the parties when only one side might be liable:

> Convincing the side who would be entitled to have one hundred to settle for seventy, or fifty, or any percentage of one hundred, in my opinion, is in contrast with the function of the judge, who has to say who is entitled to have one hundred and who has no right to get anything, or twenty to fifteen, or ten. If I believe that the claimant is right, but I try to get him to an agreement, I would clearly try to convince him to give up something that he is entitled to obtain, and this, in my opinion, is not part of the role of the judge.[22]

One young judge, however, broke the mold and stated that she did not see a problem in proposing that on party receive 70 percent instead of 100 percent to achieve a settlement.

[20] Interview with judge (anonymized due to the ethical guidelines of the study), Florence Court, Italy (Jan. 28, 2019).

[21] Interview with judge (anonymized due to the ethical guidelines of the study), Florence Court, Italy (June 14, 2018).

[22] *Id.*

The diagnostic capacity of judges has expanded from mediation orders to other settlement practices. Judges in the Florence Court are developing a sensitivity to matching the case type to the dispute resolution method. In interviews and during court observations, judges noted that certain forms of disputes correlated with specific modes of disposition (the list that follows is not exhaustive). Here, too, the perceived distinction between types of cases suited for in-court justice (according to law) and the types that are suited for out-of-court justice (mediation) is apparent:

a. In-court justice:

> **Judgment** was appropriate (a) when the *compensation asked was too high for an agreement*, such as in death or serious injury damages claim; (b) in banking disputes that involve the *damaged reputation* of the plaintiff (for being registered as a "risk"); (c) when the positions of the parties were too far apart; (d) when the matter involved inalienable rights (in which case other forms of disposition are not allowed by law). **Judicial conciliation proposals** were mentioned by judges as appropriate for: (a) corporate liability cases, since, according to one judge, "parties are very interested in a *rapid reconciliation and quick definition* of the suit, because commercial companies are dynamic entities and need certainty"; (b) public administration disputes; the judge explained: "Public administration bodies don't tend to go to mediation, since due to oversight, they must have an *authoritative stamp of approval* for their decisions"; (c) insurance claims, only if the suing party was willing to accept low compensation to receive the sum quickly; (d) banking disputes, following an expert report, whereupon the judge can easily offer a proposal, as the disputes are *technical*; (e) disputes in which liability is presumed by law.

b. Out-of-court justice:

> **Mediation orders** were mentioned as appropriate "when the case involves aspects that are outside the dispute, and it would be appropriate to mediate all issues." This includes: (a) interpersonal disputes (e.g., between neighbors); (b) contractual relations between people, as in these cases, as one judge said, "usually extra-legal issues are present"; (c) cases in which another proceeding is ongoing between the parties.

In general, as can be observed from the aforementioned, judges are becoming adept at discerning the needs present in certain case types: whether it be an overriding need for efficiency, the need for a public stamp of approval, or the need for a broad notion of justice that addresses extraneous concerns.[23]

Interviews with judges in Florence suggest that they can promote the resolution of conflicts without eroding the traditional judicial role or co-opting mediation. This may be partly a consequence of the inquisitorial nature of the trial, which does not include a long oral phase after collecting the written evidence. The simplicity and maturity of the judicial evaluation make the judges less preoccupied with risk assessment and prediction, and more interested in the substantive difference between adjudication and mediation. Such a shift may occur in systems such as in Israel, where the gravitation of the judicial process has moved to pretrial (see Chapters 2 and 3), inquisitorial practices are enabled, and an institutional substantive preference for a broad mediation concept exists. They generally preserve the dichotomy between adjudication and mediation and may try to ensure that each case is handled through an optimal process that fits the nature of the case.

5.5 Conclusion

Interviews with judges show that the seemingly innocuous concept of settlement can manifest in unexpected ways: There are widely different strategies to implement a settlement priority in court, and a large variety of unrelated and even opposing reasons for doing so. Judges may prefer settlement due to a belief that reaching justice in court is untenable or not worth the turmoil for the parties. Or they may prefer settlement to advance justice when the law does not provide a just result. In Israel, judges are motivated by the incentives given by the legal system to clear dockets through the whip of statistics on the number of closed cases. For this reason, judges may express the feeling that they are slaves of a system that places efficiency on a pedestal. In legal jurisdictions, such as Italy and England and Wales, where judges are not evaluated based on their settlement rate dispositions or incentivized to settle cases, judges express

[23] A study in the Florence first-instance court substantiates the use of the tools by judges for the year 2018. *See* Elisa Guazzesi, *I dati di Giustizia semplice*, in MEDIAZIONE DEI CONFLITTI. UNA SCELTA CONDIVISA 173 (Paola Lucarelli, ed., 2019). The social impact of the research has been analyzed by Annalisa Tonarelli, *L'impatto sociale del progetto. Una ricerca sulle trasformazioni all'interno del "campo giuridico*, in MEDIAZIONE DEI CONFLITTI. UNA SCELTA CONDIVISA 223 (Paola Lucarelli, ed., 2019).

more process choice between adjudication and mediation, or avoid deliberation on the settlement culture altogether.

The judicial attempt to bring about settlement can be justified on various other grounds as well: the increase of data and the complexity of cases, an ideology of the court as a place for conflict resolution that sustains relationships, or leadership. It can bypass the law in cases for which the judge feels the law does not have an appropriate response. We also see that, according to judges, settlement has the power both to uproot and create justice.

While judges sometimes portray themselves as neutral agents that try to lead the parties to compromise, lawyers and litigants often do not see them that way. They see the judges as having an interest to close the case quickly rather than having the parties' interests in mind, and may express a feeling that judges have exerted undue pressure on them. Sometimes, however, the intervention of the judge is viewed as a welcome shortcut in terms of cost, time, and emotional turmoil. We also saw that judicial settlement efforts can lead to the filing of spurious claims. (When the default is settlement in the courtroom, as in the pretrial family, spurious claims can be filed in order to settle on a sum. If lawyers do this, it can lead to spurious files on a large scale.)

When we seek the theoretical and conceptual perspectives that judges develop, we see that no coherent perspective that preserves the classic perception of law emerges. Judges are either enthusiastic about settlement and abbreviated proceedings as a more complex developed notion justice, or they are skeptic about its use and weary of it. They are, in a sense, bound within a pragmatic reality they cannot conceptually capture or justify. Some conflict of interest (to adjudicate is wrong; to settle is right) and ambivalence are exposed in their positions.

The case in Italy is different in that respect. There we found that judges usually maintain a separation between in-court and out-of-court justice, viewing the liability of the parties as the main factor in court and broader interests as the main impetus to take a case out of court to mediation. Thus judicial conciliation proposals are made along the lines of liability, and cases are referred to mediation if they have characteristics that are appropriate for that type of case resolution.

6

Power and Persuasion

Judicial Role as Reflected in Courtroom Observations

Judicial actions in the courtroom remain for the most part off the record and hard to discern. Moreover, judicial settlement practices in the United States, for example, can take place in judicial chambers, far from the public eye. Thus there is a need for physical presence of researchers in public hearings to understand what judges do today in the age of vanishing trials.

Researchers of this study entered courts in London, Florence, and Tel Aviv. A few of their observations can be found in the first part of this book, and the greater part of them are analyzed here, with a focus on observations in Tel Aviv, which – as mentioned in the previous chapters – belongs to the pretrial family, where the "high noon" of judicial settlement practices occur. In Israel, contrary to the United States, judges are not allowed to confer with parties in their judicial chambers. Thus, all judicial settlement efforts can be viewed in the courtroom.

The various judicial conflict resolution practices that emerged in Israel's most active first-instance court, in Tel Aviv, provide a new perspective on power in the courtroom, identifying new forms of legitimation and justice developed by judges as they perform their settlement-promoting roles. The first part of this chapter will uncover the types of settlement promotion judges employ there. The Tel Aviv Court provides an important porthole into judicial settlement practices, since these hearings are open to the public and, unlike pretrial in the United States, cannot take place in judicial chambers.

The second part of this chapter will discuss an alternative model, found in the Florence Court, where judges were only recently permitted to use settlement practices. There, the judges are supported by interns who screen cases before trial to examine whether they may be appropriate for mediation. In court, judges may offer mediation to the parties and explain their reasoning for doing so but will usually not try to settle the cases themselves.

As parties increasingly pursue legal negotiation and seek information and signals from the judges, and judges increasingly integrate settlement consideration into their roles, it is important to showcase judicial practices that diverge from the simple application of pressure on the parties. Thus, in the third part of this chapter, we will showcase the intervention styles of several Tel-Aviv judges, which offer new visions for the judicial role.

6.1 Tel Aviv: Settlement Practices Employed by Judges in the Courtroom[1]

The judicial practices identified included the use of structural elements related to the legal hearing: an ***opening statement conveying the expectation or an invitation to settle*** by the judge expressed at the start of the hearing; holding hearings by alternating adjudication ***on and off the record***, as a way of creating an informal and semi-confidential space for judges to carry out judicial settlement promoting activities; the ***lawyer–client–judge interactional triangle*** captured instances in which judges spoke directly with litigants present (e.g., in court to address their emotional reaction). In some cases, judges praised the lawyer while addressing the clients; called litigants to testify in order to interrogate them and extract evidence; and addressed business and relationship interests while directly talking to the lawyers' clients. Judges also invoke their authority when using ***court procedure and legal costs*** to persuade litigants to settle – setting a future hearing date to allow litigants the opportunity to settle, or set a relatively close date so as to pressure lawyers into preparing the case within a short period, while pointing to the possibility of settlement. They may use the possibility of mandating costs as a way of encouraging litigants to settle and avoid the financial expense of a full trial. In addition, judges may point to the negative aspects of the legal process or outcome, thus creating a ***legal aversion***. These include the high costs that a litigant may incur during the legal case or the emotional distress that may result from a publicized trial as opposed to a settlement agreement that will not be made public. Emphasizing the negative aspects of the legal process is done as a way

[1] This section derives from Hadas Cohen & Michal Alberstein, *Power and Persuasion in the Courtroom* 6 CARDOZO INT'L & COMPAR. L. REV. 767 (2023) and Ayelet Sela, Nourit Zimerman & Michal Alberstein, *Judges as Gatekeepers and the Dismaying Shadow of the Law: Courtroom Observations of Judicial Settlement Practices*, 24 HARV. NEGOT. L. REV. 83 (2018).

of encouraging parties to agree to a settlement proposal that the judge might offer, or to nudge them into negotiation rather than carrying on with the full legal process.

Following is an observed hearing exemplifying a combination of several such strategies:[2]

> The judge opened the hearing by telling the lawyers: "You are at home. I think the risk is greater than the probable gain for both of you, and an agreement can be reached." The attorney for the third-party defendant objected to a settlement, and the judge responded, "I will not force you [to settle] but I will schedule the evidentiary hearing before the Summer Recess [in three weeks]." While checking for an available date for the hearing on her electronic calendar, the judge said, "I thought you would have a constructive discussion, and reach understandings about a risk-gain trade-off. It's a waste of time and money but I will not force you." Following additional exchanges with the lawyers, the judge alluded to her potential future ruling on legal costs, which according to Israeli law are awarded at the discretion of the judge: "You should take into account . . . that pursuing a case unnecessarily – and this is not a threat – involves more than just court fees." The judge then split a piece of paper, handed each lawyer one half, and asked them to make a confidential settlement offer. After discovering that the two proposals were far apart, the judge noted, "Were the parties themselves present at the hearing, it would have been possible to settle the case."

In addition, judges engage in ***direct facilitation of litigotiation*** (i.e., the negotiation occurring between parties during the litigation process) to help parties reach an agreement. They might offer settlement proposals, ask litigants about out-of-court negotiations that may have taken place, or inquire as to what has prevented them from reaching an agreement. Judges might give a ***prediction*** of the legal outcome, either directly or by implying the strengths and weaknesses of each side's case, in order to give litigants an indication of the judge's perception regarding the legal outcome that the litigants can expect.

An explicit case of prediction and facilitation is demonstrated, in a dispute regarding realtor fees:[3]

DEFENDANT'S LAWYER (DL):	We are willing to settle the case, but they are asking for an unreasonable amount.
JUDGE (J):	How much? Let's talk about the money!
DL:	We will pay one percent plus taxes.

2 *Id., at* 102.
3 *Id., at* 107.

PLAINTIFFS' LAWYER (PL):	We are asking for 1.5 percent plus tax.
J:	Will the case be over for 60,000 shekels [approximately 16,500 USD]?
PL:	I want to consult with my client.
J:	He will not get more than that.
	[PL goes outside to call her client, and then reports he is willing to settle the case for 65,000 shekels [approximately 18,000 USD].
J:	I am not negotiating with you or with your client. This is not horse-trading. Please deliver the message to your client, he will not get more than that [which I proposed]. He should take the money now.

In addition, sometimes judges asked parties if they would like them to serve as quasi-arbitrators, employing ***procedural contract and quasi-arbitration techniques***. In such cases, judges propose that the litigants set a monetary range with a minimum and a maximum amount, between which they can reach mutual agreement. This practice is particularly pertinent in Israel, where Article 79(a) of the Israeli Courts Law allows judges to design such judicial arbitration modes if litigants authorize the judge to rule by way of compromise.

While judges have some official training in mediation, in most cases this is not as comprehensive as the training received by mediators. However, court observation revealed that judges employ a host of ***ADR techniques*** to facilitate settlements. They might express empathy toward litigants, refer to the relationship between them, or reflect on the parties' nonlegal interests. Another practice, the ***style and tone of judicial intervention***, elicited different reactions from lawyers and litigants. The same sentence spoken softly may have a very different effect if uttered harshly or with anger.

Judges can use ***humor*** as a way of creating a positive atmosphere and mutual trust. They invoke their own personal relationships when attempting to convince lawyers and litigants regarding hearing dates: "I will do everything to prevent postponing the hearing, including fighting with my wife. . ." They refer the difficulties of getting witnesses to testify: "You cannot control any witnesses, unless they are tied in your balcony, and then [we have] a completely different set of rules." Or they refer to politics as a way of demonstrating their impartiality and the futility of the conflict in question: "As Begin [a former Israeli prime minister] said about the Iran–Iraq war: 'I wish both sides good luck.'"

As mentioned previously, judges sometimes ***apply pressure,*** both mild and strong, on parties and lawyers, encouraging them to settle. As an example, a judge referred to the unreasonable length of the proceedings when opening the hearing, stating: "Either the sides will settle, or I will 'terminate' the case. . . The case has been going on since 2014, and I have no intention in having this business go on any further."

Or they might refer to the interests of powerful litigants when encouraging settlements:

> The case is unclear, and it should end in a settlement. This is exactly the type of case in which the state health services do not want me to write a verdict . . . There are good mediators who know the field, and you will be much better off going to them. Believe me, you don't want me to write a verdict here . . .

A softer way of incentivizing settlements is referring to one's own limitations in providing a suitable solution to the conflict at hand. In a case of medical negligence – the litigant's eye had been enucleated, and the litigants were not present in court – the judge almost pleaded with the lawyers:

> I ask you to implore your clients to go to mediation, since mediators have tools that I do not. The mediator can explain to the plaintiff a situation in which there is no liability . . . to say no to mediation in this case is a position that cannot be accepted. If [you will not go to mediation] the court will have to appoint a specialist . . . How can I know if a certain medical practice is common in this medical area?

At times, judges ***mirrored*** to litigants the legal situation the way they perceived it, usually before giving them a ***prediction*** of the legal outcome. In other cases, they mirrored while giving a prediction. We identified this dynamic in a defamation case, when the judge ***mirrored*** the legal situation in his opinion to the prosecutor, stating, "[W]hile the documents of the prosecution are very detailed, I do not find any basis for a defamation case in the indictment, not in terms of the damages listed nor in terms of the factual basis."

At other times, judges are hesitant when they see that the litigants and their lawyers are ready to act out on their mirroring. In a case concerning a car accident, the judge said what he thought about the facts of the case without making a prediction about the legal outcome. Based on video documentation of the incident, the judge said that he believed that the case involved wrongdoing on the part of the driver. When the lawyer heard this, he asked to withdraw the lawsuit; the judge then said that he could be wrong, and that they should nevertheless proceed with the case, as this was only his preliminary opinion.

We also detected a ***carryover effect***, which had to do with the fact that pretrial hearings (both civil and criminal) are typically held consecutively, such that a judge holds several hearings in a single courtroom sitting, usually in the morning. In such a setting, the judge's attitude regarding settlement in any given case can impact not only the litigants and lawyers involved but also those who wait in the courtroom for their case to be heard. In the other jurisdictions we studied, Italy and England and Wales, no such carryover effect existed, since hearings were scheduled one after another, while litigants and lawyers waited outside.

Figure 6.1 is a statistical representation of the recurrence of judicial practices across all observed hearings in the Tel Aviv first-instance court.

When examining the frequency of judicial practices to promote settlement, we can see that applying pressure by judges is a dominant practice. Judges also encourage the parties to reach settlement independently and to pursue litigotiation. They use prediction and mirroring to provide parties with more information regarding their case; in about a third of all cases, they used the opening statement to invite parties to settle. The use of humor is quite rare, as too is that of the lawyer–client–judge triangle. ADR practices are used, but only in less than a third of the cases. The use of judicial arbitration through Section 79(a) is also discussed with litigants and sometimes exercised. Legal aversion is expressed in 15% of the cases, and the use of legal procedure is quite common in incentivizing parties to settle. These practices are used in conjunction with each another.

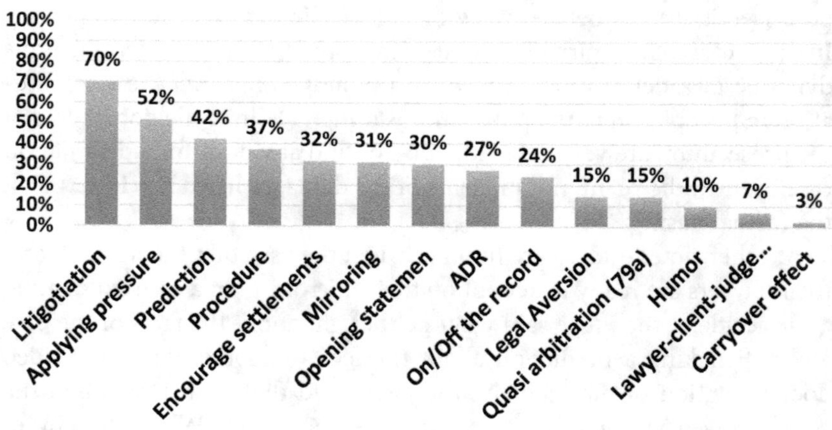

Figure 6.1 Judicial conflict resolution practices.

6.2 Florence: The Diagnostic, Adjudicative Judge

Judges in Italy, who were only recently authorized to promote settlement, took a different approach to settlement in comparison to judges in Israel and the United States. The differences as observed in court are summarized in the following.

6.2.1 Truth as a Unique Inspiration for Judicial Settlement

Judges would not rely on instinct or heuristics, as has been found in other legal systems.[4] Instead, they preferred to refer to an expert report provided by the parties or to a court-appointed expert report. Liability was central to their decision on how to proceed with the case. If the liability of the parties seemed clear from the expert report or could be presumed by law (such as in the case of watchmen when goods under the supervision have been damaged), they felt comfortable writing a judicial conciliation proposal.[5] Otherwise, they refrained from doing so.

Thus, expert reports were widely referred to in court observations and interviews as a central piece of evidence based on which a judicial conciliation proposal could be made or a negotiation to reach a settlement could be conducted. The *lack* of an expert report was also used at times to induce the parties to negotiate and settle. In court observations we found that the court-appointed expert may be mentioned in order to *induce the parties to settle.* The reasoning: Such an appointment incurs expenses upon the parties; thus, the parties might prefer to settle. For instance, in one case, the judge said to attorneys: "If you had deposited a private report on the costs of a possible demolition of the irregular garret, I could have done a conciliation proposal. Now I have to nominate a technical expert, and that means time and costs." In response, the attorneys asked the judge to set another hearing in order to verify whether the parties were willing to negotiate their dispute.

The search for liability was central from the lawyers' point of view as well. For example, in the first hearing of a case involving the collapse of a building's parking area, owners of the apartments in the building sued the architect, builders, and surveyors for damages. After the judge asked

[4] *See* Nofit Amir & Michal Alberstein, *New Families of Legal Systems in Transition and Implications for AI (forthcoming)*; James A. Wall, Jr. & Lawrence F. Schiller, *Judicial Involvement in Pre-Trial Settlement: A Judge Is Not a Bump on a Log*, 6 AM. J. TRIAL ADVOC. 27, 35–36 (1982).

[5] Art 185-*bis* C.p.c. (It.).

if they could reach an agreement, the architect's attorney said: "Your honor, I find it hard to reach an agreement here . . . It would be at least necessary to understand who is responsible for the event." The builders' attorney said: "I believe that an expert report is necessary in this case, in order to understand the exact amount of the damages and, lastly, the exact percentage of liability of the defendants." The judge did not insist on his invitation and fixed another hearing to continue the trial.

Prediction was not used when liability was not clear-cut. This contrasts deeply with the common use of prediction in adversarial systems, as early as the first hearing of the pretrial.[6] In the past, the suggestion of a judicial conciliation proposal without specific authority was grounds for recusal due to concerns regarding anticipation. Thus, 185 *bis* states explicitly that a judge who offers a judicial conciliation proposal may continue to preside over the trial.[7] However, prediction is still a marginal practice and did not take place at all in the trials that we observed.

6.2.2 *Sharp Separation between Adjudication and Mediation*

Mediation is viewed by judges as a transformative process, one which they have no time to attempt and whose place is not in the courtroom. Judges decide which cases are suitable for mediation while considering the parameters set out in the art.5(2) in Legislative Decree No. 28, 2010 (nature of the dispute, conduct of the parties) and other issues (e.g., parallel proceedings, an ongoing relationship).[8]

Restarting communication in a relationship – business or other – was a central consideration in issuing a mediation order.[9] In one case, the lawyers offered to easily end the dispute through negotiation in light of interchanges during the hearing, yet the judge insisted on mediation:

[6] *See* Sela et al., *supra* note 1, at 106–108.

[7] *Supra* note 5.

[8] D.Lgs. 4 Marzo 2010, n.28 (It.). Judges make these determinations with the help of legal interns who analyze the case.

[9] This correlates with the view that a central role of mediation is to improve communication between parties to a conflict, as clearly underlined by CLAUDIA COVATA, LA MEDIAZIONE PER LA COMPOSIZIONE DELLE CONTROVERSIE CIVILI E COMMERCIALI 497, 505 (Mauro Bove ed., CEDAM 2011) (stating that "the role of the mediator is, mostly, that of helping the parties understand both the nature and the potential of mediation, and to manage the emotions of the parties till they are able to restart dialogue and to point out all the possible shared and mutually beneficial agreements").

DEFENSE ATTORNEY: "Your honor, if you could defer the hearing so that we have time to continue the negotiation . . ."

JUDGE: "Mmh, I was not thinking about negotiation, I consider this case suitable for mediation." The attorneys gave their consent.

The judge read the mediation order out loud: "Given that an expert report would be necessary in order to verify the amount of consumption, given that, at this stage of the trial, it would be favorable to reactivate the communication between the parties, also in order to avoid the costs of the future expert report, given that the mediation could furthermore preserve the business relationship between the parties . . ."

In another instance, the judge implored the attorneys to attempt mediation to help the parties communicate and rehabilitate their relationship, yet the attorneys persuaded the judge that the relationship was so tense that a meeting between the parties would only aggravate the circumstances.

Since judges maintain a positive view of adjudication (seeing it as one of two separate dimensions of dispute resolution available to the parties), they do not usually apply a heavy-handed approach to settlement. Rather, they take the lawyers' opinions into serious consideration when deciding the suitability of the case for mediation or settlement.

In our observations, mediation was not coerced even though judges have the authority to do so through a mediation order. The use of articles 185 c.p.c, calling the parties to a conciliation hearing (usually only lawyers are present at hearings), was also often made in consultation with the lawyers, with the judge asking whether they thought bringing the parties together might advance a settlement.[10] The judge accepted their opinion, whether positive or negative.

Following these and similar findings, we find it reasonable to argue that the judges separate more sharply than do common law judges between the truth-seeking in law and the truth collaboratively constructed by the parties in mediation. They insist on the legal criteria as the sole measure for judges even when pursuing judicial conflict resolution (JCR) methods and avoid the common tendency in adversarial systems to perceive the legal truth itself as based on compromise and many times indeterminate. This dichotomy offers an interesting

[10] *Supra* note 5.

perspective on the issue of cooptation of mediation through court-annexed programs (in other countries). The concern is that court-annexed mediation is efficiency-focused and evaluative, thus compromising the potential benefits of mediation.[11] Mediation practice in Italy, though institutionalized, and monitored by the judiciary, with mediation centers approved by a designated judge, and sometimes operating within the tribunal, as in Florence, is cherished as another form of justice, and keeps the promise of dialogue and transformation.

6.3 New Sources of Legitimation?[12]

Since the law does not ascribe precisely how to promote settlements, judges are indirectly expected to fill this void themselves. In our observations, we found that while most of the judges had not developed a reflexive or coherent perspective on their new role and mostly used hard powers, a few had developed unique approaches, which can be described as judicial conflict resolution (JCR) styles, using a mix of soft power and authority-based hard power to promote settlements in their courtrooms. In contrast to applying pressure on parties, as seen from the discussion earlier in this chapter, these styles could offer potential best practices for judges who seek to integrate settlement promotion into their roles.

In this section, we outline three judicial styles as developed by a few judges, who have incorporated direct facilitation of negotiations into their practices to promote settlement. Each of these judges, working in Israel, where judges are expected to bring about settlement in pretrial (as is the emphasis of the pretrial family; see Chapter 3), is considered a champion of settlement. Each uses various aspects of judicial procedure to design a repeating "script" into which they have integrated soft types of power, sometimes combined with varying degrees of traditional hard powers, to generate new modes of legitimacy.

6.3.1 The Dispute Design Judge

This judge began every observed hearing by asking the litigants or their lawyers (if only the lawyers were present) for permission to speak off the

[11] *See* Patrick G. Coy & Timothy Hedeen, *A Stage Model of Social Movement Co-optation: Community Mediation in the United States*, 46 SOC. Q. 405, 405 (2005) (noting that "community mediation has become increasingly institutionalized and has undergone various degrees of co-optation in its evolving relationship with the court system").

[12] This section is derived from Cohen & Alberstein, *supra* note 1.

record, that is, without documenting in the protocol what he would say. Having secured their agreement (which was given in all the observed hearings), he proceeded to assess the legal and factual strengths and weaknesses, as well as the strategic advantages and disadvantages, of each side. Subsequently, he either sent the litigants and their lawyers outside to try and reach a settlement or proposed (or tried to propose) a settlement agreement "tailored" to the case discussed at the hearing. We name this style "dispute design,"[13] as it takes into account goals, stakeholders, processes, and structures in developing a systematic approach for a distinct form of disputes.

To showcase this style, we will take the case of a dispute between a contractor and a client regarding an apartment that had been sold with defects. This did not result in a final settlement, instead ending with both sides only agreeing to consider it.

The judge began the session by asking the lawyers and the litigants their names, after which he asked if they would agree to hold the hearing off the protocol and again explaining what this meant. He then went on to describe to them the structure of the hearing: "I read the file and I want to explain to you what I think about it, after which I will send you outside to talk."

He asked if the apartment had been "delivered" to the client, to which the sides answered that there was a disagreement on this matter. The judge did not get a chance to explain his interpretation of the facts, as at this point the atmosphere became charged when the litigants demanded the right to show the judge certain documents. He refused their request, angrily stating: "You will not run my hearing!"

In response, the litigants retorted that they no longer wished to have the hearing off the record. The judge started to dictate everything that had been said to the stenographer, and he had to slow down his speech significantly to enable her to record everything he said. At this point the judge stopped and told the litigants that he did not want to continue the hearing on the record, as "the pace of dictation makes it hard to continue . . . [and because] the court has limited ability to bring the sides to an agreement in a formal hearing." The judge asked the litigants to reconsider discussing off the record, as "having the hearing off the record serves both sides, and we could end this case today or continue to trial."

[13] Stephanie Smith & Janet Martinez, *An Analytic Framework for Dispute Systems Design*, 14 HARV. NEGOT. L. REV. 123 (2009).

Once everyone calmed down, the judge apologized for his earlier outburst, saying that he was stressed because he was not able to run the hearing as he saw fit. Hearing this, the litigants agreed to continue with the hearing off the record. When this was settled, the judge litigotiated by mirroring to the sides his understanding of their case's respective strengths and weaknesses, saying that the respondents would have a hard time establishing their claims. The judges further stated that the case will have further implications for other tenants in the building. He concluded that at the present time he was leaning toward the plaintiffs and that they might have a higher chance of winning – but that this could change. To even out his last statement and to dissuade the defendants from insisting on a full trial, the judge ended with a warning about the high costs of the trial experts.

At this point, the defendants stated that they previously had arrived at a settlement agreement, but that the plaintiff kept changing his mind. The plaintiff said that they had agreed on everything but one small matter. The judge asked if they would mind telling him what they had not agreed on, and that perhaps he could help. It turned out that the disagreement was on an amount of about $10,000 in compensation, and that they also were unable to agree on liability regarding a defective air conditioner. Further discussion revealed that the plaintiff's lawyer had an interest in going to full trial because he represented six other tenants in the building with similar problems. After hearing this, the judge proposed a settlement:

> Why don't you have the air condition tunnels re-examined by a professional? If the system is functional, the plaintiff will pay for the examination, and if the system malfunctions the defendant will pay for the examination and the compensation?

In response, both sides began to argue heatedly again regarding liability for the air conditioner's malfunction. In a final attempt to bring the sides to an agreement, the judge used a host of soft power conflict resolution practices. While he had earlier held out a settlement proposal, he now litigotiated in an attempt to narrow the points of contention. First, he set an agenda focusing them on the issues that need to be addressed; he then gave a general prediction; he invoked legal aversion while discussing the negative aspects of going ahead with a trial; and he finished by directly encouraging settlement: ". . . the plaintiff has an interest in going to trial because of the other tenants. There is a mere 13,000 shekels (about $4,500) difference between you . . ." The judge turned to the plaintiff:

"Proving what you will need to prove is going to be expensive . . . I think you should settle today, since carrying on will be costly for you . . ."

The judge turned to the respondents: "If you really want to end this and you don't like my offer, go outside and talk amongst yourselves. The lawyers will go over what you will decide, and I will ratify it . . ."

The litigants and their lawyers refused to do as he suggested, and the settlement discussion came to a dead end. The judge concluded: "I think that the dynamic between the litigants is positive, yet the lawyers are preventing us from settling. If they would have let me, I would have gone on. . ."

On realizing that the litigants and their lawyers were not interested in hearing his proposal, the judge ended the hearing.

This judge took advantage of the flexibility of the law, which allows him to decide what to include in the hearing's protocol. He created an informal and at times even intimate space, in which the court's hierarchy is much less rigid. He applied a simultaneous mix of soft and hard powers, attempting to influence the litigants to settle. He further used various modes of power interchangeably and a dynamic and relational manner, according to the fluctuating dynamic in court between himself and the litigants and their lawyers, and the relationship between the litigants and the lawyers.[14]

To start, the judge did not impose anything on the litigants. To the contrary, when proposing to hold the hearing off the record, he created a particular atmosphere – then used that space to influence the litigants to reach a settlement. Holding the hearing off the record also helped him establish himself as an expert on the case, which gave his predictions, invitation, and expectation to settle a much stronger effect. It came from an expert who was talking to the litigants in an informal and intimate space.

At the same time, the judge also used hard powers, even if in a much more nuanced manner than if he had adjudicated on the merits of the case and passed judgment accordingly. This happened when he spoke negatively about continuing with the trial and expressing ***legal aversion*** to further court hearings, and in the second hearing when he gave a ***prediction mirroring*** how he perceived the sides' respective legal standings. These constituted coercive forms of power, as these sentiments were expressed by the judge who would ultimately preside over the substantive

[14] Omer Shapira, *Exploring the Concept of Power in Mediation: Mediators' Sources of Power and Influence Tactics*, 24 OHIO ST. J. DISP. RESOL. 535 (2009), at 558–63.

hearing should the parties not reach a settlement. Aside from that, the judge ***applied pressure*** on the litigants to continue the hearing off the record. While he did not impose it, but rather simply said that he could not dictate quickly to the stenographer, for the litigants to refuse it would have been very confrontational. He further applied pressure when concluding that they could end the hearing that day with a settlement.

When comparing this judge with other judges who have not developed this concrete dispute design style, it becomes clear that the process he created, which became coherent for the litigants (especially for repeat players in his courtroom), maintained a balanced and legitimate exercise of power, even when the use of hard power practices was involved. The respectful atmosphere in his courtroom was preserved and protected. The boundaries between the autonomy of the litigants sent outside and the authority of the judge was clear.

6.3.2 The Trust-Building Charismatic Judge

The most distinct feature of this judge's judicial style was not the type or the order of the judicial conflict resolution practices that he used, or the specific interplay of soft powers. Rather, his unique charisma and particular sense of humor created an atmosphere of ease and trust in his courtroom, which made it easier for him to convince the litigants of his settlement attempts. He additionally ***mirrored*** and ***predicted*** what he thought would be the legal outcome of the cases, and in some cases he visited the property at the center of the dispute.[15]

The following hearing, in a lawsuit over a rental debt between a landlord and a tenant who lived in a rent-controlled apartment, demonstrates this dynamic. Throughout the hearing, the judge was very empathic toward the tenant. He began the hearing by expressing his empathy with the disadvantaged tenant, stating that he did not want the defendant to have to choose between paying rent or buying medication, and that therefore the sides should go outside and try to reach an agreement between them. Emphasizing that the issue at hand was not only the debt itself but also the matter of feasible payments, the judge said, off the protocol: "There is no doubt that the defendant owes money. The only question is what the terms of the payment will be."

[15] The quotes of the hearings used in this section are taken from Kim Yankolovitz, Judicial Conflict Resolution from the Point of View of the Judge (2019) (unpublished seminar paper at Bar Ilan University written in the framework of this research).

The litigants went outside to speak about a possible settlement. After a short while they returned, stating that they could only reach a partial agreement and would be grateful if the court helped them reconcile their disagreements. The judge responded, with a smile: "I see that I need to bring the (car) battery and the cables," evoking a metaphor of a stalled car that needed to be jump-started. This comment broke the ice, as the litigants and their lawyers all laughed. With a more relaxed atmosphere in the courtroom now, the landlord agreed to spread the debt further to help the tenant make the payments. The judge continued the hearing by creating sanctions to ensure that payment would be made. When the landlord said that she was not a social worker, the judge implored her jokingly: "I'm trying to make sure the lion will be full and the sheep will remain whole." Eventually, she agreed to the new payment schedule, and the judge personally thanked her.

Trust was created through the judge's openness and humor, which created a unique atmosphere for compromise. This also happened when the judge explained the rationale behind the sides reaching an agreement on their own:[16]

> I have a big toolbox, with hammers of various sizes, but this case needs a tweezer. Yet in my toolbox I do not have a tweezer, but you (the litigants) have a tweezer, and you need to use it.

The judge continued with his humorous remarks throughout the hearing. When he referenced the litigants' agreement to his offer, he stated: ". . . if both sides are equally unhappy with (my) opinion, it inevitably means that it is a good one."

Later, when contemplating the reliability of witnesses, he pondered: ". . . no witness is in your control unless they are tied in your backyard, and then it's a completely different set of rules . . ."

To conclude, unlike the dispute design judge who created more of a recurring streamlined model to encourage settlement as an alternative to the loss of law-based legitimacy, this judge's judicial style creates a particular ambiance that leads to more trust and less resistance on behalf of the litigants as a source of legitimacy.

6.3.3 *The Mediating Judge*

While hundreds of our court observations focused on regular pretrial court hearings, here we focus on a hearing by a different judge who regularly leads reconciliation procedures in court (which are a less

[16] *Id.*

common form of dispute resolution made available in the Tel Aviv first-instance court). Unlike regular pretrial, the judge in these hearings is not the presiding judge at the pretrial phase and consequentially will not preside over the trial itself.[17] In fact, there is a court-mandated "wall" between the judge presiding over the judicial mediation and the judges adjudicating the case in the "regular" hearings, and the two are not allowed to discuss the case. Therefore, one of the most significant hard powers of the judges – namely, the litigants' awareness that if they do not accept the judge's settlement offer, they will still meet the presiding judge at the trial – does not exist here. For this reason, reconciliation judges' power to offer incentives through prediction are limited, as they will not preside over the trial itself. It is interesting to note that in Singapore, for example, settlement judges belong to a separate category in court and cannot decide cases at all.

To this end, the style of judging uses an even more extended plethora of soft powers, drawing on mediation practices when addressing the emotional aspects of the litigants' needs for recognition of a sense of justice, and, in effect, creating a unique amalgamation of soft-power judicial practices.

In a hearing dealing with a real-estate dispute, the buyers of an apartment were not informed that a cell phone communication tower was based on the roof of the building. After buying the apartment and finding out about the tower, they sought to cancel the deal, but the sellers refused.

The judge began the hearing by stating that his goal was to bring the sides to a compromise. He then proceeded to summarize the facts of the case, ensuring that both sides agreed that he had recounted it correctly and that they both agreed on his version of events. He then noted that both sides knew each other from school, alluding to a common history, stating that in Israel everyone knew everyone and that there were very few degrees of separation.

The judge continued to frame the legal aspects of the hearing, stating:

> [T]his is not a tort hearing, since experts have not been able to determine if any damage is caused by cell phone towers. Instead, we are here to decide whether the sellers were under duty to disclose the existence of the cell phone tower, or [if] was it the buyers' obligation to try to find out themselves if they cared about such matters ... there is a contractual disagreement on the extent of the obligation to disclose in this case. This

[17] As stated earlier, in the Israeli legal system the judge presiding in pretrial will also preside in the trial itself should the litigants not settle.

> never came up in the conversations between the buyers and the sellers, and we only have the buyers' version after they found out.

The judge litigotiated when he framed the legal responsibility and the question at hand: whether the buyers had agreed to buy the property "as is" or not; and, if they had not agreed to a cell phone tower being part of the property, whether it was their responsibility to find out.

The judge sought the litigants' agreement for him to carry out ***quasi-arbitration according to Article 79(a),*** which allows judges to hand down a verdict without explaining the rationale for the decision, for which the litigants have not right of appeal. The judge attempted to convince them of a "bottom" and a "ceiling" between which he could adjudicate. In doing so, he spoke to both sides' interests:

> [F]actually there is no doubt that the buyers did not know about the cellphone tower when they agreed to buy the place... and when they did find out about it they had already committed to loan payments... They decided to sue and while the appraiser did not determine that there was actual danger from the cell phone tower, it is beyond dispute that most people do not want to live next to it and therefore the existence of the cellphone tower led to a depreciation of value.

The judge moved on the ***mirror*** to the sides their own contributory negligence: "The sellers should have disclosed but the buyers should have made sure to find out... After all this a deal of over $500,000. . . ."

Addressing the buyers, he asked: "So, what did you do to protect yourselves?"

The buyer said that he tried to have the tower removed but without success, and that if the seller could remove it, he would drop the lawsuit. When the judge asked him why he did not sell the apartment, he said that no one will want to buy it with a cell tower on the roof.

At that point the judge said that he recommended that the litigants agree to quasi-arbitration between an agreed-upon "floor" and "ceiling," or go to mediation. He added that if they did not agree to end with a settlement, the hearing would be returned to the original pretrial judge. The judge continued to narrow the gap between the floor and the ceiling, making sure that both sides agreed to the narrowing range; the sides agreed to think about it and to give him an answer within one week.

While the litigants did not leave the court with an agreed-upon settlement, the judge managed to convince them to think about his adjudicating in a ***quasi-arbitration***, and to let him know within one week. He did so using only soft powers.

6.3.4 *Three Possible Modalities of Power and Legitimation*

It seems that the lack of guidance in the law on how to promote settlements has led a few judges to informally generate new modes of legitimacy when encouraging litigants to settle.

Each judge drew on different sources, structural and personality based, and used a different amalgamation of power bases when influencing litigants to settle. At the outset, they all used environmental power to create a new atmosphere in their courtrooms, which enabled them to influence and convince rather than rely on the classic force of law to encourage litigants to settle.

The dispute design judge used legal procedure and the space granted to him by law to conduct hearings off the record. In this informal intimate space, he used different forms of power, both hard and soft, while replacing law-based legitimacy with a hearing based on a repetitive script in which authority-based top-down hierarchal power relations between the judge and the litigants were maintained. The litigants were provided with a proposed solution based on legal arguments, and were sent to reach a settlement based on a clear assessment by the judge.

In contrast, the charismatic judge created trust to promote settlement between the parties. His ability to create the right atmosphere had an effect on the negotiation dynamic, which motivated the litigants to collaborate. Thus, instead of the vertical top-down power relations invoked by the dispute design judge, he succeeded in creating a more horizontal relationship with the litigants, nudging them into accepting his settlement proposals because they identified with him and felt that he had their interests at heart. In other words, the charismatic judge relied on the litigants' willing cooperation.

The mediating judge was the most remote from legal based legitimacy, in part because he could not be presiding over the court hearings should the pretrial negotiations fail. While the hearings are external to the procedure and, as such, need to establish other sources of legitimation altogether, this mediation procedure was created by the court itself as an institutional alternative to the legal hearing. Thus, paradoxically – and unlike the other two judges, who created informal settings to generate sources of legitimation – the mediating judge enjoyed formal, system-based legitimacy. Another mediating judge, not mentioned here, used her authority to encourage listening and to extract the most important issues for each side. Such legitimacy derives from the conflict resolution expertise that such judges have, combined with their inherent authority.

PART III

Legal Metamorphosis?

7

A New Paradigm for Judicial Involvement

The role of judges has changed dramatically, yet its new nature has not brought about a corresponding shift in legal thought. As shown in the previous chapters, legal systems have harnessed judges to help accomplish the speedy disposal of cases through settlement. They do so in varying degrees, through different strategies, and the judges themselves implement the tools in different ways in each of the legal families (the trial, pretrial, and pre-filing families; see Chapter 3).

While judges are most involved in negotiating a settlement in the pretrial family, they are also authorized to help the parties reach a settlement in the other two legal families. The Florence Court, in the trial family, presented a judicial model that mainly separates between adjudication and settlement efforts: Judges diagnose cases for mediation and refer them out of court as appropriate while explaining their reasoning in writing. If judges formulate a settlement proposal, it is after they have determined liability. Unlike judges in the pretrial family, they will usually not take part in the negotiations between the parties to settle the dispute.

However, conciliation hearings, authorized by law, do take place sporadically, and then judges must be able to combine legal and conflict resolution considerations. This currently secondary role of judges in the trial family is their main role in pretrial families. Yet how should this combination be achieved? As shown in Chapter 5, judges' perspectives on their new role are diverse and do not provide a coherent understanding of the new landscape. In particular, we found that they often failed to address deeply the tension between the legal and the conflict resolution orientation in their work.

This chapter outlines the new landscape of judicial discretion in the settlement era, referring to both critical claims of law and advanced perspectives on conflict resolution. It integrates theoretical claims as to the notion of law and legal formalism together with advanced approaches to conflict resolution. It suggests a new model for judicial discretion and provides a theoretical framework to combine the principles of conflict resolution and law as they pertain to the judicial role. In addition, it shows how judges may exercise their discretion in the courtroom (rather than through a judicial verdict). We then entwine our theories and findings, constructing a training scheme suggested for judges, which integrates conflict resolution perspectives as well as normative and ethical considerations.

7.1 The Dual Concern Model of Judicial Work

When trying to capture judicial discretion and decision-making in an era of vanishing trials, it becomes clear that judges in their work respond to two distinct contexts: the legal worldview and the social conflict framework.[1] In terms of the legal worldview, judges acknowledge various limitations of rules in determining a legal case: Rules may miss the uniqueness of the individual case; they may be indeterminate; they may be meaningless without reference to their social goals; and they may reinforce inequalities in society. In terms of the social conflict framework, judges acknowledge underlying needs and interests that are deeper than the legal dispute and require unique processing. Judges acknowledge the diverse interests of parties, including their overlapping goals; they are exposed to underlying emotions and relationships, which drive the conflict and escalate it; they acknowledge the existence of unrepresented third parties; and they are aware of various social considerations. The discretion that judges exercise between legal and conflict considerations may reflect this complexity. Judges operate in the legal world and the world of conflicts and, in using their discretion, can reflect the richness of these two evolving worldviews. The dual-concern model of judicial settlement discretion includes two axes: legal considerations and conflict considerations.[2] For each settlement promotion we can articulate a concrete intersection of perspective of conflict resolution in the shadow of a perspective of law and vice versa.

[1] Yuval Sinai & Michal Alberstein, *Expanding Judicial Discretion: Between Legal and Conflict Considerations*, 21 HARVARD NEGOT. L. REV. (2016); Michal Alberstein, *Complexity and Reconstruction as Contemporary Legal Thought: Law–Conflict Interactions and Judicial Work*, in SEARCHING FOR CONTEMPORARY LEGAL THOUGHT (Justin Desautels-Stein & Christopher Tomlins, eds., 2017) 465.

[2] Sinai & Alberstein, *id.*, at 231.

Whether judges in fact acknowledge this complexity, implicitly work with it, or may deny it altogether depends on personality and legal culture. Our suggestion is to introduce this new landscape in order to expand the notion of judicial discretion to meet reality and increase understanding of contemporary judicial practices. This will provide more choices for litigants, who will better understand the limits and opportunities offered by the new judicial role.[3]

Each axis in the dual concern model graduates from a simple to a more complex rendering of the respective concern. Legal considerations (the *x* axis) graduate from the most basic form – a formal application of the law – to their most sophisticated form – promoting social justice. Similarly, conflict considerations (the *y* axis) graduate from simple bargaining to negotiating identity conflicts. Figure 7.1 specifies the different categories that lie on each axis, showing the gamut of perspectives and intersections between them.[4]

7.1.1 Legal Perspectives: The X *Axis*

The *x* axis of judicial discretion ranges from *mechanical jurisprudence* (A) to *promoting social justice* (E). Mechanical jurisprudence is often considered the ideal type of judicial decision-making and entails deciding conflicts on the basis of strict legal rules. According to this perception, conflicts are brought before judges after all negotiations have failed, and at this point judges are asked to engage in rational rule-based decision-making (A1 rubric in Figure 7.1). They decide cases mechanically assuming that bargaining attempts have failed.

A broader perception of the legal aspect of the judicial work internalizes critique of mechanical jurisprudence and includes extralegal considerations such as equity (B), precise justice (C), policy and principles instrumentalism (D), efficiency (E), and social justice (F).[5]

Critical and reconstructive arguments about law, as presented by the above-mentioned schools, penetrate the legal domain: Law students are exposed to critical thinking in their legal education, and judges are part of the legal community and develop their own judicial style in reference to various arguments and claims about law. The legal field has developed

[3] Yuval Sinai & Michal Alberstein, *Court Arbitration by Compromise: Discretion, Hybridity and Legal Pluralism*, 13 CARDOZO PUBL. L. POLICY & ETHICS J. 739 (2015).

[4] For a full explanation of the different intersections, *see* Sinai & Alberstein, *supra* note 1.

[5] Sinai & Alberstein, *supra* note 1.

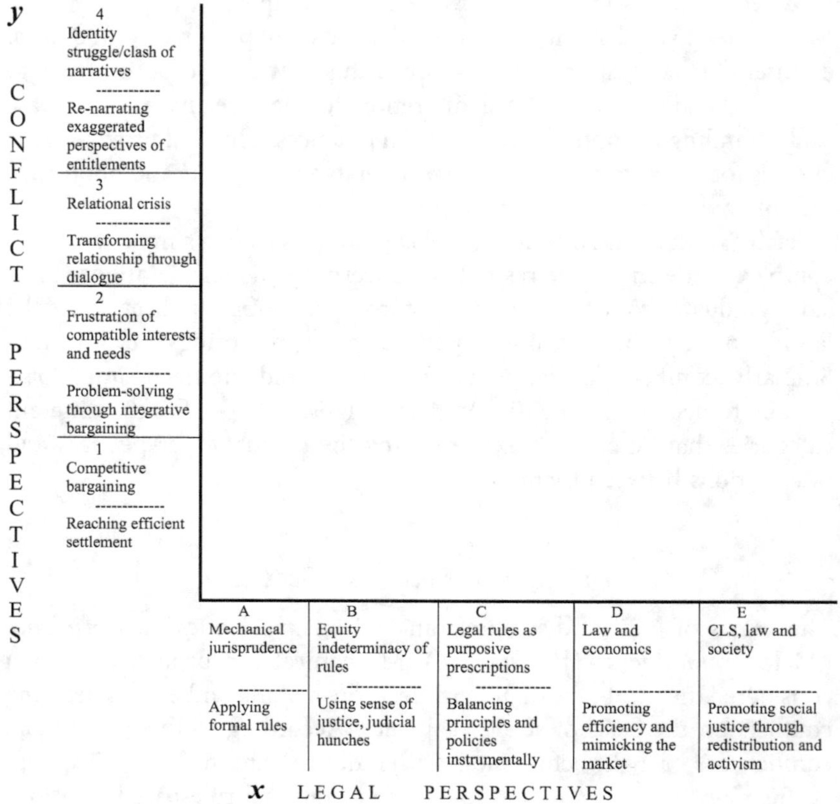

Figure 7.1 Judicial discretion between conflict and legal perspectives.

some structured responses to critical claims, such as the purposive interpretation. Furthermore, we find systematic patterns in some informal expressions of judge rhetoric in case law. The use of such reconstructive and informal frames can be measured.[6] The settlement hearing is another arena in which judges constantly use reconstructive narratives about law, and do so in the shadow of certain perspectives about reshaping social conflicts.

[6] Michal Alberstein, Limor Gabay-Egozi & Bryna Bogoch, *Between Formalism and Discretion: Measuring Trends in Supreme Court Rhetoric*, 47 HOFSTRA L. REV. 1103 (2019); Michal Alberstein, Limor Gabay-Egozi & Bryna Bogoch, *What's with Formalism? An Empirical Study of Various Predictors and Profiles of Supreme Court Rhetoric*, 30 S. CALI. INTERDISCIPL. L.J. 269 (2021).

7.1.2 *Conflict Perspectives: The Y Axis*

The *y* axis of judicial settlement discretion range from *competitive bargaining* (1) to *identity conversations* (4). The common perception of the intersection of law and conflict is that of a competitive negotiation, which assumes that the expected legal outcome will be a formal application of law. The parties bargain "in the shadow"[7] of that prediction, and their "private ordering" is a market of rulemaking in which new subrules and arrangements constitute the law in action.[8] The legal conflict setting, which is assumed under this notion, is that of competitive bargaining. This means that the goals in the conflict oppose each other, that resources are limited,[9] and that parties aspire to maximize their benefits at the expense of each other (1A rubric in Figure 7.1).

A broader perspective on conflicts may acknowledge underlying needs and interests that are deeper than the legal dispute and thereby require unique processing. Furthermore, underlying emotions and relationships that motivate and escalate the conflict may become the focus of judicial interventions (2). Sometimes judges may acknowledge and identify narratives that underlie legal disputes in order to resolve them (3). When judges exercise discretion, they may reflect this complexity and work with it while ascending the *y* axis (4).

Two sets of new conceptions emerge out of the new model when exploring the new settlement discretional landscape: From the conflict angle, engagement in conflicts can be perceived as bargaining in a competitive mode (1), negotiating for problem-solving (2), facilitating dialogue in order to transform relationships (3), and re-narrating identities within ideological struggles (4). Such conflict engagement may be carried out in the shadow of a variety of conceptions of law – from a mechanistic formal application of rules (A), to equity and intuition (B), to policy balancing and instrumental public problem-solving (C), to efficient allocation of legal entitlement (D) and social transformation and redistribution (E).

7 See Robert H. Mnookin & Lewis Kornhauser, *Bargaining in the Shadow of the Law: The Case of Divorce*, 88 YALE L.J. 950 (1979). This article provides one of the prevailing models for understanding the relationship between legal decision-making and conflicts. It assumes that prediction of the legal decision-making affects the private ordering of parties, which is based on prediction of a mechanistic application of rules.

8 *Id.* at 958.

9 ROY J. LEWICKI, DAVID M. SAUNDERS & BRUCE BARRY (eds.), NEGOTIATION (2014).

From the legal perspective, legal decision-making, either formal, purposive or promoting social change (A–E), may occur while holding various assumptions about conflict source – from pure bargaining to narrative clash (1–4). The model suggests a conceptual ideal framework, which in reality will need adaption to specific legal cultures. In Italy, for example, mechanical jurisprudence and applying black-letter law as written in the code is still considered the prevailing paradigm in judicial work, and purposive interpretation is not common in judicial rhetoric. In Israel, which can be characterized as a post-formalist culture, more reconstructive modes of law are acknowledged, and England remains overall formalist. Nevertheless, drawing the lines between the legal and conflict aspects of the conflict is required in any judicial work, and a vanishing trials era calls for more awareness of this conceptual complexity and the flexibility and choice it offers for policymakers.[10]

7.2 The Underlying Principles of Law and Conflict Resolution

The graph in Figure 7.1 shows different types of conflict resolution and legal perspectives, but it does not state the underlying principles of these perspectives. When trying to integrate conflict resolution into law, one must analyze the underlying principles of conflict resolution and see how they can meet the underlying principles of law. This process of hybridization can be conceptualized according to six recurring principles in the field of conflict resolution that are relevant to our topic, judicial conflict resolution.[11] These principles suggest different modes by which judges may help transform and reconstruct legal conflicts.

1. *Process emphasis*. A central theme that inspired the origin of the field of conflict resolution is the concept that "process matters," and that each conflict requires a focused reflection on how to engage with this process. In philosophy, the idea of process as overcoming substantive arguments is a familiar solution to old metaphysical problems. Within the American philosophy of pragmatism, this tendency is mostly celebrated when instead of determining between dichotomies such as mind and body, experience and reason, or being and not being there is a

[10] For a detailed exploration of contemporary law–conflict interactions in judicial decision-making, *see* Desautels-Stein & Tomlins, *supra* note 1.

[11] Michal Alberstein, *The Law of Alternatives: Conflict Resolution as The Art of Reconstruction*, 16 CARDOZO J. CONFL. RES. 888–92 (2015), at 879.

constant shift toward "becoming" and a use of a process that is supposed to embrace paradoxes by containing oppositional logics of the previous discourse within the new regime.[12] In jurisprudence, an emphasis on process has been introduced by various schools, such as The Legal Realism,[13] The Legal Process,[14] and by legal philosophers such as Dworkin[15] and Fiss. The process emphasis in law is usually focused on escaping the application of legal rules through reference to the principles and policies behind them and applying them in a functional mode, as discussed in presenting the policy orientation above under the legal considerations axis. From a conflict resolution perspective, the process emphasis is the idea that the legal conflict is only a superficial presentation of positions, while the real movers of the conflict are the private interests and needs of the parties.[16] The combination of the process emphasis in law with that of conflict resolution will require that private interests and needs of parties will be analyzed in the shadow of "public" principles and policies as defined by law. Stepping back from the conflict scene and reflecting on the conflict and the process are acts of judgment deferral, which may philosophically help judges constructively engage with legal conflicts. Judges can ask themselves about the goal of a certain hearing in terms of rehabilitating the offender, empowering the victims, and benefiting the conditions of third parties, such as children in criminal conflicts.[17] In civil conflict they may address existing relationships and other conflicts, complex interests, and various options that may not appear in the court files. They can frame the hearing in court as aiming to resolve the conflict or to develop a better understanding of it. They can

[12] LOUIS MENAND (ed.), PRAGMATISM: A READER (1997); MORRIS DICKSTEIN (ed.), *The* REVIVAL OF PRAGMATISM: NEW ESSAYS ON SOCIAL THOUGHT, LAW, AND CULTURE (1998); MATTHEW FESTENSTEIN, PRAGMATISM AND POLITICAL THEORY: FROM DEWEY TO RORTY (1997).

[13] WILLIAM W. FISHER, MORTON J. HORWITZ & THOMAS A. REED (eds.), AMERICAN LEGAL REALISM (1993) 326.

[14] HENRY M. HART, JR. & ALBERT M. SACKS, THE LEGAL PROCESS: BASIC PROBLEMS IN THE MAKING AND APPLICATION OF LAW (William N. Eskridge & Jr. Phillip P. Frickey, eds.) (1994).

[15] RONALD DWORKIN, TAKING RIGHTS SERIOUSLY (1977) 563; RONALD DWORKIN, LAW'S EMPIRE (1986) 470.

[16] Owen M. Fiss, *Against Settlement*, 93 YALE L.J. 1073 (1984); Tania Sourdin, *Five Reasons Why Judges Should Conduct Settlement Conferences*, 37 MONASH U. L. REV. 145 (2011).

[17] In 1999, an estimated 721,500 state and federal prisoners were parents to 1,498,800 children under age eighteen. See BUREAU OF JUSTICE STATISTICS, U.S. DEP'T OF JUST., BJS SPECIAL REPS., NCJ 182335, INCARCERATED PARENTS AND THEIR CHILDREN 1 (2000), https://bjs.ojp.gov/content/pub/pdf/iptc.pdf.

also plan and build a process to address the elements they choose to emphasize. In the training workshop we have constructed for judges, drawing a conflict map and discussing the opening statement and framing of the settlement hearing are the skills we teach judges and encourage them to practice.[18]

2. *Constructive future-oriented intervention.* In conflict resolution, process emphasis is combined with a positive mode of intervention. The choice to reject the more pessimistic, descriptive perspective on the conflict resolution field is an ideological preference not justified by objective criteria or by pure reason.[19] This gesture can be characterized as almost a Nietzschean mode in which after realizing that there is no God, no metaphysical truth, no external criteria to rely on, the immediate choice is not necessarily nihilism and despair but instead a pure will to extract the constructive picture of reality.[20] A judge who espouses a constructivist consciousness assumes that resolving the conflict amicably and helping the parties try various modes of processing is always better than imposing a formal legal solution on them. Judges who intervene in legal conflicts ask themselves how to improve their conduct (based on legal precedents) and how to improve the situation before them, not only how to decide what occurred in the past and how to punish accordingly. Moments of escalation will be framed by them as temporary relapses. Small agreements will be celebrated as important steps in building trust and reconciliation. Humor and good spirit may further increase their positive impact. Our court observations reinforced that assumption, and some of our "settlement champions" were using humor and positive framing in order to promote settlements.[21]

3. *Underlying hidden layer.* According to conflict resolution philosophy, the social conditions underlying legal disputes – those that constitute the criminal or civil conflict – are the true essence of the conflict that needs to be addressed. In criminal cases, judges should address addiction problems, welfare issues, domestic violence, mental health conditions, and other elements at the core of criminal conflict. For example, in the Israeli Penal Code there is a reference to the circumstances of the

[18] Fields of Agreement, a training workshop for judges, prepared in collaboration with The Center for Judicial Training, Israeli Supreme Court.

[19] KEVIN AVRUCH, CULTURE AND CONFLICT RESOLUTION (1998).

[20] FRIEDRICH NIETZSCHE, BEYOND GOOD AND EVIL: PRELUDE TO A PHILOSOPHY OF THE FUTURE (translated. with commentary, Walter Kaufmann) (1966).

[21] *See* Chapter 5.

offender. In addition, judges must apply theories from the world of positive criminology. In civil cases, a legal claim may be motivated by the need to promote reputation, to ventilate emotions, to succeed in another dispute, or other hidden motives. Addressing the various underlying needs and sometimes contrasting interests of the parties is a source for creativity and a deeper understanding of the conflict by judges as well as the parties. Processing them constructively may benefit society and the parties to conflicts. It may also help prevent future crimes and similar disputes. Although the hidden interests are often concealed by litigants in court, and, unlike in mediation, judges are usually not allowed to meet separately with the parties in order to learn about their true concerns and needs, acknowledging the existence of a hidden layer, and exploring some of it, may contribute to better settlements.

4. *Hybridity, complexity, and deconstruction.* Legal conflicts are typically presented in a binary, adversarial way, depicting the conflict as a win-lose situation in which one party's claim opposes the other's and reflects an all-or-nothing argument. The idea of deconstruction and hybridization as transforming conflicts begins with judges' efforts to differentiate between legal claims, to narrow controversies, and to balance arguments. In the new emerging field of new governance it is also a theoretical perspective about the right ways to promote social change through law, and to combine social forces in a mode of negotiation and joint action.[22] This philosophy continues in conflict resolution work when other issues that are not necessarily apparent on the briefs of the parties should be considered in order to deal with the conflict. Conflicts have emotional, economical, medical, and criminological aspects that need to be addressed and may affect the conflict intervention mode needed in order to process them constructively. A conflict resolution perspective aspires to address and manage such complexity. It embraces the complexity and ambivalence as sources for creativity and innovation. Facilitators of alternatives encourage disputants to deconstruct an "all-or-nothing" or "win-lose" legal framework into a multiple array of smaller, more manageable problems, interests, choices, preferences, and desires.[23] These problems, in turn, become partly resolvable through

[22] Amy J. Cohen, *Negotiation, Meet New Governance: Interests, Skills, and Selves* 33 LAW & SOCIAL INQUIRY 503–62 (2008).

[23] Robert Axelrod's game theory work on the Prisoner's Dilemma provides the basis for a famous deconstruction of this sort. He assumes a recurring, rather than one-shot, Prisoner's Dilemma, which enables each player to engage in a series of discrete, small

hybridization – that is, a creative strategy for practical bargaining and compromise in which parties agree to make incremental and piecemeal trades across multiple divergent interests and desires.[24] The phenomenon of conflict, civil as well as criminal, is always complex. The common criminal legal perspective tends to oversimplify crime by constructing it as a polar answer of guilty or not guilty. In civil cases, the perception of the dispute is of an argument about legal rights and entitlements. In conflict resolution, "complexifying" the surface of conflicts is a common mode of transforming them. Separating the interest in rehabilitation from that of prevention – balancing retribution with restoration – or balancing other interests in civil cases is a hybrid activity made possible by embracing the philosophy underlying the field. Addressing conflicts as a complex phenomenon that needs to be tackled by deploying various regulation mechanisms and modes of intervention may provide a more effective way to deal with it. Being familiar with the multidoor landscape of both civil and criminal justice today, as discussed and explored in this book, can help judges address this complexity as well by fitting the right process to each particular issue and setting the agenda for dealing with them.

5. *Relationship and emotions.* A conflict resolution perspective entails a reconstructed perception of the human subject and strives to enrich and transform the common individualistic consciousness through the emphasis on the relational aspect of conflict interactions. The

responses to her opponent's choices. Axelrod then proceeds to show how particular kinds of responses can develop rational incentives for collaboration over the course of the longer game. ROBERT AXELROD, THE EVOLUTION OF COOPERATION (1984) 27–54. Drawing on Axelrod, theorists of alternatives likewise describe the act of negotiating conflict not as a one-shot deal but rather as a series of choices or stages where parties can make small decisions to enable a growing sense of trust and collaboration. *See, e.g.*, DAVID A. LAX & JAMES K. SEBENIUS, THE MANAGER AS NEGOTIATOR: BARGAINING FOR COOPERATION AND COMPETITIVE GAIN (1986) 160 (using Axelrod's research to propose dividing the negotiation "process into a number of small steps"). *See also,* ROGER FISHER, FRACTIONATING CONFLICT, Vol. 3 (1964) 920–41, 921 (similarly proposing a number of practical advantages for conflict resolution when major conflicts are treated as "a number of small ones").

24 For a few examples, *see* ROGER FISHER & WILLIAM URY, GETTING TO YES (1981) 73–79 (describing how to use shared and differing interests to "invent options for mutual gain"); David A. Lax & James K. Sebenius, supra note 23, at 88–116 (offering lessons in "trading on difference"); ROBERT H. MNOOKIN, SCOTT R. PEPPET & ANDREW S. TULUMELLO, BEYOND WINNING: NEGOTIATING TO CREATE VALUE IN DEALS AND DISPUTES (2000) 12–15, 28–43 (offering lessons on how to identify the multiple issues comprising a problem and to leverage differing issues into value creating trades).

acknowledgment of emotions and relationship in the conflict as a significant element in human dispute is an innovation that aims to produce a new conflict self that is less individualistic, less separated, and more caring and empathetic. The judge is supposed to exercise "relationality" with the parties in the courtroom in order to promote trust, encourage compliance, and transform the conflict.

In their work, judges can refer to the reality that people are interconnected in relational networks, and can encourage constructive expression of emotions.[25] In contrast to the common legal procedure, which assumes that litigants or offenders and victims are individuals who carry legal rights, the conflict resolution–oriented judge will address the networks of relationships underlying the case.[26] They may also address in-court relationships, such as between lawyers, or between counsel and client. Judges may encourage apologies if they have the potential to amend relationships, they can regulate emptions in the courtroom and learn from them, they can contain a victim's horror, and they can give victims a voice in court while protecting them from unnecessary and intrusive cross-examination. They can make sure defendants take rehabilitative and therapeutic steps, and can encourage them do so. Judges may also consider relationships with third parties – such as children or elderly parents – when sentencing offenders or encouraging settlements. In the training we have prepared for judges we teach them to address the lawyer–parties–judge triangle in listening to laypersons in the

[25] *See generally*, JENNIFER NEDELSKY, LAW'S RELATIONS: A RELATIONAL THEORY OF SELF, AUTONOMY, AND LAW (2011) (presenting a comprehensive perception of the relevance of relational thinking for lawyers and legal work in general).

[26] Bibas writes, in that regard: "[E]ven if the state runs the process, human emotion deserves a seat at the table. Emotion is not some raw, blind passion wholly divorced from and antithetical to reason. It is in part cognitive and evaluative and can be educated. Recent scholarship has impressively defended the importance of giving emotion a role in substantive criminal law alongside reason. Emotions are an important part of what makes us human and how we understand and evaluate our fellow humans' actions. Crime excites fear and anger, empathy and indignation, sorrow and forgiveness. Victims need our solidarity; wrongdoers merit our anger but also empathy for their plight and reasons for breaking the law. This rainbow of emotions is central to appreciating and responding to all the parties' stakes in crime. While the parties have emotional stakes, they must not be judges in their own causes; neutral arbiters must reflect upon and filter the competing emotional claims in order to distill justice. It is time to extend the same emotional logic to criminal procedures. Laymen care whether criminal justice is emotionally sensitive or tone-deaf, and taking these concerns into account should bolster the law's legitimacy." Stephanos Bibas & Richard A. Bierschbach, *Integrating Remorse and Apology into Criminal Procedure*, 114 YALE L.J. 85 (2004), at 87–88.

courtroom; we exercise empathy and emotional acknowledgment as part of uncovering needs and concerns related to the conflict. We discuss the role of authority when exercising therapeutic jurisprudence.

6. *Bottom-up work.* The usual perception of law is of a top-down institution that imposes legal rules in order to enforce and reach compliance. A conflict resolution perspective assumes that learning from interdisciplinary collaboration and "not knowing" yet what exact rule should be applied in a certain conflict, is part of the right process to achieve a solution to concrete conflicts. A conflict resolution perspective espouses a "grassroots" emphasis of working from the bottom up without knowing yet the complete plan or the preferred outcome that should be achieved. Although judges are authoritative figures and have power over the parties, conflict resolution philosophy suggests that involving the parties, which are the best experts to their conflict, in the decision-making process may help in constructively transforming the conflict. Judges who show empathy for the accused or the litigants, create behavioral contact with parties, and encourage participation and choice may help encourage more compliance and creativity and improve the quality of their intervention. In the training workshops for judges we outline best practices we have identified as encouraging participation and choice. Problem-solving courts' guidelines are discussed as part of this session.

7.3 From the Inside Out: Implementing Judicial Discretion through Hard and Soft Powers in Court[27]

The dual discretion model and the hybridization of conflict and law both pertain to the internal considerations of judges. Yet, when verdicts are few and far between, how can judges implement these considerations to persuade parties to settle?

Traditionally, judges were viewed as having the ultimate authority in court, and power relations were supposedly simple: Judges give orders, with which litigants and lawyers must comply. This is a straightforward exercise of coercive power backed by procedural and substantive legal rules. In the age of the vanishing trial, however, when judicial-led

[27] This section derives from HADAS COHEN & MICHAL ALBERSTEIN, POWER AND PERSUASION IN THE COURTROOM 6 CARDOZO INT'L & COMPAR. L. REV. 767 (2023).

settlements far outnumber written verdicts, and with judicial settlement promotion institutionalized by law, this is no longer the case.[28]

The effort to settle cases during preliminary hearings and to avoid reaching the trial phase implicitly creates a negotiation between the judge and the litigants. The judges in our study had a clear interest in closing the litigation gate due to their caseload and following their institutional incentives. Litigants were in most cases interested – or at least presented themselves as being interested – in reaching the trial phase and having their day in court to assert their legal rights, and ultimately to receive a written verdict.

Since judges are dependent on the litigants and rely on their agreement to press for settlement, they are parties to a negotiation over the decision of the litigants to pursue trial and be given a written verdict. The judges must therefore convince the litigants either to agree to a concrete settlement they propose or to reach an agreement on their own. If the litigants are sent to a mediator or arbitrator, they must first agree to this, and must pay for the service.

Judges, then, cannot use hierarchal hard powers to simply order the litigants to do things that they, the judges, want, as they could do when adjudicating rather than settling cases. Thus, they may incorporate into their practices an array of direct and indirect soft powers that involve sophisticated persuasion to influence the litigants' attitudes, goals, and beliefs – to "activate" them to behave in a certain way.

Social psychologists John R. P. French and Bertram H. Raven famously characterized power as the potential ability to influence the behavior of another person through the use of force, and to bring about change in a person's behavior and opinions.[29] Their typology of power has been applied to various academic fields in the social sciences.[30] It has also

[28] See, for instance, Rule 16 of the Federal Rules of Civil Procedure stipulates that "the court may consider and take appropriate action . . . settling the case and using special procedures to assist in resolving the dispute" (FED. R. CIV. P. 16 (C)(2)(I) (1993)).

[29] John R. P. French, Jr. & Bertram Raven, *The Bases of Social Power*, in STUDIES IN SOCIAL POWER 150, 152 (Dorwin Cartwright ed., 1959), at 151.

[30] See Koslowsky & Joseph Schwarzwald, *The Power Interaction Model: Theory, Methodology, and Empirical Applications*, in THE USE AND ABUSE OF POWER: MULTIPLE PERSPECTIVES ON THE CAUSES OF CORRUPTION 195, 196 (Annette Y. Lee-Chai & John A. Bargh eds., 2001) at 197 ("The French and Raven (1959) typology of social power is thought to be 'the most comprehensive and insightful theory of social influence in functional terms or more generally'. Indeed, it has been used in a variety of fields for studying interpersonal power and influence. These include familial relations, education, marketing and consumer psychology, and health and medicine."). See also

been used to analyze mediation and to examine the complex relationship between mediators, parties, and their representatives.[31] Building on this analysis and expanding it, we use French and Raven's understanding of power to analyze the observed interactions between judges, litigants, and lawyers in court.

French and Raven defined six bases of power, broadly divided into hard and soft forms of power.[32] ***Reward*** and ***Coercive*** power are "hard" forms of power, which delineate the ability to administer positive valences and remove negative ones, or to inflict punishment.[33] When using these forms of power, there is no attempt to change or affect the other person's attitude or perception of reality, but rather to force them to change their behavior out of fear of punishment, or due to dependency and expectation of a promised result.[34] The other four bases of power delineate a more nuanced taxonomy of power relations that has to do with influence rather than coercion. They reflect social hierarchies and automatic behavior patterns based on the "mental shortcuts" that people adopt to handle complex information,[35] identification with others,[36] the obligation to reciprocate or treat and be treated fairly,[37] and more. These include ***legitimate*** power, which is based on the social perception that one has the ability to prescribe certain behaviors to another; ***referent*** power, which is based on the identification of one with another; and ***expert*** power, based on the understanding that another person holds knowledge or ***expertise***.[38] Later, a sixth source of power, ***information***, was added to the list.[39] Experts in power dynamics have further emphasized the greater effectiveness of soft powers tactics such as inspiration,

Bertram H. Raven, *A Power/Interaction Model of Interpersonal Influence: French and Raven Thirty Years Later*, 7 J. SOC. BEHAV & PERSONALITY 217 (1992), at 239–40 (noting that "[the] model was developed as a guide for research, and for an analysis of on-going interactive situations. As such, it may also be useful for those who are in positions of influence, to help them understand more clearly the bases for their own actions, and the possibilities of alternatives.").

31 Omer Shapira, *Exploring the Concept of Power in Mediation: Mediators' Sources of Power and Influence Tactics*, 24 OHIO ST. J. DISP. RESOL. 535 (2009), at 540.

32 Raven, *supra* note 30, at 218, 234–39.

33 French & Raven, *supra* note 29, at 152.

34 *Id.* at 150, 152. See also Raven, *supra* note 30, at 234–39.

35 Shapira, *supra* note 31 at 545.

36 *Id.*, at 548.

37 *Id.*, at 550.

38 French & Raven, *supra* note 29, at 152–156.

39 Bertram H. Raven, *Social Influence and Power*, in CURRENT STUDIES IN SOCIAL PSYCHOLOGY (Ivan D. Steiner & Martin Fishbein eds., 1965) 371, 372.

legitimacy, and rational persuasion for acquiring and sustaining influence.[40] Some differentiate between potential, perceived, exercised, and realized power.[41] The personal orientation of the individual, whether cognitive, motivational, moral, or negotiation skill based,[42] has a further and significant effect on the use of the various bases of power. Judges with competitive dispositions, for example, may emphasize "power over," while the more cooperative will align with the "power with" approach.[43]

In contrast to power dynamics, which aim to change people's behaviors and negotiation outcomes, persuasion aims to change people's minds.[44] Research on social influence has established that if compliance is not accompanied by private acceptance, the outcomes of influence are typically ephemeral and unstable. Persuasion is therefore a critical tool in creating lasting settlements between parties in conflict with one another.[45] In conflict resolution studies, it has been proved that the intuitive heuristic processing of conflict information, in contrast to systematic processing, introduces biases such as fixed pie assumptions, anchoring, and stereotypes.[46] The pretrial setting can be described as addressing the need to develop more systematic understanding of the conflict while not conducting the full systematic process of the trial and verdict. Judges at the pretrial stage are expected to provide litigants with a more balanced and coherent perspective of their conflict, to frame the controversial legal issues clearly, to reduce personal bias, and to gather information. This process of increased knowledge is accompanied, usually, by an indication of the expected decisions. While judges usually claim that their legal assessment is tentative and based on the current knowledge available – in other words, heuristic – litigants take this indication seriously, and will perceive it as an anchor for the judge. They may still insist on pursuing the trial if they strongly believe that a

40 Gary Yukl & J. Bruce Tracey, *Consequences of Influence Tactics Used with Subordinates, Peers, and the Boss*, 77.4 J. APPL. PSYCHOL. 525 (1992).

41 Peter H. Kim, Robin L. Pinkley & Alison R. Fragale, *Power Dynamics in Negotiation*, 30.4 ACAD. MANAG. REV. 799–822 (2005).

42 ROY J. LEWICKI, DAVID M. SAUNDERS & BRUCE BARRY, NEGOTIATION (2006) 191–192.

43 *Id*, at 192.

44 PETER T. COLEMAN, MORTON DEUTSCH & ERIC C. MARCUS (eds.), THE HANDBOOK OF CONFLICT RESOLUTION: THEORY AND PRACTICE (2014) 533–557.

45 *Id*, at 533.

46 C. K. W. Dreu, *Social Conflict: The Emergence and Consequences of Struggle and Negotiation*, in HANDBOOK ON SOCIAL PSYCHOLOGY (S. T. Fiske, D. T. Gilbert & G. Lindzey eds., 2010).

more thorough process of fact finding will persuade the judge. However, given that time is of essence for judges because they are allocated more cases than they are able to adjudicate on the merits, and since systematic and thorough decision-making requires much more time, judges will try to persuade the parties that their current legal assessment is solidly founded.[47] Persuasion techniques may further address psychological aspects, sometimes unconscious to the litigants themselves, such as a fear of settling, the search for fairness, the need for sense of choice, and an inviting atmosphere. In terms of the judge as a party to the negotiation over admitting the trial for full adjudication, persuasion entails settlement praise and more information about the costs of a trial.

Going back to the analysis of the power that judges hold, by the nature of their position and as granted by the law, judges have ***coercive*** power embedded in their authority to give verdicts and potentially to bring about negative outcomes for the litigants in the cases they are trying. Coercive power derives from high social status, physical strength, or control over resources, as well as from the expectation that failure to comply will result in punishment.[48]

Nevertheless, exercise of the judicial role is backed by the legitimacy of the law, which provides a reason to obey, and is not considered brutal force.[49] Judges have ***legitimate*** power, reflecting the rule of law, which is the governance of law and not men. When writing legal opinions, judges are considered to be expressing reason and authority, rendered to them by the people. They are also backed by their perceived legal expertise.[50] In the courtroom, judicial legitimacy power manifests in the judges' ability to compel testimonies and impose decisions that affect the lives of the litigants before them. The judge can impose sanctions, control behavior, and decide about the process. The stronger the potential punishment – or even the mere threat of it – the stronger the coercive power the judge holds.[51] Yet, this power is backed by the legitimacy of the law. As judicial decision becomes rarer, legitimation of power

[47] This statement is based on unofficial conversations with ten Israeli presiding judges, in which they told us that they would not have been able to write full verdicts in all of their cases due to time constraints – one of the reasons why they encouraged settlements.

[48] French & Raven, *supra* note 29, at 157–58.

[49] See also JOSEPH RAZ, THE AUTHORITY OF LAW: ESSAYS ON LAW AND MORALITY (1979).

[50] In his philosophical discussion of the notion of the authority of law, Raz defines it as providing a reason to obey on the basis on expertise. See Raz, *id.*

[51] French & Raven, *supra* note 29, at 152.

becomes more interdependent and is not founded on pure legal reasoning. The judge's expertise is also not in settlement promotion or conflict resolution. This is another cause of diminished legitimacy. In what follows, we will draw on the practices that we identified in court to analyze that coercive and reward powers that judges use, along with persuasion techniques.

When promoting settlements, judges forego their legitimacy power to decide by law, and instead use coercive powers in one of two ways, for which they rely indirectly on the rule of law. First, judges can directly ***apply pressure*** on litigants and their lawyers to agree to a settlement offer proposed by the judge. They can also threaten the ***legal costs*** (which is part of the legal ***procedure*** judges apply to encourage settlements) that the litigants will incur if they do not settle. For example, in a case between an insurance company and a private person, the judge explicitly told the insurance company's lawyers that he did not side with them: "... great judges did not accept argument as the ones you put forth, even though I must say that you have done a great job doing so ..." The judge went on to explain the reason for his opinion: "... You go from one jurisdiction to another, 'forum shopping' for the judge who will give you the verdict you want ... and I am telling you ... [pointing to the defendants' lawyer] I am inclined to side with them ..." In this case, coercive power operates in the background, owing to the fact that if the parties do not settle, they know that the judge could eventually use coercive power in the trial that will ensue. In this sense, the coercive power held by judges is a horizon of a potential future of negative implications, either real or imagined, that could materialize should the parties refuse to settle.

The second way judges use power within the settlement hearing is much less direct. It takes place without an explicit assertion of power, and it stems from the mere possibility of the judges using it. This occurs because litigants know that the same judge who made the settlement offer at the pretrial stage will also preside over the trial should they not settle.[52] Refusing a settlement offer, especially if the judge is the one who made it

[52] See RCA 288/89 *Ushiyot Insurance Company v. Cohen* PD 43(4) 427, 432 (Isr.) (noting that under Israeli law, the pretrial and trial phases are considered separate procedural units, such that the presiding pretrial judge will not necessarily preside over the trial); see also Israeli Rules of Civil Procedure-1984, 40; CSA 1168/02 Falah vs. Civil Service Authority PD 56(6) 197, 202 (Isr.) (noting that the general rule is that "all hearings should be held before the same judicial panel, as much as possible"); OMBUDSMAN OF THE ISRAELI, JUDICIARY OPINION 04106 CHANGE OF JUDGES 3 (2006) [Hebrew], www.justice.gov.il/Units/NezivutShoftim.

and even if the judge "only" encourages that they accept it, has threatening implications that are part of the hierarchy of the courtroom. This dynamic is exacerbated in the Israeli legal system, where judges have authority over all procedural and dispositive decisions, as there are no jury trials.

Applying pressure or predicting then relies on a form of legitimacy that derives from the authority that judges have in court to apply sanctions should the sides find themselves unable to settle and the case will end in a trial. The indirect use of coercive power relies on legitimate power based on the rule of law, since it alludes to the possibility that the judge who proposed the settlement will preside over the trial if the sides do not agree to her suggestion for settlement. The rule of law becomes a source of coercion rather than of legitimacy in this sense. The perceived and remote nature of the application of legal rules makes it less legitimate and more coercive. Accordingly, applying pressure, imposing costs, combined with prediction and mirroring, manifested regularly in our observations.

Rewards power, similarly to coercive power, stems from control over resources and potential outcomes. It is also a direct form of power; however, unlike coercive power, it holds the ability to bring about a positive outcome.[53] Judges use it to motivate litigants to make concessions that they otherwise would not have made. Usually, judges use ***court procedure and legal costs*** as a ***rewards*** form of hard power. They often point out to litigants that settling at that point would save the litigants money, as they will not have to pay the lawyers, the costs of the other side, or court fees, stating that the risk is now worth it for them. (Sometimes, they also threaten to impose more costs, as noted earlier with reference to coercive powers.) As one judge said, "This is not a case for which you should stand on your back two feet [be stubborn] and insist on litigating. You might end up losing a lot here . . ." The saving of

[53] Jan Bruins, *Social Power and Influence Tactics: A Theoretical Introduction*, 55 J. SOC. ISSUES. 7, 12 (1999), at 9 (suggesting that the difference between theories that focus on the bases of power and theories that focus on influencing tactics is that the first approach represents a move from theory to facts, i.e., a theory is developed and then tested by empirical research, while the latter approach represents a move from empirical findings on methods of influence to an explanation of these findings by a theory). Each approach has its advantages and disadvantages, and the ideal is to integrate the advantages of both. Influence tactics sometimes serve to enhance the bases of power and increase the effectiveness of influence attempts.

costs becomes the reward the judges flag up to motivate the litigants to settle.

These two forms of hard power are very dominant in the settlement scene. Judges do not usually consider them as "hard," since they perceive them as the legitimate persuasion and incentivization of litigants to close the case. Still, this is a hard tactic that they exercise in the negotiation in which they are parties with strong interests: the interest to close the case. They use the hierarchy that has been given to them as a legitimized judicial power to decide, to influence an outcome in a negotiation in which they do not have the power to decide. The parties are free to pursue the trial and to ask for it; judges close the gate to them by applying these hard powers. They do not motivate the parties from within by using these tactics, but rather from the outside by offering sticks and carrots. French and Raven's understanding of soft powers, on the other hand, underscores a much more subtle taxonomy of power relations that counts for the indirect effects on those that they are applied upon. These powers can help judges negotiate more effectively and to encourage more trust and compliance by and between the parties.

Of these, the first form of power is **expert** power. This is based on the perception, be it false or real, that the one who holds power has superior knowledge and experience.[54] Experts automatically have this power attributed to them because of the psychological and mental shortcuts that assist them in processing large amounts of information quickly.[55] Judges are perceived as experts in law by virtue of their position and their experience. As a result, statements made by judges are more likely to be perceived as correct without close examination, and could therefore go a long way in convincing litigants to agree to settle.[56] This would be especially the case if the judge is perceived as an expert in the particular field of law in which the case is being litigated, such as labor law or patent law. Sometimes, judges might demonstrate their expertise by referring to minute details of a case, referring to parties and lawyers by name, or showing mastery the nuances of the legal dispute and its development. In a manner that goes beyond the status attributed to judges by law, judicial expertise is continuously constructed and maintained in court hearings, based on the dynamics that they create in the courtroom, their

[54] French & Raven, *supra* note 29, at 163.

[55] ROBERT B. CALDINI, INFLUENCE: SCIENCE AND PRACTICE 6–7 (1993).

[56] *Id*, at 8, and ERWIN P. BETINGHAUS & MICHAEL J. CODY, PERSUASIVE COMMUNICATION 71–72, 125–33 (1994).

personality, and their charisma. Consequentially, such attributed expertise equips judges with more psychological leverage when attempting to convince litigants to settle. A drawback experienced by judges in the settlement scene is that they usually are not experts in conflict resolution and mediation, and are not perceived by the litigants as such. Therefore, the litigants rely on the judges' legal knowledge but do not perceive them as informed enough to exercise it during the preliminary hearing.

The following judicial practices, which we identified in the courtroom, demonstrate the use of expert power. First, judges encourage ***litigotiation*** when speaking from a position of experience and knowledge, assessing the risks for litigants if they do not settle at the pretrial stage and continue to a full trial. They further identify and evaluate the litigants' interests, offering a new solution or making a unique settlement proposal for the matter at hand. This occurred in a defamation case determining whether the reputation of a piano teacher had been damaged. The judge used expert power when summarizing the legal strengths and weaknesses of the case to the litigants, and followed with a proposal for judicial arbitration:

> ... this is not a simple case – on the one hand there was an invasion of privacy, but then again while it was fully proven that the responsibility was the defendant's, the damages were not proven. Therefore, I propose you settle by 79a [judicial arbitration] and allow me to decide on the compensation, which will be between a minimum of ₪[New Israeli Shekels] 2000 and a maximum of ₪ 6000 ...

Here, the judge established expert power by showing that he knew the case thoroughly enough to determine the partial liability of the litigants while setting realistic expectations for them that will help them accept his proposed settlement. The judge further wielded coercive power by subtly insinuating the verdict that he would give, should the sides choose to continue to a full trial rather than settle, when stating the range of the minimum and maximum damages that he will decide. When the plaintiff's lawyer exclaimed that the damage incurred had been extensive, the judge said that this had not been proven, explaining: "You can ask for a verdict, but please remember that you could lose everything and have to pay expenses."

Following the judge's demonstration of a mix of coercive and expert power, the two sides agreed to the judge's proposal for arbitration.

The judge's statement is extremely significant, once analyzed with French and Raven's typology of power relations, which is contextual and relational. As such, power operates differently in different settings; while such a statement might seem neutral if said between equals, it holds very threatening implications if said by a person in a position of authority, such as a judge.

Strong ***opening statements*** are another tactic used by judges to establish their expertise directly and indirectly, by underscoring the details of the case and guiding the direction of the hearing toward settlement. A judge used this tactic in a case pertaining to the mishandling of an apartment sale. He began the session by stating that he had read both sides' pleadings carefully, as well as their affidavits – including the last one, submitted just the day before. After making sure the litigants had acknowledged that he was up to speed with the case's details, he asked if the mediation they participated in had succeeded. When they told him it had not, the judge asked if they were ready to settle, given that the only relevant question for him was whether the defendant did his job and now could tell the purchasers of the apartment how much they had to pay. In this case, the judge used soft power in his opening statement when suggesting a settlement and framing the hearing in that tone. In doing so, he established his expertise by demonstrating detailed knowledge of the case and its legal aspects.

Judges further establish expertise when holding part of the hearing ***off the record***, when discussions are not documented. Judges use this informal space, in which what is said remains only between them and the parties involved, to clarify to the litigants their position regarding the legal and the factual aspects of the conflict, or tell the litigants what part of the factual story they deem relevant to the hearing. Due to the informality of such exchanges, a more intimate setting is created, one that has less of a hierarchy framing it. Consequently, whatever the judge reflects regarding the case, their position is perceived as coming from an expert on the matter – but without the forceful and top-down aspects, and thus more likely to be received. The discussion remains heuristic and off the record, but nevertheless increases persuasion by providing more knowledge, including on the judge's interstitial legal perspective.

Another form of indirect power is ***referent power***, which one has when another person identifies with the power that they hold, or if one find common points of likeness with them.[57] Referent power motivates the individual to obey and follow the power holder because others identify

[57] French & Raven, *supra* note 29, at 161–62.

with them, or because they are charismatic.[58] In the courtroom, judges come to wield such power when they ***use humor***, or if they express empathy with the litigants' hardships. In common with the off-the-record dynamic, this creates a sense of closeness with the litigants, which breaks down the judge–litigant hierarchy. The trust created in the courtroom persuades the litigants to give more weight to what the judges advise, and persuades them to become more cooperative and less resistant to attempts to influence them to agree to settle.[59]

Another form of soft power that judges hold that is not directly coercive but nevertheless is not as nuanced as referent or expert power is ***legitimate power***. This power is inherent to the judge's position; litigants must comply, as by law they are obliged to do what judges request.[60] During pretrial, judges have the authority to determine the scope of the claim, to eliminate issues, to hear testimonies, and to decide facts after hearing the litigants. Therefore, their legal power as a judge can be used at the pretrial stage in the traditional sense; in fact, it can be argued that they conduct a circumscribed trial.[61] There are several other types of soft power that are part of the legitimate power held by judges. First, judges have ***position*** power, deriving from the role they hold and stemming from their position as ascribed by law and enforced by social norms. This type of power mandates them to hand down verdicts, to order litigants to testify, or to refrain from doing certain things. Judges can use this power in a sophisticated and less apparent way, by demonstrating that they have specific knowledge of a certain field relevant to the case, alluding to their expert power as discussed before, and sometimes to a settlement expertise.

The ***power of equity***, which is based on the idea of fairness and the right for compensation if one has been wronged, is used by judges when attempting to influence litigants or their lawyers to act.[62] When parties refuse to settle on a fair resolution, the judge might invoke this power dynamic in order to influence them to accept a settlement proposal or to agree to a concession. The ***power of weakness***, another form of indirect soft power, is based on the ingrained responsibility one has to help those

[58] Raven, *supra* note 30 at 221. Conversely, we tend to reject advice given by someone we find repulsive.

[59] Such practices in mediation have been researched: see Deborah M. Kolb, *Strategy and the Tactics of Mediation*, 36 HUM. REL. 247 (1983), at 19.

[60] Raven, *supra* note 30, at 220–21.

[61] Nora Freeman Engstrom, *The Diminished Trial*, 86 FORDHAM L. REV. 2131 (2018).

[62] Raven, *supra* note 30, at 220–21.

who cannot help themselves or those dependent on others.[63] While these two forms of power describe a dynamic that exists between the litigants, judges use them to convince parties to settle in different cases, such as when a witness connected to one party or the other is particularly vulnerable, by noting that continuing to a full trial would harm them. There is a famous saying that judges have "no sword and no purse"[64] and therefore are weak within the social sphere, possessing only the legitimacy of the law and the trust of the people. In the pretrial hearing, it can be argued that they even have less power, given that they cannot apply the law fully yet. Nevertheless, we did not witness a significant or explicit use of the power of weakness within the settlement hearings that we observed, although judges did mention it during our interviews. The only use we found was with reference to the weakness of the litigants. In some situations, judges stated that the easiest way forward for them would be to decide the case and use the authority and reason of the law; still they preferred the hard way of encouraging consent-based dispositions.

These two forms of power played out in a case in which a Holocaust survivor sued the German government for compensation. The survivor sued his previous lawyer, demanding a refund of part of the lawyer's fee. During the hearing, an exchange between the lawyers became very heated when the judge attempted to have them agree to a settlement. The judge used the judicial conflict resolution practice of ***mirroring*** each side's disadvantages in the case, at some point exclaiming in exasperation:

> Calm down! Please respect the fact that the litigant is a Holocaust survivor who has gone through very difficult ordeals in his life. Look at how calm he is! And now, let's talk about the risks you will take if you decide to go ahead with a trial . . .

In emphasizing the hardships experienced by the litigant as a Holocaust survivor, the judge employed the powers of ***weakness***, ***equity***, and ***reciprocity***. Given the centrality of the Holocaust in Israeli society, mentioning the litigant's history invoked not only his weakness as someone who had suffered trauma but also the responsibility ingrained in Israelis to respect that collective trauma and to honor survivors.[65] As we have seen,

[63] *Id.*

[64] ALEXANDER HAMILTON, THE FEDERALIST PAPERS NO. 78 (1788).

[65] TOM SEGEV, THE SEVENTH MILLION: ISRAELIS AND THE HOLOCAUST (1991); Yael Zerubavel, *The Death of Memory and the Memory of Death: Massada and the Holocaust as Historical Metaphors*, ALPAIM 10 (1994), 42–67.

the judge alluded to the power of equity, and indirectly to the power of reciprocity, directed especially at the lawyer of the other party, who was asked to behave "properly" given that someone who had suffered much more could behave calmly.

The last type of soft power used by judges that is also related to reciprocity, weakness, and equity is ***third-party power***, in which judges rely on the existence of a third party, neither a litigant nor a lawyer representing them, and who is not necessarily in court to influence them.[66] Judges do so, for instance, when mentioning professionals, such as a mediator who is a retired judge and who could use his professional experience to help the litigants resolve not only the matter at hand but also other conflicts linked to the main one that brought them to court, and who can "really resolve the conflict." At other times, judges may invoke third-party power by mentioning vulnerable parties associated to the litigants, who would suffer if the parties go ahead with a full legal process.

Different from legitimate power stemming from the position that judges hold, ***informational power*** has to do with information judges have that could help them convince litigants to settle.[67] Such use of information could be direct or indirect; it could involve applying strong pressure by directly giving ***predictions*** regarding the legal matter at hand, stating the weaknesses of each side. While the sides independently decide whether to continue to settlement or to continue to trial, they are nevertheless heavily influenced by the information they receive from the judges.

Another form of soft power employed by judges is ***environmental*** power,[68] which affects the atmosphere in the courtroom and in turn helps them steer litigants into responding to their settlement efforts. This type of power plays out in the courtroom when judges directly intervene and influence the negotiations between the litigants in order to encourage them to settle. Without handing down verdicts or directly using strong powers, judges control the legal procedure when deciding which aspects of the legal conflict they will address, how much time will be spent on each topic, and the issues they will focus on.

[66] Raven, *supra* note 30, at 222 (when they discuss invoking an external third party as a way to influence the power relations between the parties who are engaged with each other).

[67] Raven, *supra* note 30, at 221–22.

[68] *Id.*

An example of the use of a mix of strong and soft powers can be seen in a damages lawsuit following the death of a garbage car worker, who was crushed to death by a car while uploading it onto a garbage can. The parties had to determine responsibility for the accident between the municipality, the truck manufacturing company, and the worker – the last sharing this responsibility with the municipality. The judge proposed mediation, agreeing to set the next hearing 120 days hence. When the lawyers asked whether the judge would agree to postpone the hearing if they ask for this, the judge answered: "Only if you have already begun mediation, otherwise we will move immediately to the evidence hearing."[69]

Here, the judge explicitly conditioned the option of postponing upon the litigants beginning mediation, which could lead to a settlement agreement. The atmosphere created by the judge was only encouragement and not designed to force the parties to settle. Still, the judge used his ***control of procedure*** to send a very clear message regarding his expectation that the sides should negotiate a settlement.

7.4 Training Model for Judicial Conflict Resolution: Fields of Agreement

When integrating the conceptual perspective on judicial work together with actual perceptions of judges as emerging from interviews and practice, the need for a new role definition emerged quite dramatically from the judges themselves.[70] If judges' main goal is not to decide cases blindly by using a scale of justice, what is their new goal? In legal literature, it was Hercules of Dworkin, who during the 1980s replaced the formalistic judge in classical legal theory and inspired the image of the activist judge who exercises judicial discretion, and balances policies and principles that underlie the legal rules.[71] Should we call the new judge Aaron or Hillel – a priest and a sage who pursue peace and are praised for relational leadership?[72] Should judges aspire to be activist peace seekers?

[69] *Id.*

[70] Such calls emerged during trainings provided for judges as part of the research project in various occasions.

[71] RONALD DWORKIN, LAW'S EMPIRE (1986).

[72] For elaboration on the peace pursuer role in Jewish culture and its relationship to the biblical Aaron, see DANIEL ROTH, THIRD-PARTY PEACEMAKERS IN JUDAISM: TEXT, THEORY, AND PRACTICE (2021).

This question is most acute in legal systems that belong to the pretrial family (see Chapter 3), but they pertain to the other two legal families as well. When discussing the judicial role with judges in Israel (which belongs to the pretrial family where the adjudicative and settlement functions of the judge are most likely to be combined), it became clear that several ethical dilemmas emerge from the settlement culture in which they operate. For instance, is pursuing a normative legal solution still a valid motive? There are no guidelines for judges today for sorting out the "visible trial" in order to generate new legal norms.

Another question rises as to the boundaries of judges' intervention: How far should they explore the parties' broad interests? Is it their role to try and reconcile them? In some legal cultures, designated judges are responsible for mediation and do not conduct authoritative decision-making.[73] In others, there is a clear separation between the judge who promotes settlement and the one who presides on the case. Their level of exploration of the conflict may depend on their location on the conflict resolution scale, and in some cases the parties themselves may endorse them with the authority to decide their cases by way of compromise while using conflict resolution considerations.[74] However, judges may exert undue pressure on parties to settle, and parties may feel obligated to settle to keep on good terms with the judge who has much authority on their case. In addition, the fact that judges have an interest in settling the case due to institutional incentives makes them a party to the negotiation rather than neutral brokers. As shown in our interviews, this can weaken parties' faith in the system and cause them to question whether the judge has their interest in mind.

Judicial training should reflect these questions and set ethical standards for judicial promotion of settlement. Understanding the issue of judicial conflict resolution in depth should begin with the theoretical underpinnings showcased in this chapter: the dual concern model, the integration of underlying principles of conflict resolution and law, and the implementation of judicial discretion through hard and soft powers in the courtroom.

We maintain that the boundaries of law and conflict should be constantly drawn and discussed in reference to judicial practices and written

[73] See the situation in Singapore as discussed in Jean-Francois Roberge & Dorcas Quek Anderson, *Judicial Mediation: From Debates to Renewal*, 19 CARDOZO J. CONFLICT RESOL. 613 (2018).

[74] Sinai & Alberstein, *supra* note 1.

judicial opinions in order to improve the judicial work of settlement and to frame it as a new form of social order,[75] that of judicial conflict resolution, which has coherence and cause. Following that we have developed a model training for judges that is based on the research findings.

The main judicial process that the model develops is the preliminary hearing – which would be the pretrial or settlement magistrates hearing (in the pretrial family) or the first hearing (in the trial family). Although we created the module of training for civil judges, we believe it can be further adapted to the criminal setting. The training is based on milestones that any judge should follow when conducting a settlement hearing and follows a movie prepared by us and conducted by a well-known director and real actors. It is based on a real courtroom observation that we have conducted and was filmed in a courtroom. The first milestone is *The Preparation for The Hearing*. Judges as conflict resolution experts should examine the conflict they intend to settle by using a conflict map that examines the various aspects relevant for the resolution of the case: type of relationship, interests and goals, barriers to conflict resolution, alternatives to the courts, and creative solutions. At this stage judges can sort out the different issues that underlie the conflict, diagnose the controversial issues, and devise a process to deal with the conflict in a constructive way. The second milestone is providing an *Opening Statement*. The first impression for the litigants is given by an elaborate explanation of the judge in court about the goals and sequence of the pretrial (settlement) hearing. The judge sets the expectation, and we practice with judges different modes of opening, discussing their effect on expectations and the progress of the case. The third milestone is *Promoting the Litigotiation*.[76] This section of the training is dedicated to teaching the judges various tactics of mediation and negotiation that can help them. We discuss strategies and manipulations in negotiation and elaborate on the importance of depersonalization and positive psychology. In particular, we speak about the importance of empathy, the building of trust, and the use of the existing regulation to incentivize the parties to settle.

[75] KENNETH I. WINSTON (ed.), THE PRINCIPLES OF SOCIAL ORDER. SELECTED ESSAYS OF LON L. FULLER (2001) 81–206.

[76] This notion is taken from Marc Galanter, *Worlds of Deals: Using Negotiation to Teach about Legal Process*, 34 J. LEGAL ED. 268 (1984).

The next milestone we discuss is *The Judge–Lawyer–Client Triangle*. The unique setting of the negotiation within the court preliminary hearing is related to the presence of the litigants (who are present at hearings in most of the cases and jurisdictions) and the fact that it can contribute to the resolution of the legal conflicts. Should judges speak directly to the litigants? What should be the purpose of their talk? Enabling clearning of the air or extracting information and evidence? How can lawyers be empowered within the courtroom settling? What is the right technique for listening to litigants, and what should judges do with the knowledge they accumulate? These questions are discussed with the judges during training, and a few guidelines are suggested at the end of the session.

We dedicate a focused discussion to the next milestone, *Emotional Regulation in The Courtroom*, and invite an external expert to this session. The judges learn about the role of emotions in conflicts within this session and practice the constructive use of them while transcending the old-fashioned image of the dispassionate judge. A separate session is dedicated to the *Conflict–Legal Relationship* milestone within the settlement hearing. In this part we return to some of the dilemmas discussed in this chapter and in interviews with judges. How should judges integrate legal with conflict considerations? What is the role of apology within a legal setting? What are the ethical boundaries of promoting settlement, and does the pursuance of a normative outcome create a conflict of interest? We discuss these issues with judges while offering our conceptual framework and use their best practices and examples to refine our guidelines. Finally, we present the end game of *Getting to Yes* through the use of authority and discuss possible ways to close the hearing by integrating authority with empowerment of the litigants and their lawyers. Judges who have taken the training have reported on a significant impact on their practice and perspective, and we perceive it as contributing to the reconstruction of the new judicial conflict resolution role of judges.

The above model is just one among many that can be used, taking into account the specific legal culture and legal family (in this case the pretrial family). It can be adapted or revamped to train judges to help promote settlement while maintaining their traditional role. In the Florence Court (Italy belongs to the trial family, as described in Chapter 3), judges promote settlement in a way that more or less maintains the traditional judicial role. Judges issue settlement proposals after determining liability and taking it into account. They have a significant diagnostic role, fitting cases to forms of dispute resolution while for the most part avoiding negotiating the case themselves. They provide reasoned decisions on referrals to mediation according to the circumstances of the case. In addition, they adjudicate a relatively high percentage of cases (more than 40%), seeing them through to a verdict. This type of judicial role or variations of it can be taken into account and trained for accordingly. Training for criminal judges that addresses the multidoor nature of the criminal justice system and deals with the unique lay participants in criminal conflicts – the defendants and victims – is also very much needed in order to reconstruct the public conceptual framework for judicial work.

8

New Horizons of Mediation

8.1 Mediation Goes Mainstream: Authority-based and Public

The journey of mediation as a nonauthoritative process into the court system has come full circle with one utterly different model emerging in contemporary times. As mentioned in the previous chapters, mediation has inspired hybrid judicial roles and settlement promotion and introduced consent as the foundation for many hybrid legal processes. Yet this hybridization has worked both ways, affecting mediation as well.

Authority-based mediation is emerging as an advanced judicial process that *generates public norms*. This new sophisticated model for dealing with *polycentric* legal problems while preserving soft qualities of the process and keeping a narrow focus on a legal outcome is, in fact, a novel form of private adjudication.

Legal disputes, such as major environmental litigations, which involve multiple stake holders, complex diverse interests, and long-term possible effects are mostly dealt with today through unique forms of consensus building and mediation, combining legal knowledge with negotiation in the shadow of the court. Such cases, which are becoming more common as complexity increases, offer negotiated norms as a better regulative solution to hard cases, and contribute to the decline of adjudication. Instead of mediation being considered a private alternative that works in small cases, when the normative framework is clear, it becomes a public tool for norm generation, for which adjudication is a pale substitute. We will describe and analyze the growing phenomenon of "authority-based mediation" and explore its theoretical foundations, as well as a possible role in transforming adjudication.

The origins that formed the foundations for the new model have been both external and internal. Externally, the new perception of courts regarding mediation created the need for a mediation procedure that is outcome oriented (rather than process oriented). On the internal level, the model has developed through mediators' evolving ability to use authority within mediation procedures, as a result of their interactions with the parties. This development involves trial and error, as well as the inclusion of basic elements of formal legal jurisdiction. The mediation is conducted in a way that examines the law as well as possible legal outcomes, the agreement is approved by the court, and might even set a precedent for negotiations that concern similar circumstances or in negotiations that involve the same parties.[1] This model is suitable to represented parties whose lawyers are present in the mediation room. It incorporates authoritative elements that correspond with the dynamic that typifies many courtroom encounters where a judge aims to bring the parties to an agreement, even though he has the authority to make a judgment.[2] Retired judges and senior lawyers, such as those who are members of the JAMS organization, have found this model useful and utilized it successfully.

In this model, the parties and their attorneys are required to arrive at mediation in the same state of preparedness as they would have arrived at an evidentiary hearing at court. This is mainly since most cases end in an agreement at the end of the first meeting.[3] Contrary to other models of mediation, within authority-based mediation the parties are required to submit to the mediator all relevant legal materials, and they may additionally be asked to relate to specific aspects through position papers that are submitted to the mediator to allow for an informed and balanced evaluation of the dispute. Litigants arrive for this session prepared to be able, to the best of their abilities, to present their arguments and interests, and ensure that those who have the authority to approve an agreement are present.

[1] See lawyers' comments in the court hearing transcript in TA (Tel Aviv District Court) 65143-12-15 *Alias v. Verint systems LTD*., (16.11.16) (unpublished transcript, copy with authors), in front of Hon. Judge Hannah Pliner: "We have heard the court's comment with regard to referring the case to mediation before the mediator [. . .] that already dealt with a similar case (Galamidi)." This case ended with an agreement following mediation on Oct. 10, 2017.

[2] KARNI PERLMAN, DISPUTE RESOLUTION – THERAPEUTIC AND NON-ADVERSARIAL JUSTICE (2015) (Hebrew). *See also* Yitzchak Zamir, *Mediating Public Conflicts*, 7 LAW & GOV. 119 (2004) (Hebrew), in which he discusses whether Israeli law allows retired judges to serve as mediators.

[3] From data collected along the years of practice of one of the book's authors, and analyzed for the purpose of explaining the new model suggested in here, we have found that more than 90% of the cases resulted in an agreement, and in 80% of these cases and agreement was reached after only one session. For example, between the years 2012–2015, 344 agreements were signed following only one mediation session, out of 430 cases that were referred to this process.

Part of the authority of the mediator, vis-à-vis the attorneys, apart from his or her complete familiarity with the legal materials, is the conducting of an open, rational,[4] intellectual discourse, and developing their trust. Such discourse may lead to an outcome that is completely different from what they themselves have anticipated at the beginning of the legal process. The insight that may result from such realization turns the lawyers into the mediator's long arm, and the mediator may even define them as such before the parties. That way, once the attorney is convinced that the mediator's evaluation and proposal is based on a deep understanding of the law and of the facts of the case, they can reflect to their clients the authority of the mediator, thus increasing their own trust in the process and in the mediator.

Observing authority-based mediation revealed some common elements that enabled this process to work:[5] The *opening statement* of the mediation usually entails some elaboration on the rational intellectual nature of the project; there will be an honest dialogue, enriched with modesty, in which legal reasoning and values will be relevant, and there will be a consensual ending that will answer the parties' anticipation and expectation as expressed in the *long period of waiting* for this advanced process. During the mediation, *authority will be established* through reference to previous cases handled by the mediator, to his or her expertise, to the familiarity with the lawyers, and the appreciation by the court. It is quite common that *a normative value-based perspective is established* as an integral foundation for the mediation. The mediator can declare, for example, that discrimination based on religion cannot be tolerated and facilitate the conversation based on this premise. In a class action, the mediator can develop new causes for action based on a new legal perspective he or she perceives as justified and as corresponding with higher legal principles, in contrast to the common critique of mediation and settlement as eroding the public sphere (which is most commonly ascribed to Owen Fiss).[6] The authority-based mediator

4 We use here the term "rational" discourse to describe a process in which reason is used as a tool through which aspirations and desires can be explored. One of the main tools of authority-based mediation is reason, as reason can lead individuals to a significant change of consciousness, and can create a shared language between the parties and the mediator.

5 For elaboration on each element of the mediation, *see* Amos Gabrieli, Nourit Zimerman & Michal Alberstein *Authority-Based Mediation*, CARDOZO J. CONFLICT RESOL. (2018).

6 See Owen M. Fiss, *Against Settlement*, 93 YALE L.J. 1073 (1984); Tania Sourdin, *Five Reasons Why Judges Should Conduct Settlement Conferences*, 37 MONASH U. L. REV. 145

encourages legal normative debates that are not formalistic and invites the parties to accept his or her normative interpretation.

In parallel to the legal emphasis and the professional dialogue with the lawyers, and sometimes in sharp contrast to this emphasis, a mainly soft relational discourse is developed with the parties. Apologies are expressed, emotions are acknowledged, pain is addressed. These *parallel spheres* of law and mediation enable the process to culminate in a mediation agreement following a nonrecoverable *mediation proposal* that is later framed into a complex binding legal document ending the dispute. The document is submitted to the court for approval and endorsement as a verdict.

When considering the relationship of the authority-based model of mediation to other evolving models in the field of conflict resolution, it becomes clear that it is closest in principle to the legal world. Advanced models of mediation, such as transformative mediation, take large strides away from the legal world, and even from the pragmatic concept of problem solving. In such models, including narrative mediation, restorative justice, and humanistic mediation as well, the third party is conceptualized as having therapeutic features.[7] The importance of the intervention is in empowering the parties – emotionally, morally, and sometimes even spiritually[8] – and in strengthening their ability to have a constructive dialogue and to reach decisions with minimal intervention on behalf of the third party in the practical solutions the parties may reach. Such procedures are very distanced from the legal world and emphasize a true, meaningful, and transformative alternative.[9]

It is possible to think of the development of the authority-based mediation model as a reaction to the distance between the world of conflict resolution and the legal world. The internal development of the field of conflict resolution, while maintaining the primal motivations of

(2011); David Luban, *Settlements and the Erosion of the Public Realm*, 83 GEO. L.J. 2619 (1995).

7 MICHAL ALBERSTEIN, ALTERNATIVE JUSTICE: MEDIATION, RECONCILIATION AND TREATMENT USING LEGAL MECHANISMS (2015).

8 Ted Lewis & Marc S. Umbriet, *What Is a Humanistic Approach to Mediation? An Overview* (2015), www.mediate.com/articles/LewisUmbreit1.cfm.

9 Robert A. Baruch Bush, *Mediation and Adjudication, Dispute Resolution and Ideology: An Imaginary Conversation*, 3 J. CONTEMP LEGAL ISSUES 1 (1989); HOWARD ZEHR, CHANGING LENSES: A NEW FOCUS FOR CRIME AND JUSTICE (1990); ROBERT A. BARUCH BUSH & JOSEPH P. FOLGER, THE PROMISE OF MEDIATION: THE TRANSFORMATIVE APPROACH TO CONFLICT (2nd ed. 2004).

its founders to present an alternative model to legal procedures, has led to more complex procedural models, which deal with challenging types of conflicts: crises in relationships, harms that involve criminal aspects, as well as identity-based conflicts.[10] In many ways, the focus on these types of conflicts and advanced models have driven lawyers – who mostly deal with practical disagreements – away from the world of mediation.

One such example would be the narrative mediation model, first developed by Winslade and Monk,[11] which promotes an interpretive paradigm of mediation and redefines the role of the mediator. This model presents a dynamic process, with no structure, rules, or program that are known in advance. The mediator listens to the parties and responds to their narratives and actions providing attentiveness and reflection.[12] The main characteristic of narrative mediation is its focus on language and discourse, and the main role of the mediator is to build trust between the parties (which is defined as "intervention"), deconstructing the original disputed narrative and creating an alternative narrative in which the conflict is diminished or even disappears. The goal of narrative mediation is to lead the parties through an educational process in which they will learn to challenge their own perceptions of entitlement within their cultural environment. This model requires cultural thinking, deep social discourse, and a rejection of traditional social paradigms.

In contrast to these developments, the evolvement of authority-based mediation offers an alternative that grows from within legal grounds in search of legal solutions that incorporate the parties' consent and their extralegal interests. The encounter of authoritative mediators with the world of dispute resolution is grounded in their identity as lawyers and legal experts. At the heart of the development of authority-based mediation is therefore the creation of tools and solutions that stem from the world of dispute resolution but at the same time maintain a close dialogue with the legal world. The willingness of parties to depart from their original claims is explained by the unique authoritative elements of this process: the creation of commitment toward achieving an agreement,

[10] Michal Alberstein and Jay Rothman *Individuals, Groups, Intergroups: Theorizing about the Role of Identity in Conflicts* 28 OHIO ST. J. DISP. RESOL. 631 (2013).

[11] JOHN WINSLADE & GERALD MONK, NARRATIVE MEDIATION: A NEW APPROACH TO CONFLICT RESOLUTION (2000).

[12] For a more detailed discussion of this model, *see* MICHAL ALBERSTEIN, THE JURISPRUDENCE OF MEDIATION, 292–397 (2007) (Hebrew).

and the acceptance of the mediator's authority in that regard; the incorporation of legal elements; and emotional discourse and soft dialogue between the mediator and the parties. We have defined this new notion of authority as relational.[13]

The unique characteristics of authority-based mediation – which differs both from traditional mediation and from the manner in which judges conduct settlement-oriented procedures in the shadow of their judicial authority – create a new outlook regarding the relationship between mediation and adjudication, and the role of authority in promoting consent-based legal outcomes.[14] It reflects a move from approaches that view authority as external to mediation and as having no role within it to viewing authority as an important tool within mediation, one that expands this process and its limits until it redefines mediation altogether.

8.2 The Self-Help Individualized Notion of Mediation

While inside the legal system the authority-based model can deal with complex and advanced large-scale legal conflicts that generate normative implications, most of the cases that burden the legal system are small and "not worthy" of entering the court system. In addition, legal systems integrate strategies to prevent many cases from reaching trial or even the filing stage (see Chapter 3). One effect of the drive to settlement and the shift of many legal systems to earlier stages of the judicial process is the search for a mediation-oriented approach for cases before they enter the courts.

In our research we found that the prevailing trend in contemporary legal systems is to shift the gravity of the judicial work to the pretrial stage while focusing on settlement promotion. The next stage is to encourage litigants, by monetary and technological incentives, to settle before even entering the court or meeting a judge. Such a shift to the prefiling stage, as it happens in England and Wales and begins to happen in Israel,[15] requires new paradigms of justice for the majority of cases as

[13] See Gabrieli et al., *supra* note 5.

[14] *Id.*

[15] See Nofit Amir & Michal Alberstein, *New Families of Legal Systems in Transition, and Implications for AI*, 33(1) TRANSNATIONAL LAW & CONTEMPORARY PROBLEMS (2024).

well as small non-litigable disputes that in the past have always remained unsettled.

Our approach is to increase mediation sensitivity and awareness for the majority of cases by developing an AI-based recommendation system based on conflict resolution features. Such an application can guide human litigants before they even meet a lawyer.

While court systems worldwide are investing much effort into increasing efficiency, a human-centered approach, which takes into account litigants' needs, interests, and emotions, is lacking. Thus, an innovative intake screening recommendation system (which we call MultiDoor) can integrate each litigant's (or potential litigant's) specific needs, interests, and emotions, the features of the case, and the predicted case trajectory in the legal system, resulting in a diagnostic recommendation (e.g., mediation, arbitration, adjudication, out-of-the-box solutions). This application is currently under development and is undergoing a crowdsourcing experiment to accumulate data on users' satisfaction with conflict resolution–oriented processing of their disputes; developing forecasting models for user satisfaction and a machine learning–based recommendation system. The system's benefits include developing a new domain of conflict resolution machine learning via collaboration among data scientists and legal and conflict resolution experts; advancing a personalized conflict resolution–oriented response to disputes, including to small non-litigable disputes; promoting public trust and social well-being by ensuring that parties – including those from disenfranchised sectors – are informed and supported to self-determine how to resolve their disputes; and answering the current drawbacks of online dispute resolution (ODR) systems, which focus mostly on legal issues rather than on the interests of the parties.

The name of the platform and the inspiration for its development come from the idea by Frank Sander, founder of the ADR movement, who introduced the notion of the multidoor courthouse and set the vision for the court as a conflict resolution center in which conflicts are triaged to the proper door following an interview with a screening clerk.[16] Sander and Goldberg, together with Rozdeiczer, defined the role of the ADR lawyer as "fitting the forum to the fuss" and developed

[16] Frank E. A. Sander & Stephen B. Goldberg, *Fitting the Forum to the Fuss: A User-Friendly Guide to Selecting an ADR Procedure*, 10 NEGOT. J. 49, 68 (1994).

several intake questionnaires that can identify parties' needs and barriers to settlement.[17] Sander's idea was to educate the lawyers to become conflict resolution agents and to advise clients as to the right door they should use when processing their conflict – mediation, arbitration, negotiation, or other hybrid processes. This idea has not materialized within the co-opted institutionalization of mediation, as discussed earlier, and many lawyers keep pursuing litigation as the first option without inquiring about broader interests and goals of their clients. The proposed application will overcome this deficiency by approaching parties before they reach a lawyer and while they consider their path by themselves. It will inquire about their needs, emotions, goals, and principles and ask them to rank their experience. It will collect broad data on their conflict and their personal features. It will diagnose their type of personality and conflict resolution style. Then it will provide them with a personalized recommendation of a door to proceed with. They will also get a legal assessment of their claim in court if they choose adjudication, but the main value of the intake process will be to open for them new perspective on their conflict and the most effective ways to deal with it.

After constructing the recommendation system that can advise people as to the right door to choose their conflict, we will validate the platform and integrate it with a legal outcome forecasting model that will provide prospective litigants with a reality check as to the adjudication door. We believe that this platform will help foster the spirit of mediation by approaching litigants before they frame the conflict in a legal manner, and will help de-bias and de-escalate conflicts before they enter the court system. This horizon of mediation as a self-help AI-based recommendation system is another consequence of the receding legal process due to efficiency-based legal reforms worldwide.[18]

8.3 The Jurisprudence of Mediation and the Consensual Horizons of Law

As the two contemporary mediation models described in this chapter suggest, as legal systems approach the possibility of a "vanishing third

[17] *Id.*

[18] On the new typology of legal systems based on the emphasis on trial, pretrial and prefiling, *see* Chapter 3.

party,"[19] new horizons of mediation emerge and require a more nuanced architecture of the boundaries between public and private. First, the mediation discourse has become rich and diverse, containing different models guided by various worldviews, and can be used in different contexts and levels. Mediation as practiced within the transformed legal system may carry different jurisprudential values – pragmatic balancing of personal interests alongside public policies, transformed legal perspectives as a consequence of a relational dialogue, or a rearrangement of legal identities based on rewriting the narrative of conflict and challenging entitlement perspectives through introducing cultural critique. Since the more advanced notions of mediation and even the generic pragmatic one usually do not attract significant interest within the efficiency-driven contemporary court system, we noted two developments that may indicate new horizons. One is the generation of new norms and soft law through authority-based mediation. Another is the coaching of potential litigants in mediation-oriented thinking while developing a personalized recommendation system based on conflict resolution. Such an emphasis may encourage more attention to the more developed notion of mediation – the transformative and the narrative.

Second, as we examine the effect of the development of mediation on the horizons of law, it can be argued that deep conflicts regarding societal tensions such as state and religion, nationalism and universalism, pro-life and pro-choice, and many other deep divides related to constitutional values, such as the Jewish and Democratic tension in Israeli constitutional formula,[20] can be resolved today through sophisticated models of consensus building and mediation, and the search for compromise may become a legitimate horizon with strong philosophical foundations in an age of vanishing trials and claims regarding the politicization of the judiciary.[21]

[19] *See* ORNA RABINOVICH-EINY, THE 'VANISHING THIRD PARTY': ACCESS TO JUSTICE, PROCEDURAL JUSTICE AND SUBSTANTIVE JUSTICE IN THE AGE OF DISPUTE RESOLUTION AUTOMATION, EUROPEAN RESEARCH COUNCIL (ERC) CONSOLIDATOR GRANT PROPOSAL (2021). See also https://dralab.haifa.ac.il.

[20] See the project developed at Bar Ilan University together with Shahar Lifshitz on "Embracing a conflict resolution approach for the Jewish-democratic diad." This project, supported by the Israeli Academy of Science, has included gathering a group of postdocs and a senior lecturer to build a conflict resolution perspective to address national debates, and culminated in a three-day international conference that included Supreme Court Justices, and is expected to yield a special volume on this subject in *Bar Ilan Law Studies*.

[21] *Id.*

9

The Law – End or Turning Point?

As described in Chapter 3, legal systems seem to be gravitating from trial to pretrial to pre-filing while preventing litigants from pursuing later stages in the legal process. Faced with the trajectory of legal systems today, policymakers can now contend with perhaps the most critical choice of our times. Will they continue down the road to the end of law or will they renew its role? Will they choose the legal family that is most appropriate for their constituents or let the gravitational pull toward the privatization of disputes decide for them?

Our research has shown a general erosion of the status of law and the existence of three contemporary legal families (see Chapter 3). In the trial family, adjudication is still a main route for disputes, and the judge implements the law to decide disputes in a formalistic fashion. However, in the pretrial family, the judge uses a mix of law and heuristics, both with a strong bias toward settlement, as a means to help settle the case. In the pre-filing family, the role of law is obfuscated further, since judicial involvement is a distant, often unrealistic prospect: The parties are, in general, on their own. Whether negotiations revolve around the law when the "shadow of law" recedes so acutely is unknown due to the private nature of dispute resolution in the pre-filing family. Parties may choose not to negotiate or abandon their claims without a realistic option for pretrial or trial.

One might claim that if law has such an obfuscated role – especially in the pre-filing family – why not displace it altogether through AI-based decision-making? Indeed, we show in our research that the pre-filing family may be the most conducive to AI-based dispute resolution (see further on in this chapter).

Yet one might choose to look at the remarkable changes that legal systems have undergone in recent decades as a mark of flexibility within legal systems – and potential for growth. As of today, the underlying motive for change has all too frequently been saving time and money for the legal systems themselves. However, if this underlying motive is moderated and retuned to respond to the *needs of the individual litigant*, changes of a different nature are possible. Indeed, one of the results of our research is the call for human-centered design.[1]

We here differentiate between (1) the individual litigant – who is often oblivious to the changes that legal systems have undergone and steps unknowingly into the dispute resolution system (often with only a movie-inspired notion that is not anchored in reality) – and (2) repeat litigants – banks, governments, large companies – that are aware of the changes in the legal system and know what to expect due to the large volume of lawsuits they are party to.

While this gap has always been considerable, it is even more so in pretrial and pre-filing families, which are in fact new types of legal systems of which individual litigants are not usually aware and cannot assess the implications. To them, the experience of being prevented from pursuing trial in the pretrial legal systems or even filing a case in the pre-filing legal systems can be akin to that of the "man from the countryside" in Kafka's *Before the Law:*

> In front of the law there is a doorkeeper. A man from the countryside comes up to the door and asks for entry. But the doorkeeper says he can't let him in to the law right now. The man thinks about this, and then he asks if he'll be able to go in later on. "That's possible," says the doorkeeper, "but not now". The gateway to the law is open as it always is, and the doorkeeper has stepped to one side, so the man bends over to try and see in. When the doorkeeper notices this he laughs and says, "If you're tempted give it a try, try and go in even though I say you can't. Careful though: I'm powerful. And I'm on the lowliest of all the doormen. But there's a doorkeeper for each of the rooms and each of them is more powerful than the last. It's more than I can stand just to look at the third one." The man from the country had not expected difficulties like this, the law was supposed to be accessible for anyone at any time, he thinks.[2]

So how does one create a human-centered legal system within the constraints of pretrial and pre-filing families? This leads us to factors shaping legal agency and choice.

[1] Nofit Amir & Michal Alberstein, *Designing Responsive Legal Systems: A Comparative Study*, 22 PEPP. DISP. RESOL. L.J. 263 (2022).

[2] FRANZ KAFKA, *Before the Law, in* THE TRIAL 148–49 (David Wyllie trans., 1925).

9.1 Level of Individual Agency and Choice

Level of individual choice refers to the components affecting the ability to choose the procedure that will be used for one's dispute.[3] As mentioned, it is important to distinguish between litigants that are repeat players (banks, insurance companies, government agencies) and litigants who are individuals (human litigants).[4] Most of the lawsuits that individual litigants are a party to include a non-individual player.[5] Unlike repeat players, which often have ample accumulated data to reach optimal decisions, individual litigants lack the experience and resources to obtain such data. Even with the help of an attorney, individual litigants often do not have access to information on possible case trajectories and the projected consequences of their choices.

It is important to note that the tension between individual agency and collective interests is inherent to democracies, such that individual agency is balanced with other social considerations.[6] In addition, individual choice can be manipulated (by default biases, etc.). With these caveats in mind, individual choice and agency are often considered core values of democracy, allowing for a sense of participation and bestowing legitimacy upon public institutions.[7] The lack of them spurs masterpieces of despair, such as those of Kafka and Camus, denoting government as an arbitrary entity detached from the individual, and based on power rather than on legitimacy.[8]

[3] *See* Donna Shestowsky, *Disputants' Preferences for Court-Connected Dispute Resolution Procedures: Why We Should Care and Why We Know So Little*, 23 OHIO ST. J. DISP. RESOL. 549 (2008).

[4] *See* Paola Lucarelli, Nofit Amir, Dana Rosen, Hadas Cohen & Michal Alberstein, *Fitting the Forum to the Fuss While Seeking the Truth*, 36 OHIO ST. J. DISP. RESOL. 213 (2020), at 18.

[5] According to our study, only 7% of cases in the Tel Aviv first-instance court included a claimant and a defendant who were individual litigants; 58% included an individual litigant and a non-individual litigant; 35% included only non-individual litigants.

[6] Linda Mulcahy, *The Collective Interest in Private Dispute Resolution*, 33 OXFORD J. LEG. STUD. 59 (2013); *see also* David Beetham, *Theorising Democracy and Local Government*, in RETHINKING LOCAL DEMOCRACY 28 (Desmond King & Gerry Stoker, eds., 1996).

[7] Sherry R. Arnstein, *A Ladder of Citizen Participation*, 35 J. AM. INST. PLANNERS 216 (1969); Jaclyn Barnao, *In Pursuit of Settlement: Deciphering Judicial Activism*, 18 GEO. J. LEGAL ETHICS 583 (2005), at 593 ("Although aggressive techniques might convince a wary party who is being unrealistic about the chances of their case on the merits to settle, it may not leave that party satisfied with the justice system in general because they felt pressured into making such a decision.").

[8] Arnstein, *id.*, at 217.

Some central factors influencing individual agency and choice differed between the three legal systems, and some were shared. The following is by no means an exhaustive list, but rather a portrait of main research findings regarding individual agency:

9.1.1 Transparency

The ability to make informed choices requires transparency regarding the different options, including expected trajectory of cases, the rate of settlement according to case type, and, when possible, the content of agreements (which can be anonymized) reached in mediation or approved by the court.[9] In all three legal systems, as well as in the United States, the study faced transparency challenges, but to very different extents (see Chapter 4). The study was able to bridge some information gaps through a mixed-methods approach. Repeat players such as banks and insurance companies may also find ways to surmount transparency challenges by influencing and tracking the outcomes in their own cases.[10] The individual disputant, however, does not have the resources to do so.

The lack of information, especially regarding the expected outcome for each choice and prospects of reaching the trial stage, creates disparities for individual litigants who cannot gather this information by themselves.[11] It also provides a false picture of the court's real engagement and overload.[12]

[9] See MARCO VELICOGNA, EUROPEAN COMM'N FOR EFFICIENCY JUSTICE, REPORT NO. 24, USE OF INFORMATION AND COMMUNICATION TECHNOLOGIES IN EUROPEAN JUDICIAL SYSTEMS 177 (2016).

[10] *See* Lucarelli et al., *supra* note 4, at 18.

[11] *See, e.g., id.* (recalling that access to this database is limited to the legal community and that the authors specifically requested permission to access this article).

[12] *See, e.g.,* Chen Maanit, *How Busy Your Judge Is Can Decide How Much Money You're Awarded, Israeli Study Finds*, HAARETZ (Jan. 13, 2022), www.haaretz.com/israel-news/.premium-how-busy-your-judge-is-can-decide-how-much-money-you-re-awarded-israeli-study-finds-1.10536071. For example, there is a common claim the research team heard from the previous director of the court administration in Israel: About one million cases are filed each year in Israeli courts and are treated by the judges. Yet if only half of the cases filed ever see a judge, this claim may be challenged. *Id.*

9.1.2 Costs

In England and Wales, trial is still considered an option "for the very rich or the very poor."[13] The very rich can afford to pay for services, and the poor have access to legal aid.[14] One of the focal points of English and Welsh legal reforms was lowering costs of litigation to enable access to justice.[15] The proposal emphasized proportionate costs (litigation costs that are proportionate to the value of the claim) overseen by a judge with active case management tools.[16] In our observations, judges took this task seriously; they often cut costs by reducing the number of witnesses and experts or called for a junior-level advocate instead of a senior-level advocate to represent the case. However, costs of litigation remain very high, and it is widely agreed that they have not been reduced due to a frontloading of costs to fulfill pre-action requirements.[17] Thus, most disputants who do choose trial are unrepresented.[18] For the most part, these disputants present their cases weakly, requiring the judge to inter-

[13] LORD WOOLF, ACCESS TO JUSTICE: INTERIM REPORT TO THE LORD CHANCELLOR ON CIVIL JUSTICE SYSTEM IN ENGLAND AND WALES 4 (1995) (quoting H. HEILBRON & H. HODGE, CIVIL JUSTICE ON TRIAL: A CASE FOR CHANGE (1993)). *See* PENNY DARBYSHIRE, SITTING IN JUDGMENT: THE WORKING LIVES OF JUDGES (2012), at 4 (commenting on the impact of the reforms: "What was not achieved was a reduction in cost, because of front-loading of preparation and the exchange of information, plus the satellite insurance costs and success fees of no-win no-fee agreements which replaced most of civil legal aid . . . Sadly, the rules did not include Woolf's plan for fixed costs in the fast track. Lord Justice Jackson said in 2011 that the English and Welsh costs regime was 'the laughing stock of the world' so I think some of these problems are peculiar to England.").

[14] WOOLF, *id.*, at 4.

[15] But *see* John Sorabji, *Austerity's Effect on English Civil Justice*, 1 ERASMUS LAW REV. (2015) (noting that the rationale for court fees in 1982 was that the courts provided a service to consumers who were expected to pay for those services).

[16] *See* CPR, 2021, part 3.1(m) (Eng.). Darbyshire, *supra* note 13, at 1 ("In most cases, there is a massive imbalance of power between the parties. Therefore, to ensure speed and fairness, the court must manage cases strictly and speedily, and not leave it to the powerful party to exploit the weaker party by failing to cooperate, using delaying tactics, and racking up costs.").

[17] *See, e.g.*, Darbyshire, *supra* note 13, at 4 (noting that reduction in cost was not achieved with the Woolf Reforms).

[18] *Id. See* RABEEA ASSY, INJUSTICE IN PERSON: THE RIGHT TO SELF-REPRESENTATION (2015). *See also* Sorabji, *supra* note 15, at 164 (commenting that cuts to legal aid for many types of cases would lead to "significant increases in individuals having to litigate without legal advice or representation").

vene and help fulfill basic court requirements.[19] In our observations, unrepresented litigants seemed oddly out of place, outsiders to the law in a legal setting.

In Israel and Italy, efficiency (i.e., managing the caseload with speed) rather than costs is the center of attention.[20] Costs are not perceived as an unsurmountable barrier to litigation in academic scholarship or public discourse, and parties have access to courts as evidenced by large caseloads.[21] Yet, continuing to trial from pretrial may not be cost effective; the median case value in the Tel Aviv first-instance court, according to the statistical analysis performed in our study, was only around 25,000 NIS. Whether the parties have the financial means to continue from pretrial to trial in Israel should be explored; the fact that litigation costs have not garnered much attention implies that they are not prohibitive or that the prevailing rhetoric does not explore this issue.[22] In addition, judges consider power imbalances between parties when deciding on whom to levy costs (e.g., an individual vs. a corporation).[23]

9.1.3 Mandatory Processes

Mandatory pre-filing requirements include investment of time and cost, making trial less practical. In addition, mandatory or highly incentivized mediation (i.e., incurring cost sanctions if refused) may encumber parties to the point that they settle, not because they have had a fruitful dialogue but rather because trial has been too difficult to attain.[24] Mandatory mediation may in some cases "save parties from themselves," preventing a long, painful trial.[25] Other mandatory mediations are a source of

19 ASSY, *supra* note 18.

20 *See* Marco Gubitosi, Andrea Tortora della Corte, Sara Colombera & Claudio Schiaffino, *Legal Systems in Italy: Overview*, THOMPSON REUTERS PRACTICAL L. (Apr. 1, 2021).

21 *See, e.g.*, Maanit, *supra* note 12.

22 *See* Issi Rosen-Zvi, *Decentralization of the Judicial System in Israel: The Hidden Role of Civil Procedure Regulations*, MISHPATIM 717, 728 (2018) (Hebrew).

23 Theodore Eisenberg, Talia Fisher & Issi Rosen-Zvi, *When Courts Determine Fees in a System with a Loser Pays Norm: Fee Award Denials to Winning Plaintiffs and Defendants*, 60 UCLA L. REV. 1452, 1457 (2013).

24 *See, e.g.*, HAZEL GENN, P. FENN, M. MASON, A. LANE, N. BECHAI, L. GRAY & D. VENCAPPA, (2007). TWISTING ARMS: COURT REFERRED AND COURT LINKED MEDIATION UNDER JUDICIAL PRESSURE. MINISTRY OF JUSTICE RESEARCH SERIES 1/07 (2007) 1–215.

25 *See* Giovanni Matteucci, *Mandatory Mediation, the Italian Experience*, REVISTA ELETRÔNICA DE DIREITO PROCESSUAL 16, 189 (2015) (noting this is most poignantly

tactical information gathering.[26] In Israel, mandatory pre-mediation information hearings (*mahut*) after filing (for cases above a certain sum) often become a stage in the adversarial pursuit of trial.[27]

Additionally, when parties receive the impression that settlement is their only option during pretrial (through the statements of the pretrial judge), the path *to higher instances of appeal* is effectively blocked. Even if a pretrial judge gives a decision through judicial arbitration – an abbreviated method for resolving the case – this decision usually cannot be appealed.[28]

9.1.4 The Length of Trial

In Italy, apart from a mandatory introductory mediation meeting for around 10 percent of civil cases, parties are free to choose the mode of dispute resolution for their case.[29] However, the legal proceedings are relatively lengthy.[30] The length of trial also has implications for individual agency and choice.[31] Delay tactics by parties with deep pockets can cause weaker parties to desist from trial and settle because they require a final decision.[32] In the past, Italy was condemned by the European Union time and again for the length of trials,[33] probably influencing its

in family cases, which are not examined in our research, to enable a more collaborative approach, especially if conducted before the filing of the case).

[26] *Cf.* Fred Carr, *What's Said In Mediation Stays In Mediation, Right?*, PLAINTIFF MAG. (Sept. 2013), www.plaintiffmagazine.com/recent-issues/item/what-s-said-in-mediation-stays-in-mediation-right.

[27] Dan Yishayahu, *Perspectives of Lawyers and Mediators in Israel on Pre-Mediation Effect* (M.A. thesis in Hebrew) (on file with the authors).

[28] *See* Rosen-Zvi, *supra* note 22 (stating that the legal system has become decentralized, and decisions are now made mainly in the lower courts due to judicial case management and stricter restrictions on appeal).

[29] *See* Gubitosi, Tortora della Corte, Colombera & Schiaffino, *supra* note 20.

[30] *Id.*

[31] *See* Human Rights Act of 1998, art. 6 (Eng.) ("[E]veryone is entitled to a fair and public hearing within a reasonable time by an independent and impartial tribunal established by law.").

[32] Darbyshire, *supra* note 13, at 1.

[33] For instance, in 1999, the Grand Chamber of the European Court found in several cases that the systemic delays in the Italian judicial system constituted an administrative practice that was incompatible with the Convention. *See Ferrari v. Italy*, no. 33440/96, 28 July 1999; *A.P. v. Italy*, no. 35265/97, 28 July 1999; *Di Mauro v. Italy*, no. 34256; *Bottazzi v. Italy*, no. 34884/97, 1999. In 2004, the court found in the case of *Apicella v. Italy* that the compensation provided by Italy for undue length of proceedings was "derisory." *Apicella v. Italy*, no. 64890/01, 2006. *see* FREDERIC EDEL, LENGTH OF

introduction of civil reform, including mandatory mediation and judicial settlement tools in 2010.[34]

9.1.5 The Alternatives to Trial

While the focus of this study was the judicial role in an age of settlement and the processing of cases in court, it is important to note that individual agency and choice are affected by the quality and accessibility of alternatives to trial. The emphasis on the pre-filing phase in England and Wales correlates with a preference for settlement and ADR.[35] While often a bargaining process, court-annexed mediation is subsidized, and mediation is accessible by phone.[36] Arbitration, which is not usually individual litigants' preferred choice due to cost (though they may participate in arbitration due to arbitration clauses in contracts), offers a relatively complete solution because arbitrators are allowed to issue interim injunctions.[37] This strengthens arbitration by preventing manipulation of arbitration proceedings by the parties that renders arbitration toothless.[38] Courts issue arbitration-related injunctions only with the arbitrator's approval and when necessary (i.e., when injunctions upon third parties are requested).[39] Moreover, the emphasis on ADR in England and Wales has resulted in a bigger role for emergency arbitrators

COURT PROCEEDINGS IN THE MEMBER STATES OF THE COUNCIL OF EUROPE BASED ON THE CASE LAW OF THE EUROPEAN COURT OF HUMAN RIGHTS (3rd ed. 2018) (providing more recent examples).

[34] Michele Taruffo, *Ideologie e Teorie della Giustizia Civile*, 247 REVISTA DE PROCESSO (2015). *See* Giuseppe Conte, *The Italian Way of Mediation*, ARB. L. REV., 6 Y.B. ON ARB. & MEDIATION, 180 (2014) (providing background on the lack of a mediation culture in Italy). *See also* Paola Lucarelli & Giuseppe Conte, *Mediazione e Progresso: Persona, Società, Professione, Impresa*, UTET, 235 (2012).

[35] *See* Chapter 3.

[36] Nationwide Mediation Academy, *Mediation as a Court Annexed Service*, *in* MEDIATION METHODS FOR MEDIATORS & PARTY REPRESENTATIVES 29 (5th ed. 2006).

[37] *See The Difference Arbitration Makes: Losing Party Pays Costs of Nearly 3 Times Sum Advanced to Cover Legal Fees by Funder*, WITHERSWORLDWIDE (Sept. 26, 2016), www.withersworldwide.com/en-gb/insight/the-difference-arbitration-makes-losing-party-pays-costs-of-nearly-3-times-sum-advanced-to-cover-legal-fees-by-funder; JUSTIN WILLIAMS, HAMISH LAL & RICHARD HORNSHAW, ARBITRATION PROCEDURES AND PRACTICE IN THE UK (ENGLAND AND WALES): OVERVIEW 18 (2019).

[38] Rachel Kent & Amanda Hollis, *Concurrent Jurisdiction of Arbitral Tribunals and National Courts to Issue Interim Measures in International Arbitration*, *in* INTERIM AND EMERGENCY RELIEF IN INTERNATIONAL ARBITRATION, 87, 104 (Diora Ziyaeva, Ian A. Laird, Borzu Sabahi & Anne Marie Whitesell, eds., 2015).

[39] *Id.*

(EAs), who can be accessed by parties even before an arbitration proceeding has been initiated.[40] In Israel, court-annexed mediation seems to be mainly evaluative, though parties often sit in the same room for a large part of the mediation. Regarding the arbitrator's authority to issue injunctions, the law is ambiguous—however, lower courts have interpreted it as conferring exclusive authority to *courts* to issue injunctions (prohibiting arbitrators from doing so, and thus weakening the arbitration alternative).[41] In Italy, facilitative and transformative mediation seem relatively common, though this needs further exploration.[42] The Code of Civil Procedure was recently amended to allow arbitrators to issue interim injunctions.[43]

9.2 Suggestions for Human-Centered Design

The above-presented components of human agency and choice point toward ways of increasing human-centered design, as will be described here. Yet it is important to note that one primary way to remedy litigants' experience of feeling locked out of court or trial is to recognize the value of trial in certain cases, for example those that involve norm-making or clarify the alternatives to trial. This is especially important in a technological age that provokes new and unforeseen normative questions.[44]

[40] *Id.*

[41] *Id.* at 89.

[42] Luigi Cominelli & Claudio Lucchiari, *Italian Mediators in Action: The Impact of Style and Attitude*, 35(2) CONFLICT RESOL. Q. 223, 234 (2017) ("This distribution seems to contradict anecdotal experience, according to which most mediations are evaluative rather than transformative, as well as the literature which established the prevalence of goal-oriented mediators over relationship-oriented mediators.").

[43] C.p.c. art. 181 explicitly prohibited arbitrators from issuing interim injunctions before the amendment.

[44] Aharon Barak, *On Mediation*, 3 SHAAREI MISHPAT 9, 10 (2002) (Hebrew) ("There are cases in which an agreed solution between the parties is not an achievable goal. Judicial decision is necessary. In other cases, an agreed solution is feasible, yet it is more desirable that the case be decided by the court to create a precedent that will be applied to the general public."). On the possibility of mediation agreements being used as precedent (especially multi-party complex mediations that may be more suitable for authority-based mediation than for litigation), *see* Amos Gabrieli, Michal Alberstein, Nourit Zimerman, *Authority-Based Mediation*, 20 CARDOZO J. CONFLICT RESOL. 1 (2018) (noting that the backdrop of court is essential to bring the parties to the table and stating that "shadow of the law" is becoming fainter) ("[T]he legal system is driven by strong efficiency considerations which incentivize judges to avoid as much as possible complicated judgments that involve high costs to the system. Therefore, it is not that simple for the parties to recognize the 'shadow of the law,' which often becomes the shadow of the

For example, a judicial decision was recently given in favor of a claimant who had been sexually harassed on Twitter. She had requested that Twitter delete the tweet and was refused until threatening court action. This set a norm by which Twitter cannot evade responsibility in such cases.[45] Had the claimant accepted a settlement offer, the public would have lost this public norm. Pre-action protocols for media and communications claims in England and Wales, which include an exchange of letters between the parties, indeed specify a relatively short standard time period for response to the letter of claim (fourteen days instead of up to three months for complex claims),[46] reflecting a nuanced handling of disputes. However, cost sanctions for unreasonably refusing to mediate apply to these types of disputes as well. This means claimants would take a great (institutionally imposed) risk to go to trial instead of feeling free to choose this option – even if a precedential issue is at stake.

At present, there is not much prioritization of precedential cases for trial[47] – mostly, only parties that are recalcitrant and have the means go to trial in England and Wales. Personal injury claims for damages in England and Wales, however, are an example of deliberation on the types of claims that might require facilitation. Such claimants are exempt from the general "loser pays" rule (unless the claim was spurious), increasing both the likelihood of trial and a reasonable settlement because these claims usually involve a power disparity between the claimant and the defendant (e.g., an insurance company).[48]

One of the implications of not bringing precedential cases to trial is that people learn about the prevailing norms through public settlement agreements. This seemed to be the case in a gender discrimination lawsuit against the El Al airline, which ended in a widely covered

shadow since again and again the court will refer them to mediation, or to try and reach an agreement on their own – and in general, ask them to forgo a judicial ruling.").

45 *Linoy Bar Gefen vs. Twitter Inc* (Civil Case No. 19-08-31612). *See also* article on the early stages of the case in *Ha'aretz* (Sept. 14, 2020) Israeli judge accuses Twitter of sexism, orders it to pay expenses in sexual harassment case www.calcalistech.com/ctech/articles/0,7340,L-3849691,00.html

46 *Pre-action Protocol for Media and Communications Claims*, U.K. MINISTRY JUST., www.justice.gov.uk/courts/procedure-rules/civil/protocol/prot_def

47 However, personal injury claims for damages are made possible by exempting claimants from the general "user pays" rule (unless the claim was spurious). *See* CPR, 2021, part 44.13(1) (Eng.); ANDREWS, *supra* note 32, at 140.

48 *See* CPR, 2021, part 44.13(1) (Eng.); ANDREWS *supra* note 44, at 140.

settlement agreement facilitated by the judge.[49] The settlement agreement included training for El Al staff to deal with gender-sensitive situations among passengers and a commitment to be more sensitive in the future.[50] Some mediation agreements regarding child support, as well as in other areas, may offer nonbinding precedents. The publication of settlement agreements, if encouraged, can expand the public norm-making sphere. However, because the process leading to the agreements is confidential and the mediator cannot impose norms on the parties, this type of norm-making has its limits. It is not certain that a norm made through mediation between Twitter and the claimant would have had the same impact. By deciding the case, the court may have prevented such future disputes and the possibility that they may reach court.

By slightly changing the view of litigation to a more positive one, selective encouragement of trial can be created, giving disputants the sense that trial is available when needed. Thus, while legal systems might emphasize different stages of the legal process, they can "fit the forum to the fuss," limiting the obstacles to trial or encouraging negotiation or ADR accordingly. While generalizing trial as a last resort or limiting most cases to pretrial may offer temporary alleviation of case backlog, norm-setting facilitates settlement and the prevention of disputes.[51]

In addition, a formulation of the types of cases that should receive encouragement to go to trial can contribute to a positive view of trials by the judges themselves. This more refined view can be supported by changing the measure of judge's efficiency (from number of cases closed to recognition of judicial decision-making as an important part of their role). This view can trickle down to litigants, who will have more faith in the legal system.

In the case of mediation, rhetoric can be better aligned with reality. If mediation is mainly a form of assisted bargaining, this should also be conveyed. If, on the other hand, the values of consensual resolution are important to legal systems, court-annexed mediation programs should allow for more joint sessions, encouraging a broad perspective of the dispute and not relying too heavily on caucusing.

49 Hadas Cohen & Michal Alberstein, *Multilevel Access to Justice in a World of Vanishing Trials: A Conflict Resolution Perspective*, 47 FORDHAM URB. L.J. 1, 33–35 (2019).

50 *Id.*

51 William P. Lynch, *Why Settle for Less: Improving Settlement Conferences in Federal Court*, 94 WASH. L. REV. 1233 (2019), at 1237–38 ("When too many cases settle, the parties are deprived of the supply of precedent that sets the framework for their private negotiations.").

These are but a few possibilities that can be applied to a variety of legal systems. Another option, as demonstrated by Italy's legal system, is to create two separate forms of institutionally promoted justice: (1) an adjudicative form that is present in courtrooms, which includes judicial conciliation proposals that rely on liability (much like judicial early neutral evaluation in England and Wales) and (2) a mediator-led form of justice that is provided in mediation agencies officially approved by the Ministry of Justice and emphasizes joint sessions – in other words, consensual resolution.[52]

Arbitration can also be made more palatable by distinguishing between arbitration mandated by terms-of-service agreements between two parties with disparate power (such as a communications company and a consumer)[53] and arbitration decided through free consent of parties. Courts may intervene in the former (mitigating the power disparity so that terms-of-service contracts are not an arbitrary tool in the hands of the powerful) while giving mostly free reign to the other, including the authority to issue interim measures, so that it can offer a complete solution.[54]

9.3 Finding the Way from Kafka to Utopia

Consider this scenario, based on the opening Kafka quote (our changes are in bold):

> In front of the law there is **a virtual information officer**. A man from the countryside comes up to **this virtual information officer** and asks for

[52] A recent reform in Italy includes guidance on mediation, recommending joint sessions. See Gianfranco Gilardi, *Introduction. The Civil Justice Reform: From the Legislative Decree 1662/S/XVIII to the Delegated Law of 26 November 2021*, 206 Gazettta Ufficiale Della Republica Italiana (Nov. 29, 2021).

[53] Such agreements are often not accepted at face value by courts. *See* Linda S. Mullenix, *Gaming the System: Protecting Consumers from Unconscionable Contractual Forum-Selection and Arbitration Clauses*, 66 HASTINGS L. J. 719 (2014).

[54] Thus, in PCA 5860/16 *Facebook Inc. v. Ohad Ben Hamu* (May 13, 2018), a court in Israel decided that arbitration would take place in the user's country of residence despite an arbitration clause in a terms-of-service agreement. In other cases, where substantial consent is given to arbitration, the best support by courts for arbitration is usually nonintervention. In the United States, this includes granting disputants the choice to receive emergency relief from an arbitrator rather than from the courts. *See also Bowers v. Northern Two Cayes Co. Ltd*, 2016 WL 3647339 at p.2 (W.D.N.C. Cir. 2016); *Yahoo!, Inc. v. Microsoft Corp.*, 983 F.Supp. 2d 310 (S.D.N.Y.2013); *Johnson v. Dentsply Sirona, Inc.*, 2017 WL 4295420 (N.D. Okla. 2017).

> entry. But **the information officer explains to the man that he has other alternatives as well and asks him to consider them. The advantages and disadvantages of each option are laid out before him, taking into account the characteristics of the case and the man's self-described priorities.** The man thinks about this, and then he asks if he'll be able to go in later on **if he first tries mediation.** "**Sure,**" says the **information officer**. The gateway to the law is open as it always is, and the **information officer** has stepped to one side, so the man bends over to try and see in. When the **virtual information officer** notices this, he laughs and says, "If you're tempted to give it a try, try and go in, **they're pretty considerate in there, the judge will listen to your case and will try to help you resolve your conflict. In the meantime, I can provide you with a reliable time and cost prediction related to your case, including probable mode of disposition and outcome for each choice you make – settlement, verdict, or any other relevant door inside the courthouse.**" The man from the country had not expected **such affability**. "The law **is** supposed to be accessible for anyone at any time," he thinks. **"Maybe I'll try mediation first, and if that doesn't work, I'll come back."**[55]

This adapted scenario deals with many of the issues raised in this book and holds the ingredients of a responsive, human-centered legal system: one that focuses on individual litigants – recognizing the discrepancy between individual players, who drift through legal systems without important data, and repeat players who have enough data to make optimal decisions. Such a human-centered legal system would encourage individual agency through flexibility, provide information and satisfactory options transparently, and focus on the needs of litigants and the nature of the case. These ingredients have a large overlap with institutional interests (e.g., public trust, access to justice) as well as the aims of ADR.[56] Furthermore, a large investment may not be required to realize many of them.

A conscious process of deliberation by policymakers is needed: What stage should be emphasized by the legal system (considering a host of sometimes clashing considerations)? Relatedly, do judges have a central role in dealing with disputes? Should adjudication and settlement roles be combined, and in what manner? What is the legal system's view on trial? How far will the legal system go to increase individual agency and choice?

55 *See* KAFKA, *supra* note 2, at 148–49.

56 *See* Shestowsky, *supra* note 3, at 551 ("[The] self-determination goal of ADR could be further advanced if courts granted disputants more autonomy to exercise their preferences."); Frank E. A. Sander & Stephen B. Goldberg, *Fitting the Forum to the Fuss: A User-Friendly Guide to Selecting an ADR Procedure*, 10 NEGOT. J. 49 (1994).

Should alternative modes of norm generation based on settlements develop following the decline of written public reasoned verdicts?

All approaches can be improved to create human-centered legal systems using tools that are becoming widely available. Digitization of legal systems can facilitate distribution of relevant information to potential litigants, thus rendering statistical analysis by court administration simpler if sufficient data are reliably entered. The COVID-19 era has caused many legal systems, including those studied here, to increase the use of videoconferencing and telephone sessions in court, arbitration, and mediation.[57] If legal systems allow it, the digital age will increase transparency of legal systems (including the alternatives to trial) and provide ample data to litigants for the making of informed choices. Judicial training and legal education compatible with an age of settlement can make the court experience more human-centered by including soft approaches and ensuring pressure is not exerted on litigants to avoid trial. Because judicial pressure to settle can be accompanied by negative portrayals of trial, its replacement by other approaches would be beneficial to litigants, judges, lawyers, and society in general – thus enhancing individual agency, improving the reputation of the legal profession, and increasing public trust.

Lastly, standing "before the law" in a more responsive legal system in most cases may not even require reaching the gate of the court or its doorsteps. A responsive human-centered approach to law can educate parties about their rights, empower them by providing information on choice and conflict resolution options, focus on prevention and healing, and encourage organizations and institutional players to design responsive mediation-centered dispute systems in house. Avoiding the courts may not mean escaping the law altogether and privatizing society, but rather internalizing legal norms and increasing transparency, thus offering litigants sufficient information on their options and prospects.

9.4 Artificial Intelligence

AI technology, which is the machine analysis of large quantities of data to optimize outcomes (with the aim of creating human-like or even superhuman intelligence), is already in use in legal systems for administrative

[57] Brooke Meyer, *Judges Shift to Videoconferencing to Keep Justice System Moving Amid Coronavirus*, INSTITUTE FOR THE ADVANCEMENT OF THE AMERICAN LEGAL SYSTEM (Apr. 3, 2020).

purposes,[58] and in law firms for the purpose of legal prediction and legal analysis.[59] There are AI-supported initiatives to help parties assess their alternatives.[60] Expanding AI to adjudication has also been attempted.[61]

AI in the dispute resolution context means a machine-based analysis of a massive pool of data on disputes, disputants, law, and a wide variety of other factors to support the legal process.[62] Currently, the end result is *not* for the most part a judicial decision – that is, an AI verdict – but one cannot ignore attempts in that direction. A binding decision created through AI would dramatically change core concepts of legal systems.

The too-complex-for-comprehension component of AI has already led corporations using AI to claim that they have no oversight regarding outcomes, including discriminatory ones.[63] The "shadow of law" may be altered in ways unknown to legal actors and disputants, for how much

[58] U.S. Fiscal Year 2022 Update: Long Range Plan for Information Technology in the Federal Judiciary 6, Sept. 2021 ("A standard set of development and integration platforms are being adopted within the administrative support arena. The platforms include low code, robotic process automation with artificial intelligence, service bus for application programming interface centric integration, business intelligence and workflow solutions. The goal is to leverage these tools to reduce historical custom code complexity and replace it with standards-based platforms that enhance security, improve quality, provide consumer-friendly user experiences, and reduce the time to market for administrative support products and services.").

[59] Ayelet Sela, *Can Computers Be Fair: How Automated and Human-Powered Online Dispute Resolution Affect Procedural Justice in Mediation and Arbitration*, 33 OHIO ST. J. DISP. RESOL. 91 (2018), jury selection Ferguson, 2015; K. Medianik, *Artificially Intelligent Lawyers: Updating the Model Rules of Professional Conduct in Accordance with the New Technological Era*, 39(4) CARDOZO L. REV. (2018).

[60] Francisco Andrade et al., *Using BATNAs and WATNAs in Online Dispute Resolution*, JSAI INTERNATIONAL SYMPOSIUM ON ARTIFICIAL INTELLIGENCE (2009).

[61] In Holland, an E-court was established to adjudicate cases between consumers and health insurance companies based on a machine learning algorithm. This resulted in numerous complaints of unfair judgments and judicial attempts to intervene in the decisions. *See* Leny De Groot-van Leeuwen, *Pushing Cases Away from Judges*, Nimjegen Sociology of Law Working Paper Series (2019).

[62] For instance, a recommendation to disputants on how to pursue their disputes, taking into account legal prediction, the interests and emotions of the disputants, and more. Such a platform has received EU funding for development. *See* MICHAL ALBERSTEIN, MULTIDOOR, A DIAGNOSTIC SCREENING PLATFORM TO FACILITATE CONFLICT RESOLUTION, ERC PROOF OF CONCEPT GRANT (2022) chrome-extension://oemmndc bldboiebfnladdacbdfmadadm /https://erc.europa.eu/sites/default/files/document/file/erc-2021-poc-results-list.pdf (last accessed Dec. 3, 2022).

[63] *Id.* at 10 ("...Lufthansa's prices for flights within Germany increased up to 30%. Lufthansa's response to an enquiry from the German consumer protection organization was that the algorithm acts autonomously and beyond the company's direct control.

law would AI-based dispute resolution utilize in proportion to other factors? Since the AI decision-making process is largely autonomous and not premeditated in a way that can, without intervention, retain control over the result, the shadow of law could be transmuted to something altogether different than what we recognize today.

Efforts are being made on the institutional level to deal with the ethical aspects of AI-based judicial decisions, such as the 2018 European Ethical Charter on the Use of Artificial Intelligence in Judicial Systems and Their Environment, which has presented five general principles to be adhered to while using AI for judicial decision making.[64] Yet translating general principles into on-the-ground autonomous machine learning has proved to be complex.[65]

Disposing of disputes in legal systems with a pre-filing emphasis already (1) marginalizes the roles of humans that have traditionally been involved in the case, such as judges, magistrates, and court clerks; (2) reduces access to courts and moves dispute resolution largely to the digital space (e.g., negotiations between lawyers are today often conducted by email or WhatsApp; ODR); and (3) mystifies the role of law, since the parties are left to themselves to negotiate without a realistic court option hovering in the background (the shadow of law recedes).

However, while these factors (lack of judicial presence, lack of access to courts and relatedly the digitized geography of disputes, and the obscure function of law) have much in common with potential AI-based dispute resolution, the main aim of the legal system is significantly different. The

At the time of writing, Apple and Goldman Sachs are under investigation by New York's Department of Financial Services for discriminatory decisions made by the application system used in their newly launched credit card; male applicants for the card received significantly higher credit limit than their female spouses, even if the latter had higher credit scores. When applicants tried to appeal these credit limits, the response was that the algorithm makes the final decision and its actual decision-making system is a black box that cannot be challenged."); *see also* Iria Giuffrida, *Liability for AI Decision-Making: Some Legal and Ethical Considerations*, 88 FORDHAM L. REV. 439 (2019).

[64] COUNCIL OF EUROPE, EUROPEAN ETHICAL CHARTER ON THE USE OF AI IN JUDICIAL SYSTEMS AND THEIR ENVIRONMENT (2019), www.coe.int/en/web/cepej/cepej-european-ethical-charter-on-the-use-of-artificial-intelligence-ai-in-judicial-systems-and-their-environment

[65] Andreas Theodorou & Virginia Dignum, *Towards Ethical and Socio-legal Governance in AI*, 2 NATURE MACHINE INTELLIGENCE 10 (2020); Frank Pasquale, *A Rule of Persons, Not Machines: The Limits of Legal Automation*, 87 GEO. WASH. L. REV. 1,1 (2019)("Due process depends on narratively intelligible communication from persons and for persons that are not reducible to software. ... To preserve accountability and a humane legal order, these reasons must be expressed in language by a responsible person.").

lack of court intervention features dominantly in both, yet the main aim of AI is a binding decision – hearkening back to trial – while the main aim of pre-filing is settlement. Indeed, a swift computerized process made possible by AI may make the prospects of settlement slim indeed.

In this book we have seen a gradual chipping away of the authority of judges – by, first, introducing additional means to resolve disputes in the trial family; second, turning judges into settlement promoters with very little binding activity in the pretrial family; and, third, giving them only marginal presence in the pre-filing family. The end result, in the pre-filing family, is a vacuum of authority. AI can more easily fill a vacuum than compete with perceptions of the necessity of the judicial role.

This is not to say that AI-based dispute resolution cannot occur in pretrial and trial families, only that the conditions seem more conducive in the pre-filing family. In all three families, digital communication to resolve disputes has received a significant boost due to the coronavirus pandemic. Disputants may have become more accustomed to the idea of handling disputes through the Internet. To disputants sitting in their living rooms, the leap from a virtual hearing with a real judge or a mediator to an automated one might seem smaller than the leap from a courtroom hearing to an automated process. Thus the concept of AI-based dispute resolution is a formidable challenge for all three legal families.

Conclusion

This book examined the transformation of the courts across legal cultures, and the changing roles of judges as reflecting this transformation. We show that the decline of adjudication and the vanishing trial phenomenon, together with the rise of the ADR movement, have resulted in diffused and reconstructed legal families, in new notions of judicial discretion and justice, new models of mediation and conflict resolution have emerged, and new promises for access to justice and transparency can be fulfilled.

The different sections of the book oscillated between unveiling the entirely new legal reality in which trial has largely vanished in many countries, along with classic notions of legal justice, and the new emerging perspectives of new justice such as new legal families, new perspectives of compromise justice, new mediation models, and emerging conflict resolution technologies. Our conclusion is that the elasticity embedded within legal culture is a double-edged sword – it can either promote the development of notions of justice or lead to their demise. The present reality on the ground as well as the ideals described in this book are in no sense a part of mainstream knowledge today or publicly acknowledged by judges, lawyers, and academics. Therefore, it is important to spread them among the legal community, to keep developing the jurisprudence of settlement, to incorporate new ideas of conflict resolution justice into legal education and training, and to translate the new principles into legislation and ethical codes. We also suggest, where needed, to reconstruct trial so that it is viewed in a positive light by judges and legal systems – not an option to be avoided but rather a tool that is appropriate, and might even be encouraged, under certain circumstances.

As legal and technological developments occur at a fast pace and require timely analysis, a gravitational continuum along which prefiling, pretrial, and trial families are currently moving can prove critical to understanding and predicting trajectories of legal systems. The gravitation to an earlier emphasis affects core aspects of legal systems. The function of law changes dramatically, as does the judicial role and its centrality. Access to justice is also transformed by the move to an earlier emphasis, resulting in divergent interactions between access to trial and access to ADR. The main aim of civil justice changes from judicial application of law, to settlement with court involvement, to the private ordering of disputes.

We have offered this study and its new classification of legal families and gravitational continuum in the hope that it may contribute to a conscious effort by policymakers to influence the movement of legal systems rather than to succumb to laws of gravity and slide toward the privatization of the legal system. By opening a portal to the study of these laws of gravity, together with new models for judicial discretion and mediation, we hope to initiate a process that will help predict the future of legal systems.

Ultimately, we hope this will lead to the design of legal systems that serve the individual disputant – consciously placing the disputant at the center of concern rather than following a gravitational trajectory driven by efficiency as an aim rather than as a means to help disputants. Standing "before the law" in a more responsive legal system in many cases may not even require reaching the gate of the court or its doorsteps. A responsive, human-centered approach to law can educate parties as to their rights, empower them by providing information on their options, and focus on prevention and healing. Legal systems can thus aspire to place a focus on the human and relational aspect of the law without barring the gate to the courts, allowing access to the different forms of justice.

INDEX

For EU product safety concerns, contact us at Calle de José Abascal, 56–1°, 28003 Madrid, Spain or eugpsr@cambridge.org.

www.ingramcontent.com/pod-product-compliance
Lightning Source LLC
Chambersburg PA
CBHW071822030626
46129CB00004B/181